Kathy,
To a worthy and
distinguished stand.
Barrie.

THE FINALITY
OF YOUTH

A Study Of Runaway And Homeless
Adolescents In Great Britain

BY BARRIE M. BIVEN

Fairway Press
Lima, Ohio

THE FINALITY OF YOUTH

FIRST EDITION
Copyright © 1992 by
Barrie M. Biven

The names of youths referred to in this book have been changed to protect their identity.

7908 / ISBN 1-55673-449-2

**For
Lucy, Peter and Laura**

Acknowledgements

This project would not have seen the light of day without the solid advice and guidance of Mr. Lloyd-Jones of the Department of Education and Science, and Mr. Dennis Howell, the then Parliamentary Under-Secretary of State for Sport and for the Youth Service. I appreciate the vital role of the sponsors of the project; Countess of Albemarle, D.B.E.; Lord Hunt, C.B.E., D.S.O.; Rt. Hon. Sir Elwyn Jones, M.D., Q.C.; The National Association of Youth Clubs and the University of Sussex, all of whom, in their varied capacities, grabbed hold of a very unusual species of nettle and hung on to the very end.

Dr. W.G. Stone, the former Director of Education for Brighton, deserves special mention in helping us gain acceptability among the established social agencies.

There are a number of individuals and organizations that I would like to acknowledge for their support and practical assistance during the whole life of the project. Specifically, Peter Duke of the National College for the Training of Youth Leaders; Alan Gibson and John Ewen, past Directors of the Youth Service Information center; Fred Parrot, H.M.I., Richard Mills of the Gulbenkian Foundation; Harold Haywood of the National Association of Youth Clubs; Jack Tinker of the Daily Mail and Dr. Shadforth of the University of Sussex Medical Center.

The University of Sussex turned out to be a cornucopia of volunteers in that 200 played an active part in maintaining the project from day to day. In particular, I wish to mention Terry and Pat Sexton, John Simmonds, Barry Wood, Annie Reed, Miriam Wiltshire, Rod and Carol Kedward, Wendy Long, Joe Walsh, and Roger Kitchen.

From Brighton College of Education a small hard-working group of students remained in contact with the project throughout its life. Here the project is indebted to John Boler, Ken Worpole, Carolyn Silvers, Paul Hitchens, Stuart Reed, and Dan and Denise Jones.

Personnel from the Sussex Police Authority were able to find time to meet various members of the team in search for ways of improving cooperation. I am grateful to the late Chief Constable Williams, Superintendent Probyn, Inspector Hall, and Chief Supt. Rostron. Without the support of dozens of churchmen from all denominations the team would not have been able to run the emergency shelter component of the project and I thank them and the Friends Center for the extensive use of their buildings.

Unsung heroes on the sidelines were John Chapman, the project treasurer; Derek Sparrow, our solicitor, and Queens Counsel, John Alliott. They thoroughly deserve the gratitude of all staff for their constant protection.

This is also the place to thank those individuals in Brighton who agreed to serve on the "responsible body." Many did not understand from the outset that they were a responsible body that would not **direct**, but that their accumulated expertise would be used to **advise** and support. This difference in understanding, (no doubt attributed to lack of clarity on my part), caused a number to resign before the project had barely begun. Nevertheless, I thank them all for their willingness to give of their time freely without prejudice. They are as follows: Mr. G.L. Brown, (Temporary Treasurer) Bank Manager; Mr. R. Cavey, Chief Constable of Brighton Police; Alderman Deason, Education Committee, Brighton; Dr. K. Gough, University of Sussex Health center; Mr. R. Gould, Principal, Youth Employment Office; Mrs. A. Harper, Homemaker (voluntary worker with drug addicts); Mr. D. Howard, Lecturer, College of Education, Brighton; Mr. C. Lowe, Director of Further Education, Hove, Sussex; Mr. C. Payne, Principal Probation Officer, Brighton; Mr. K. Rawdon, Principal youth Officer, Brighton; Miss Richards, Brighton Social Service Center; Mr. G. Bennett, Brighton Social Service Center; Mr. T. Sexton, Lecturer, University of Sussex; Mr. P. Steadman, Pharmacist; and Miss O. Symons, Sussex Association of Youth Clubs.

I would like to make special mention of Vic Robinson who gave untiring supervision and encouragement to an embattled

6

staff. And without a doubt we were blessed with a uniquely talented team of full time staff. With affection I wish to thank Eve Ross, Leo Jago and Nick Ashwell for their patient and enthusiastic contributions — it is they who enabled us to have a viable project that survived tremendous onslaughts. In addition they all assisted in the writing of this book with their contributions of notes, log books, memorandums and case histories. Finally, it is my pleasure to acknowledge the enormous contribution to the success of the project made by Dr. Josephine Klein. She was a source of boundless energy and clarity when all seemed chaotic. She was a constant presence, sometimes leading, sometimes cajoling, other times content to let others set the pace. She was critical yet always helpful. The project is as much a tribute to her leadership as to mine. However, the inevitable weakness and omissions in this account are all of my own making. None of the previously mentioned individuals should in any way feel responsible for these faults. I thank them all for being a part of an historic moment, albeit of modest pretensions, in British Youth Work.

A special thank you goes to Patrick Adams, photographer of the cover photograph of this book.

Preface

This book examines the phenomenon of homeless and itinerant youth in Great Britain. As founder and Co-Director of an experimental project, the Brighton Archways Ventures (1966-1970), the author provides a history of the project and the development and delivery of services to youth deemed distinct from "unattached" youth.

Runaway youth present a multitude of problems to voluntary and statutory social service agencies and to society at large. Perceived as a new phenomenon, existing agencies were not targeted to youth "on the road." The author examines the difficulty of responding to the wide variety of individual, family, legal, medical and cultural problems presented by itinerants. Such a complex response suggests the need for establishing specialized facilities to provide for the multiple psychological and practical needs of these young people. The author also illustrates the obstacles to provision of these services, from other agencies, scattered community resistance, and finally the chronic handicaps of the individuals receiving the services.

For the reseach component within this experimental project, an "action" research method was utilized. This approach to collecting data was necessitated by the workers need to develop individual relationships with the young people. We understood, prior to launching the project, that we would learn very little about these youngsters if we could not meet some of their needs. The nature of itinerant youth, their suspiciousness of the establishment, their physical and psychological deprivations, and their instability, made quantitative research methods unsuitable.

The findings are based on reports and documents compiled during the life of the project. The reports of the youth workers and self reports of itinerant youngsters represent a major source of information. The history and development of the project is based on documents from committee meetings, letters exchanged with the local government, and project records. This data is reviewed from the standpoint of the special needs of itinerant youth and with regard for the requirements of youth workers who intend to be of service to these youth.

The results of this analysis suggest, in contradistinction to a growing contemporary school of thought, that running away or being

9

itinerant is rarely a healthy, progressive developmental step for a young person. The thousands of adolescents who made contact with this project required both short-term and long-term intervention strategies ranging from shelter to psychotherapy.

The author concludes that a project targeted to such youth requires specialized staff and must contend with adverse community reaction. The staff is beset by conflict between the youth, the community and at times between the various goals of other youth workers and voluntary service agencies. The role of the youth worker can thus be very stressful, beyond the demands of the collective needs of itinerant youth. The community reaction is adverse, to a large extent, due to a negative perception of the youth serviced. Sometimes this is a misperception. However, any project of this type must anticipate such a reaction and build broad based support during the planning stages in the project's development.

In summary, the author contends that runaway and homeless youth have special daunting needs which necessitate specially trained staff operating in protected and autonomous locales. Existing social and youth service agencies frequently exclude itinerant youth. Even if they were more accepting of these youngsters it is doubtful whether the youngsters themselves would find the agencies goals conducive to their lifestyle.

The Brighton Archways research project terminated more than two decades ago. However, very little in this book is dated as the same problem of homeless youth remains. In fact in a recent article by a trio of American social workers (Kurtz, Tavis, Kurtz; 1991) they suggest that the prognosis for homeless youths is "grim." So, it is to be hoped that this book will be a nagging reminder of a forgotten army of wanderers who have few friends to plead their case.

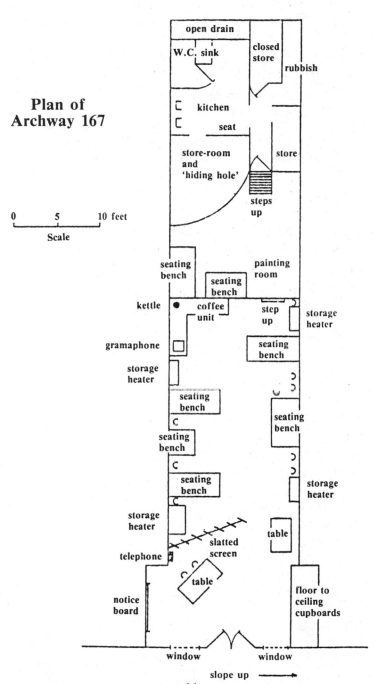

Plan of Archway 167

open drain

W.C. sink

closed store

rubbish

kitchen

seat

store-room and 'hiding hole'

store

steps up

0   5   10 feet
Scale

seating bench

painting room

seating bench

kettle

coffee unit

step up

storage heater

gramaphone

seating bench

storage heater

seating bench

seating bench

seating bench

seating bench

storage heater

storage heater

table

telephone

slatted screen

notice board

table

floor to ceiling cupboards

window

window

slope up ⟶

Table Of Contents

Chapter 1
Introduction

In the decade prior to 1966 there was increasing concern about outbreaks of violence in seaside resorts at Bank Holiday weekends. There was a great deal of publicity about large groups of young people attacking each other and bystanders, throwing stones and chairs, damaging property, breaking shop windows, and generally behaving in an antisocial manner. The police were described as being unable to restrain the youngsters. The arrests and heavy fines, of sometimes up to $200 for a breach of the peace, were said to have little effect on the young people. It appeared that nothing would control the trouble. Holiday makers became sufficiently distressed and embittered not to want to be pleasant to anyone who appeared to be a potential troublemaker.

The press publicized these disturbances in terms of antipathy shown between two groups of young people called "mods" and "rockers" and an excellent account of this aspect of events has been written by Dr. S. Cohen in his book "Folk Devils and Moral Panics." The difference between these two groups of young people was that the "rockers" rode motorbikes and dressed in black leather, and the "mods" were usually without transport, apart from a small group who rode motor scooters.

The incidents that occurred in Brighton were usually between the "mods" themselves. Few "rockers" became involved because only a few ventured into the town knowing that the "mods" would be hostile to them and that they were heavily outnumbered. There had been several television programs and newspaper reports before the disturbances which played on the difference between a "mod" and a "rocker," so when the disturbances occurred in the seaside resorts, they became known as "Mod and Rocker" riots.

These incidents were described as fights, since they appeared rather terrifying to the onlookers, though many clashes were just wild play to the young people. A bystander reported that a group of 100-200 "mods" were milling together on the beach, when for no apparent reason, they divided and pelted each other with pebbles. After a few minutes, the two groups moved off together again. Another reported a "rocker" on his motorbike attempting to ride through East Street which was then packed with many "mods." He was pulled from his moving bike and beaten up. Most of the incidents could be described as "running fights" and were mainly located in an area to the West of the Palace Pier, either on the beach or seafront, though at times the crowds split into West Street and East Street.

In response to this violent excitement, many hundreds of policemen lost their weekend leave, and were posted to seaside resorts such as Brighton, Clacton and Margate, in order that a large enough stand of authority could be made against these unruly groups of youngsters. In addition, helicopters and airbuses were kept in readiness to transport extra police to any town. The excitement was increased further by the press printing several photographs of the strength of this emergency force.

Brighton is attractive to young people. Throughout the country there are posters advertising Brighton as a seaside resort. Brighton has had a reputation for being one of the seedier, lively towns in England; this is a tradition which began long ago in the days of the Prince Regent. There are many theaters and cinemas, several of which now have late-night shows. There are numerous clubs and pubs, some of which are on the lower promenade at beach level. There are two piers which sport side-shows and many slot machines; candyfloss, ice cream, rock, hot dogs and beach toys, are all sold along the busy part of the seafront. More recently, Bingo has been growing in popularity in other parts of the town. There is a rather shabby amusement arcade in West Street with shooting galleries, and slot machines. Close to the entrance of the Palace Pier is the Aquarium to which was added a Dolphinarium, the Motor Museum, and "Louis Tussaud's" — an imitation of the famous Madame Tussaud's wax works in London.

There are a large number of cafes in the central area of the town, which is recognized as the area concentrated around

West Street and Queens Road. These two roads link Brighton railway station with the sea, and many thousands of people pass along both during the holiday season. During the holiday season, and at Bank Holiday weekends, these cafes sell poorly cooked fried foods such as fish and chips.

At Bank Holiday weekends there is a strong smell of hot dogs, onions and fish and chips, which wafts along the promenade, particularly in the evenings. Litter lies on the pavements and on the lower promenade. Generally, there is a sense of low quality and high prices about the town. However, in 1966, the Rank Organization opened an entertainment center, consisting of a luxurious dance suite, a bowling alley, an ice rink, model-car racing, and a restaurant. This provides a more sophisticated type of entertainment for young people. The prices are high, and yet the entertainment is of a good quality and so it has become popular with young people. Later on in 1969, the once shabby amusement arcade in West Street was completely rebuilt as a family center. This offered more up-market slot-machines and games for the young affluent adult. A large bar built in the style of the "Music Hall" was opened at the back of this center in July 1969.

Brighton has not been able to provide adequately for, either families or adolescents, and it certainly does not provide for the action that young people are seeking as an outlet for their energy.

It is difficult to say exactly why any young adolescent would come to Brighton. What later emerged was that there was little evidence to support the possibility of a conscious decision to go to Brighton to cause havoc. Though some young people were obviously only interested in the chance to meet some of the thousands of other young people, many were well behaved and took no part in the troubles. One incident in West Street illustrates this well. A well-dressed gentleman of about 40 was attempting to get out of the line of action of a group of "mods" who were fighting in West Street. In doing so, one of the "mods" barged into him. The man's surprise was that the "mod" stopped to apologize to him.

Many adult holiday makers appeared to be on the whole unaffected by these incidents, except when they sometimes moved closer to a fight to get a better view.

It is difficult to establish precisely how the disturbances were precipitated, but it became obvious that the respectable day-trippers, the police and the townspeople had as much to do with it as the young people themselves.

It seemed that many young people were looking for lively excitement, probably of an intensity that no town was willing to lay on. They had chosen Brighton amongst others like Margate and Southend, because these were the towns which had a reputation for catering to day-trippers. Yet, when they arrived in Brighton in large and often frightening numbers, the town was ill-prepared for them. The town fathers tried to handle the situation by discouragement and threats.

These tactics were manifested in two very distinct ways. A number of townspeople refused to serve young people in cafes and pubs, and many landladies refused to give them accomodation in the guest houses. There were also scenes on Brighton Station of policemen meeting the youngsters off the trains and putting them on a returning one. Some young people were even taken out from the center of the town, dumped on the outskirts, and told to go home.

On the other hand, but equally discouraging, many of the trading people in Brighton realized that they could make a considerable amount of money from the young people. At the Bank Holiday weekends, many pubs and cafes put up their prices. One young person talked of having paid 13 cents for a pint of beer instead of the usual 7 cents and a married couple spoke of a landlady who had offered them bed and breakfast at 5 dollars each, provided they pay in advance.

The sea-front traders, who are the people with whom the young people probably have most contact, speak resentfully of the young people's presence in Brighton. They maintain that the large numbers of young people tend to frighten off the family groups who used to come to Brighton for a quiet holiday. The traders are caught in the bind of wanting to attract the young people for their considerable custom, particularly since the trade from the family-type group in Brighton has been dropping for several years, and yet not wanting them around their stalls. These ambivalent feelings are clearly conveyed so the young people feel they are being exploited.

The press coverage was sensational, so that holiday-makers who came to Brighton at a Bank Holiday weekend were ready to see trouble occur. The young people who came were also ready for it, and so were the police. With so many people in the town waiting for something to happen, it was hardly surprising that incidents eventually did occur. Consider such scenes as a large crowd of holiday-makers leaning over the balustrade of the upper promenade watching, with an expectant air, a large group of young people sunning themselves on the beach below. The whole situation was too much like that of stage and audience, and so the young people began to act. Other incidents flared up when policemen handled some situations tactlessly or provocatively. And, of course, there are always a few who exist in any large disorganized gathering who use the safety of a crowd to provoke violent incidents.

Beginnings And Limitations

In later sections, a great deal will be said regarding the response of statutory and voluntary youth agencies to this situation. By way of a brief introduction we merely wish to state that a motley group of part-time and full-time youth workers were able to respond to the young peoples' difficulties with a generous grant from the Department of Education and Science, in London. This group formed the Brighton Archways Ventures, an autonomous project funded from special monies earmarked for experimental projects. The project was founded by Barrie Biven who co-directed operations with Josephine Klein. The three paid workers were Leo Jago, Eve Ross and Nick Askwell. For the purposes of this introduction a few words on the ideology and philosophy of the group are in order.

That there existed a philosophy, which was meaningful to all the workers, has never been in doubt. The problem has always been to identify and define this "philosophy," in language which we all understood. We felt we needed to know what the others thought and felt.

Although it was not apparent in the beginning, we wanted to feel secure in the group and to be able to trust without question the actions of the others. This highly personalized view of the work was probably due to a recognition of the demands and pressures that we knew we would have to face and the realization that we would only be able to lean on each other for support.

In the many group discussions, both formal and informal, attempts were made to discover whether it was possible for us to think in terms of a philosophical statement which would assist others in their assesment of our work. We were never able to do this in the sense that we drew up a document which we were all able to agree on. But from time to time each of us expressed our feelings and thoughts, either in reports or in discussion.

It was accepted that our beliefs and the reasons for being on the project are to be found in the dim recesses of our own life histories but such events have little relevance to the project work on a day to day basis.

We would also ask the reader to accept that we are and were aware that each of us sought our own salvation through a concern for others. We recognize that we are driven like all other men and women, to search for significance in our lives. However, we also saw ourselves as professionals. That is to say we consciously and consistently balanced this need of ours against the provision of the best possible service to the advantage of others. It matters little that the chosen group were young people or that many of them were seriously disorganized and in ill-health. The selected group certainly reveals where the talents of the workers reside and gives some indication of their interests but the ideological orientations disclose an important facet of the agreed policies and methods, which were ultimately to play such a vital role in the future of the project.

In order to bring the project into being we had to accept that we were making assumptions about a group of people and on the basis of those assumptions, admittedly founded on some considerable collective experience, we were setting up a service which would in part seek to modify the behavior of other individuals. Perhaps we used the word "accept" rather loosely here for we were deeply concerned and interested in influencing the social situation in which we found ourselves. Whether we have had any influence for better or for worse is not easy for us to decide. We have our views but feel it is better for the work to be judged in part by our report and partly by what others have observed.

Similarly, we have no way of knowing what influence this report might have upon those whose unenviable task it is to decide upon and, in turn, influence national policies on youth. There has consistently been the danger that our report would either be too esoteric or too simplistic and general to bear little relation to the nub of the work.

For in fact, the center point of the project philosophy and ultimately the work itself, was the conflict between wanting to influence and modify other's behavior through the ministrations of a service and the desire to study and inform ourselves about the extensiveness of itinerant youth movements and associated problems. Since the grant from the Department of Education supported both these aspects there was always the question of who was influencing who. In many ways we often failed to discriminate between prediction and advocacy. We hope this failure is at a minimum since a part of the philosophical atmosphere was a desire to create a moral and intellectual integrity which would enable us to report our observations objectively. But I would stress that it is not the purpose of this section to try to convince the reader that we have lived up to the fine sentiments that are uttered from time to time in the pages that follow. What we did feel was that in our work an admittance of insincerity was the same as saying that we were inefficient and dissatisfied. On many occasions we did not know the truth in ourselves nor the genuineness of others. But by building into our method the attempt to find such truths we quite deliberately formed a basis upon which our philosophy could grow and reveal itself.

I would remind the reader that this section is a retrospective essay on the philosophy of the project. It would have been useful to have been able to record our agreement on the philosophy during the opening days of the work and then later compared this to our final thoughts. Unfortunately, although we were aware that we were in considerable agreement it was not possible to clarify this into some useful general statements. It was perhaps inevitable that not only would our experiences in the work lead to the development of a kind of theory of pragmatic strategies but that they would find a home in a developing philosophy.

We were also affected by the acceptance of the professional role, that of a worker in a personal service agency. This very acceptance imposes a psychological discipline on each worker. It is a discipline which helps the worker guard against distractions, helps to develop moral and intellectual integrity and a self-scrutiny which ultimately leads to greater objectivity.

Thus, it can be seen that a definition of "the" philosophy is not possible but a great number of our attitudes, feelings and observations are described from time to time which indicate the general philosophical base from which we worked.

Working With Young People

Many critics have labelled the Archway young people as "spongers," "layabouts," "grots," and have asked the Archway staff why they should want to work with the people, who are totally unworthy of any assistance. The workers felt primarily that no one was unworthy of assistance, and secondly, that it was likely that those who appeared unworthy of assistance were probably those most likely in need of it. Other people, more aware of the problem, have asked a similar question, "why don't you leave them alone? — perhaps there are some

22

people in the archway who don't want to be worked with.'' The workers realized that there were many young people who did not want to have conversations with the workers, and yet they were equally aware that these young people still felt the need to use the archway. The workers were certain that this was a working situation. The young person who had come to the archway for some reason was obviously benefitting in some way. The worker in helping to create an atmosphere which was appreciated, was indirectly ''working'' with that young person.

From the start of the project the workers realized that the young people who were attracted to the archway needed careful handling. Those who came to the archway did so for a reason, and whereas it was not essential that the worker should find out what the reason was, it was important that the workers should be able to provide and facilitate once a youngster indicated an interest. This meant that the workers had to be sufficiently sensitive to recognize when the young people were sending out signals to them. Some of these usually ambivalent signals are reasonably easy to recognize and understand. For instance, when Jamie first arrived in Archway 141, she threw herself around the arch, treading on people, falling over their feet, charging straight into them, screaming abuse at them and generally making herself a thorough nuisance. She needed attention from the group; she wanted people to feel concerned and annoyed with her and she usually succeeded. Hiawatha used to tell quite fantastic stories about his past life, and about what he was going to do to improve the arch. This seemed like a request from the workers to provide him with something useful to do, and could therefore have been a desire to be recognized as a useful person. Other signals that were sent were less easy to sort out. What was the young person trying to communicate to you, when he refused to talk to you?, and what about the man who suddenly decided to scrub the kitchen floor — what did that mean?

When wanting to start a conversation, the workers have been aware that their conversation starters should not appear to be questions. They were always sensitive to the possibility of being seen as intrusive. Many ways of starting conversations were explored but one of the more successful methods has been simply to sit beside a person and say nothing.

The staff was sure that most of their most useful work was achieved by informal direction, advice and counselling. It was necessary to establish the purpose of conversations. It was vital that the conversations were confidential to the young people.

In time some of the young people in the archway learned that the workers were keeping record sheets on each individual person, and some young people suddenly became very suspicious of the project. But it was decided from the outset not to make a secret of this fact. It was explained that this was a necessary requirement of funding.

The workers were clear in their own minds about the case histories, and made certain that their own ethical considerations hindered future conversations as little as possible. Conversations with the young people were therefore of a natural pace, and nondirectional. All information that has been gained from the young people has come from casual conversation. Conversations were structured so that the young person gained most from the conversations; building up the case histories of the young people was secondary to the counselling at the point of contact.

Work with the young people has meant providing a means whereby the young people in the archway can talk more easily with each other and with the workers. No simple task.

An important part of the technique of working with the young people was the subject matter to which the workers were prepared to listen. The workers realized that many of the young people who came to the archway had in some ways rejected the statutory services: e.g. they would scoff at the idea of going to the probation offices for advice. It was important to understand how it was that the workers were able to be in a position to contact the young people, when the statutory agencies had failed.

Many of the young people wanted to talk about themselves, perhaps with an ideal that they would clarify some of their own ideas about themselves, or because they had a specific problem to solve.

The workers realized that they must set an atmosphere in which the young people felt less constrained and withdrawn. The workers knew, or had a fairly clear idea about which learning process some of the young people needed to go through for their personal benefit, and so they would direct the converation in such a way as to encourage the person to start the learning process. In other words direct informal teaching and counselling was the primary aim when simply attempting to meet a clearly stated physical need. The workers made full use of each other and of the supervisor, to be more certain of the degree of psychological interference that they were having on different people.

It is not possible to say with any certainty when it is "right" to speak to any young person. But the workers were more able to say with considerable certainty that "it was right to say that, to that person, when it would have been wrong two minutes earlier or ten seconds later." In this way the workers relied considerably on their intuitions in working with the young people. The workers were able to support their intuitive moments with the young people by discussing those incidents with the other workers and with their supervisor.

From the start of the project, the workers recorded as much as they could remember about an evening's work. Many of the records are simply a diary of events of a day in which things relevant or irrelevant are recorded. Whereas much of this information could have been considered as unimportant at the time of it happening, the work with the young people has proved to be of such a sensitive nature that on occasions it was necessary to build up a complete picture of one specific evening in the Archway as a basis for planning. This made it necessary to record much of what happened.

In attempting to write about the types of young people who have used the Archway scheme, considerable difficulty was experienced by the workers in coming to some acceptable, meaningful and clear ideas of the categories by which to describe the young people. The workers found that a clearer idea of the type of young people who were using the Archway was possible when consideration was given to the situations in which the worker and the young people became involved, rather than attempting to put sociological and psychiatric labels to the young people. This labelling would have been too confusing and probably inaccurate because we were not in a position to make such precise diagnoses.

Much of the contact with the youngsters was dominated by a felt need on the part of the staff to distinguish when they felt they were "working," i.e., pursuing a project aim, and when they were not. It is possible to see how working situations in the archway setting could also exclude the workers. If the worker was able to encourage other groups to form and talk with each other, then this too was a working situation helped by the worker. In these cases, it is unnecessary to attempt to distinguish between the influence of the worker or the atmosphere within the arch, in forming these groups. Each of these situations will be dealt with in more detail and examples of individuals will also be given.

To conclude this introduction the author presents a detailed history of the founding months of the Brighton Archways project. The aim is to provide the reader with some appreciation of the social and group dynamics in operation during the life of the project. It is expected that these insights will be useful in an understanding of the review of the body of knowledge and the chosen method of study.

During the summer of 1964, two detached youth workers, the author, and Paddy McCarthy, discussed the regressive impact of the "mod" and "rocker" troubles, on their clients. Their reasoning was that some of the difficulties between the town, the police, and the young people, could be seen as being caused by large numbers of young people wandering about the town all night, cold, irritable and hungry. Contacts were made with the University of Sussex and with the East Sussex Constabulary. The basic idea was that the Army would provide cliff-top tents and catering facilities.

Biven moved to Brighton in late August 1965, as a student at the University of Sussex. He shared a mutual interest in

26

adventure playgrounds with a student, Dan Jones, and they soon met, but the major topic of conversation was the possibility of setting up a Bank Holiday project. It was agreed to arrange a meeting with two or three other people in the town who might be interested in the idea.

The Brighton group soon met to discuss how they should involve themselves with the National Association of Youth Clubs who were keen to run a project in Brighton in the coming year. The Brighton group — Dan Jones, (a school teacher), Derek Harper, (A YMCA organizing secretary), John Coldbrook, (a teacher who died in 1966), and Biven — decided that it would cooperate with the NAYC group. It was unclear at that stage what either group intended. However, it was apparent that the NAYC placed more emphasis on the provision of an Information Center while the Brighton group favored an accomodation scheme. There did not seem any reason why these two services could not be combined. It was envisaged, even at that early stage, that it would be possible to administer the accomodation scheme from the same premises as the Information Center.

Paddy McCarthy did not think he could give his time to the scheme due to mounting neighborhood clashes between young blacks and whites. Tragically, he was to be killed in 1970 in Belfast in the sectarian troubles.

After three or four short meetings, the local group was clear about their involvement in the project scheme. It was decided to meet the NAYC, to work out how to coordinate the joint efforts. The first meeting was amicable and preparations for the joint project were begun in earnest. However, two of the more experienced local groups were a little concerned about the NAYC tradition of using adolescents for volunteer work. It was felt that the projected tasks were far too difficult and demanding to be left solely to a sixteen-year-old. The local group felt that some experienced people were needed to be responsible for each accomodation center. Unfortunately, this point was not taken with any enthusiasm by the NAYC group who felt it was a service by the young for the young. This

27

posture reflects one of the fundamental tenets of this NAYC service. It was to be the cause of some later difficulty when the Brighton scheme developed into a full-time project.

However, as it had been previously agreed to make the local group responsible for the rota and placing of the volunteers, it was quite a simple matter to invite experienced youth workers and put them in charge of a center.

The preparations of the weekend took longer than expected, and it was reluctantly agreed that it would be more sensible to plan for a Whitsun opening rather than Easter of 1966. In actuality, Biven had to take six weeks off from his studies as it became increasingly obvious that the group would not be able to meet the Whitsun deadline.

Early that year two lecturers from the University of Sussex, Barry Wood and Jo Klein, learned of the project from Biven and joined the local group in preparatory discussions. They were both to play a most important role in the expansion of the project.

It was known by Dan Jones that the local Youth and Community Office held the lease to a sea-front archway which was not in use. It was ideal for an information center and an administrative office. This Archway (190) was eventually loaned to the group after meetings and phone calls between the NAYC, Dan Jones and the Youth Office. The understanding was that the group could use the arch free of charge for the Whitsun Bank Holiday and other Bank Holiday weekends, provided the group damp-proofed the walls and decorated the arch. Students from the Brighton College of Education spent many weeks painting, building shelves and tables, and making good the electrical circuits. It is safe to assume that so much time would not have been spent on the arch if the local group had known that they would not be able to use the arch after the weekend as promised.

The youth office loaned crockery and pieces of office equipment to make the arch more comfortable. Although the Brighton group was grateful for this help, they all felt that the youth officers were not particularly interested in the aims of the project. The project was tolerated but not encouraged.

A similar reaction was felt when the group discussed their plans with other people in the town whom it might have been assumed would be interested and able to help. Most of the local volunteer help came from students at the College of Education and the University of Sussex. And some of the more practical work such as printing of leaflets and painting of signboards was done by the NAYC in London, instead of by a local firm or through the suggestion of a local person. Regrettably the project seemed to be supported by those groups in the community who could be classed "outsiders, temporary residents, politically left of center," and so on. Although this was not perceived by the local group in the beginning, it was to be a constant source of misunderstanding with the town and their elected council.

Except for an unused hotel, all the accomodation centers were church halls. This was not deliberate policy, but more the result of the lack of interest and, on occasions, open opposition to the scheme from the statutory and voluntary youth agencies in the town. Most of the local government organizations in the town center with premises suitable for the scheme were contacted, but none were able to offer their facilities. Some of the youth leaders were opposed to the idea, while others who favored it were not able to gain support from the club management committees.

So the best alternative was the use of church halls. Here the group met with an enthusiastic response, particularly from the non-conformist churches, such as the Salvation Army, and the Unitarians.

Biven then sent out invitations to a number of youth workers that he had known from his days in London as a youth worker. It was considered that since there were so many aspects of the scheme which could not be predicted with any certainty, it was better to staff the scheme with known competent people who had proven ability to work well in such settings.

Dan Jones, who had a wide range of friends in teaching and the Arts, was also able to bring people into the scheme who were interested in helping the project on a number of levels. The archway had to be painted, and the layout of the furniture had to be planned. Posters and information handouts had to be designed to capture the interest of a particular age group. These and a number of other essential jobs had to be discussed, decided upon and coordinated by a group of people who had not previously worked together.

Since this was a motley group of people with varying degrees of training and expertise it was not always easy to make decisions. This inevitably led to frustration and only those with the highest investment in the project were able to survive this phase and bring the project to fruition.

The preparations did not always go as smoothly as they should. Sometimes it was discovered that four of the five planners were working on the assumption that the fifth was attending to a job they had all agreed he would do, but in fact it had been forgotten. This led to delays, misunderstandings and irritation for the others. The group was further hampered by the apathy, and sometimes hostility, of many of the representatives of the traditional social service and youth agencies. The police were also concerned about the scheme and the Chief Constable of Brighton refused to meet a representative of the group to discuss its plans. The hostility and apathy could be summarized as the belief that by providing such facilities for the out-of-town youngsters, the scheme was attracting more of them to the town. It was expressed on a number of occasions that Brighton did not want the "louts" and "riff-raffs." A number of people said they did not want any young people in the town as it was not for them.

Another problem during the weekends which had not been envisaged in the planning was the fanatical interest that the local press found in the prospect of young men and young women sleeping under the same roof. The group had expressed its willingness to talk about the weekend and the project, but it was felt that a camera-man and a reporter in the centers was a violation of the right of the visitors to privacy and peace. In a sense it was felt that the project was a form of an inexpensive hotel, and few hotel guests wish to be interviewed and photographed in bed.

The press, however, were not prepared to accept this interpretation and two reporters disguised themselves as young visitors. Fortunately, their disguise was weak and the scheme's communication system was strong. After they had appeared at the archway trying to discover where the sleeping centers were, the word was passed to the other centers by telephone. One of the organizers then raced across the town to warn the other centers and just beat the reporters to the door by a few yards. There was an angry scene and only by sheer weight of numbers of volunteers at the entrance, were the two reporters kept out.

These sorts of problems had not been anticipated as the organizers had good experiences with the press in their home towns. No plan had been made to counter such difficulties. The success of this first weekend was due to the high calibre of center organizers who were, in the main, trained youth workers with considerable experience of working in informal unstructured settings.

By the Friday evening of the first Bank Holiday weekend, Biven had been accepted as the person with overall responsibility for coordinating all the various aspects of the weekend. Other members of the original organizing group ran the archway reception area and organized the accomodation centers.

One further major difficulty remained unresolved. Biven felt that the NAYC group was not able to cope with the demands of the weekend in any organizational capacity. On the whole, the NAYC weekenders were young people from other parts of the country who, in a youth club setting, would undoubtedly be competent and useful members, but in the archway scheme, they were subjected to demands that did not exist back home. There were two connected reasons why Biven felt they should assist more experienced youth workers in the centers, and do leafleting work, rather than take on an organizational role.

Firstly, they did not appear to accept the need to maintain a quiet restrained atmosphere in the sleeping centers. Like some of the visitors, they were boisterous and noisy, which in itself is no problem, but from volunteers with responsibilities in a sleeping center, it had an unsettling effect on many of the young people. They seemed more concerned with what they could get out of the weekend. This was understandable and could be accepted from young people of 16 and 17, but it meant that they were prone to operate on a whim rather than adhere to a plan which had been formulated for the good of the majority. Secondly, Biven was concerned that their vulnerability would lead them into situations which they would not be able to control. The organizers were aware that there would be many young visitors who would be taking drugs, or who would be violent.

These then were the two major concerns facing the local group in its relation to the NAYC volunteers. It was further exacerbated by the desire of the NAYC organizer to use the weekend as a broad-based education process for the weekenders and his belief that young people ought to be given greater responsibility. Unfortunately, at that stage of the project, it was undesirable to regard it as a training ground. What was needed was to provide a service, however basic, and assess from the experience of that weekend what kind of action research project to set up for future weekends. These fundamental differences in approach to the project rarely erupted into open disagreement. Both parties tacitly agreed to work together in the best way they could.

After this first weekend the need for a full-time scheme was quite apparent and Josephine Klein and Barrie Biven began to discuss how to bring this into being. The numbers of young people who used the weekend scheme, both from Brighton and other towns supported the view that it would be essential to aim for the appointment of three full-time workers. One to work with "itinerant" youngsters; another to work with the local young people; and a third to handle all administrative matters and the collection of data.

Josephine Klein, an internationally known sociologist, and Barrie Biven, made an ideal match for the task of combining a research method with a service project. Klein possessed the research training and depth of knowledge, Biven had the youth work training and experience. The academic and the practitioner were of one mind with regard to the method of study. Klein's experience of group research and Biven's work in informal settings for youngsters were complimentary. They enjoyed mutual respect and admiration.

Chapter 2
Review Of The Body Of Knowledge

Review Of The Literature In The United Kingdom

Prior to the establishment of Brighton Archways project most experimental youth work in Britain had been concerned with stable neighborhood groups of delinquent male adolescents. Much of this type of work had been carried out by voluntary groups rather than a service provided by statutory authorities. In order to fully appreciate the background to this research the author has included in this chapter a brief history of the Social and Youth Services in Britain as they specifically relate to the whole field of youth work innovation.

When surveying the literature on traditional youth work, quite aside from the more progressive experimental fringe, one is impressed by the paucity of documentation. What does exist, except for a few classic reports mentioned elsewhere in this study, are specialized products for the general public. Although these books provided a wealth of information on deviant youth, they were not considered worthy, scholarly documents. This may have been due to the publishers packaging of data considered titillating. All the ingredients for high sales were in the package. Teenagers, sex, drugs, violence and a courageous hero who tames the wild ones against all official prediction. The lurid titles left little to the imagination and misleadingly denied such books a respectable place in academia. *Generation X*, (Hamblett and Deverson, 1964); *The Big Beat Scene* (Ellis, 1961); *Blackboard Jungle* (Hunter, 1955); *The Shook-Up Generation* (Salisbury, 1958); *Turn Me On Man* (Bestic, 1966); *The Cross and the Switchblade* (Wilkerson, 1962); and *Roaring Boys* (Blishen, 1955), were but a few of the best selling books written by schoolteachers, preachers and journalists.

If a graph were to be drawn indicating numbers of publications correlated with dates, it would clearly show a steep incline immediately after 1960. There is a simple explanation. During the 1950s substantial numbers of teenage males had violently rebelled against the comforts of the affluent welfare state. This violent delinquency reached its zenith with the murders of two London policemen. Such acts were unprecedented and the general public clamored for governmental action. The quick response was the Albemarle Report (1960) and the equally rapid establishment of a National College to train large numbers of youth workers. Funds were provided to build clubs and leisure centers and to provide staff for experimental projects. Thereafter, the field of juvenile delinquency was opened up to a wide range of professionals and scholars and given the government's official seal of approval. The change in the establishment attitude was in stark contrast to the posture toward the early experimental youth projects. The voluntary groups who set up such fringe projects tended to be viewed in much the same light as their chosen clientele.

The Archways Project, and a handful of other experimental youth work schemes (Smith, Farrant and Marchant, 1972; Goetschius and Tash, 1967; Ince, 1971; Cox, 1970; Holden, 1972), were responsible for helping to change this attitude. Funding through central and local government offices for experimental youth work was commonplace by the early 1970s.

Review Of The Literature In The United States Of America

The author surveyed the books and papers stored at the Graduate Library of the University of Michigan. The author also made a computerized search of articles, magazines and newspaper reports, and books under nine different key words with five selected combinations from the original nine. For example, a search was made of items "Runaway," "Itinerant," "Hippie," "Youth" and "Teenager," with varying combinations of these descriptive items. A similar picture to the situation in the United Kingdom was revealed. That is to say, a few articles and books prior to 1960-1965 with an upsurge in the early 1970s.

However, unlike the United Kingdom there were unpublished doctoral dissertations from the 1970s dealing with drug abuse, runaways and delinquency issues. Although a few dissertations dealt with the problem of runaways from a service perspective, usually written by volunteers in safe houses and shelters, there were a few dissertations dealing with diagnostic issues, and it was not common to come across a combination of the two. The obvious explanation is suggested by the fact that a doctoral candidate does not usually have the time, funds, resources or inclination to carry out a fully-fledged action research project.

The author turned up the same classic books and papers in the computer search, and on the shelves of the University Library, that had been widely read by the British experimental youth workers in the 1960s.

The reason for the absence of documentation for the 1940s and 1950s can only be surmised. It is not within the scope of this study to look at this in depth but the author assumes that World War II and the Korean War account for a relative plateau in delinquency and a subsequent cooling of interest in the perennial problem of crime.

Chapters 1-3 of this study together provide a comprehensive review of the background to this research project. The major point that the author wishes to convey at this juncture is the idea that itinerancy as a social problem of youth did not exist prior to 1965. Running away has only in the last 20 years been perceived as a problem on a national scale both in the United States and the United Kingdom. Although the literature conveys no consensus as to the contemporary causes of itinerancy or running away, some general themes occur with noticeable regularity. Sex crimes against the young, school failure, drug addiction, the absence of appropriate family structure and guidance, the failure of the church as a socializing agency are but a few encountered in many reports.

The author reviewed one hundred and twenty psychological abstracts, 16 social science items, 23 newspaper and magazine articles and 20 sociological abstracts. Shellow's monograph

(1967) on suburban runaways of the 1960s came closest to the studied groups in the Brighton Project. He found that runaways could be classified into two types; a small group whose running away was bound up with their individual psychopathology and a large group whose running away did not seem necessarily to reflect psychopathology. The Brighton Project results would reverse this review. The author's study found that the overwhelming proportion of Archway users showed that their itinerancy or running away was bound up with psychopathology.

A review of the body of knowledge would not be complete without some appreciation of the changes in youth services provision from its infancy in the 1930s to the period immediately prior to the setting up of the Brighton Archways Ventures.

A Brief History Of The Social And Youth Services

While clear development of the Youth Services began in 1939 with circular 1486 under the Board of Education, attention to the need for social services begins much earlier. Social services began as voluntary provisions of charity to needy individuals. The problems of the poor were believed to be traceable to individual shortcomings, generally of a moral nature. Even as the state assumed responsibility, the focus on the individual remained.

The last 90 years have witnessed a social revolution. We have seen the coming of the welfare state, the rise of commercial entertainment, and an increase in the social and economic importance of the working-class adolescent. The young person now has sufficient economic resources to utilize a large part of the expanding field of commercial entertainment. Indeed the entertainment moguls behind this field have responded to the new teenage demand by creating sufficient supply to satisfy it, and inevitably, creating a demand to increase profitability. Moreover, on the tail of this economic freedom has come a growing social freedom. With this freedom the young person no longer has to submit himself to a set of beliefs, ideals, and values which he may not believe in. Faced with these changes, the youth service, or a large section of it, responded by burying its head in the sand. A large, unattractive, draughty hall with games equipment and a record player is not enough to draw young people into a club.

The economic problems of the 30s brought a recognition of structural contributions to the cause of poverty and unemployment. The introduction of social insurance measures greatly expanded the clientele of the social services and laid the foundation for the modern welfare state. Characteristic of this change was a shift in focus from selective provisions of service to more universalistic principles. Universality was still limited, however, by aid provided to categories of individuals. Defining such categories, although representing an expansion of services, meant that some who did not fit into the categories were not included.

One aspect of the expansion of services within the context of the changing economic structure was an awareness of the problems of young people as a special category. While the concern for youth began earlier with voluntary associations like the Boys Brigade, the YMCA, YWCA, and Working Boys and Girls Club, the industrial revolution and unemployment led to a concern for measures to deal with "idle youth." Many voluntary youth workers were concerned with raising the voluntary school-leaving age in an effort to deal with an expansion of the leisure time of young people and to keep them off the streets and out of the pubs.

The specific provisions of one response to this situation, circular 1486, were grants to support voluntary organizations, provision for the appointment of youth officers, and the setting up of local committees with representatives of statutory and voluntary parties (Milson, 1970:9). At this time (1939) there were about four million young people between the ages of 14 and 20, but only five hundred thousand were associated with voluntary organizations. The advent of World War II disrupted funding and attention from the problems of youth. During the

50s the Teen Canteens reactivated interest in youth but attracted mainly those young people, 14-16, who were bright and closely associated with the existing educational system.

The single most important and lasting impact on Youth Services was the Albemarle Report (1960). The Albermarle Report recognized the widespread social changes in the mid twentieth century and their impact on youth. The awareness of a growing economy, increasing numbers of young people, mass consumerism, and a developing "youth culture," stimulated new interest in youth and youth work. The special problems and moral conflicts involved in being in a rapidly changing, increasingly technological society required professional, specialized youth workers. In response to this report, more money and more attention, including grants and university training programs, were devoted to youth work. The expectation that Youth Service should have a "custodial, socializing, moralizing, and reformative role" (Milson, 1970:29) was maintained by attention given to special need groups. Half of the projects funded in 1969 for example, were for special need groups, including handicapped and "unattached" youth.

The Albemarle Report stated that some youth "find it difficult to come to terms with society and whose social incapacity can take many forms, from shyness to compulsive exhibitionism and crime. The Youth Service is there to help them, too, but at present this group is found principally among the 'unattached.' " (p. 105) The report also noted the limitations of the Youth Service for dealing with this group of young people. On the one hand, reliance on voluntary workers and the general nature of professional training limited work with such youth. On the other hand such "unattached" youth tended to view youth organizations as "Establishment" institutions and irrelevant to their needs.

Attempts to work with youth described as "unattached" had been made prior to the Albemarle Report. The Barge Boys Club, described in M.L. Turner's "Ship Without Sails," (1953) opened in 1949. This club ran for six years and provided the nucleus for another experimental club for "unclubbables" known as the Anvil Club. The purpose of the Anvil Club was firstly to be an experimental organization to help older, unclubbable adolescents, secondly, to explore methods of approach to such boys, and thirdly, to discover the reasons for their rejection of orthodox clubs and good leaders. The Anvil Club saw its role as providing a "real contribution to make in a sphere which is **not** covered by other statutory or voluntary youth organizations." **(The Anvil Club**, 1960:8) The youth it hoped to attract had in fact been terrorizing another youth group. The Anvil Club differed from orthodox youth clubs in offering few organized events and in not making many demands on the members. At the conclusion of the Anvil Club experiment, it was thought that such a club was, "possibly the only way of approaching these boys through small groups with a professional worker to help them, as individuals, to cope with their emotional difficulties in a more mature way and to modify some of their attitudes and values." **(The Anvil Club**, 1960:52)

The importance of the Barge Boys Club and the Anvil Club cannot be overlooked in any study of experimental youth work. A substantial number of the original committee and the youth workers went on to play a most significant founding role in a number of other projects throughout the '50s and '60s. In turn these more recent projects attracted other talented workers and committee members who themselves founded experimental youth schemes. Derek Shuttleworth, Hyla Holden, Peter Kuenstler, Phyllis Gerson, Peter Massie, Josephine Klein, Barbara Ward, Barrie Biven are some of those who worked through the '50s and '60s.

It is abundantly clear that the experience provided the worker with new insights into client needs. In taking a stance closely allied to the young person, and separate from the authority of the teachers and social workers, workers in experimental projects were forced to re-examine the relevance of much orthodox educational and social provision, and to question the assumptions upon which much youthwork and social welfare provision is based. They were forced to look at their motivations and suitability for the work in circumstances very different from the more clearly defined authority roles.

The point I wish to make about the positive gains from experimental work follows from this. The staff placed in these new positions were freed from the constrictions which previous roles had placed upon them; they were able to act with a new freedom once they had come to terms with the consequences of separating themselves from the well-defined role of case-worker, club-leader, or teacher. But workers found the blurred role-set uncomfortable. Nevertheless it undoubtedly permitted positive intervention and support in situations where occupants of more clearly defined roles would have been at a disadvantage. Young people were able to define the worker in terms acceptable to themselves, **without having to maintain the role of client.**

Experimenters changed their tactics and their concerns, consistent with the cultural changes at large. By the end of the Anvil Club and the emergence of the Hoxton Project (1972) young people were seen as increasingly rebellious and violent. The violence of these young people became headline news with the vandalism and fighting which came to be associated with the Rock-and-Roll music of Bill Haley and his Comets, and their many followers. The adult world was horrified by the killing of a policeman by two young men, one only in his teens, and by several other crimes of violence involving the young. For the young person outside the milieu of the uniformed group or the church youth club there was the street, the cinema, the pub, the dance hall and the cafe.

To some seasoned workers it did not seem as if there had been an increase in the violence, merely it had moved out of tightly policed ghettos. Teenagers in the late '50s and early '60s had large sums of money to spend on leisure pursuits, and it was to be expected that they would take with them to the inner city and the middle class areas, their traditional values.

The Albemarle Report was, in fact, the consequence of a government commission set up under public pressure to examine the causes of juvenile delinquency and associated problems. Interestingly the very special problem of juvenile violence of this time had been predicted by psychologists and sociologists immediately after World War II and confirmed by Wilkins (1960) in his paper "Delinquent Generations." He says:

> *Children born between 1935 and 1942 have been more delinquent over the whole post-war period than those born in any other seven year period . . . Moreover the highest delinquency rates have occurred among those children who were four or five years old during some part of the war, and this suggests the possibility that disturbance at such ages may have a particularly harmful effect. The interest of these findings is increased by the fact that they apply in a similar way to both Scotland and England notwithstanding that the rates of crime at different ages are not the same in the two countries and that the type of disturbance caused in Scotland by the war was different from that in many parts of England.*

> *Another finding of this generation is that youths aged between 17 and 21 in 1955 onwards, who would be expected because of their years of birth to be exceptionally delinquent, have in fact been even more delinquent than could have been foretold by their years of birth analysis.*

By the early '60s experimental youth work started to move in directions other than the cafe and coffee bar. Working on the streets without the emcumbrance of premises was favored by increasing numbers of youth work committees. It was also not as expensive. Street work had been established as a viable youth work method in the United States during the '50s. However, the American workers had borrowed a neglected approach used by many social and youth workers in the slums of Britain's largest cities for the past half century.

Other youth work committees experimented with Arts Laboratories and some workers contracted formal agreements with commercial discotheques and public houses. The results of these different approaches seemed favorable.

The statutory youth service increasingly funded these experimental schemes. While this enabled many a worthy project to survive the exercise of control over the use of funds by traditionally minded statutory bodies it placed a limitation on workers trying to respond to the here-and-now needs of youth. Voluntary bodies had tended to be more understanding and were free of the necessity of accountability to a city or county auditor. Additionally by the very nature of long term planning and budgeting, inherent in local government, the statutory services cannot quickly respond to the outgrowth of new phenomena, whether it be in terms of research, provision, man power or materials.

As a consequence the youth services were caught off guard again in the mid '60s with the emergence of the "Underground." The anonymous aging inner city attracted critical, discontented and alienated young people, and provided a milieu where they could adopt a lifestyle quite remote from their more conventional home background. A lifestyle marked at one extreme by extended intellectual criticism of present-day society, and at the other by an escape into a variety of deviant social behavior. It is possible to identify a highly heterogeneous network of young people attracted by Underground values and lifestyles. In addition to serious exponents of the "alternative society" there are "Hells Angels," rockers, hippies, academic dropouts, members of ethnic sub-groups, mods, skinheads and "grammar boys." A potential clientele very far from the "corner-boy culture" from which most of the early experimental youth projects drew their clientele. The underground was the first time that working class and middle class youth combined in a social movement around central moral issues. Nuclear disarmament, drug usage, anti-intellectualism, anti-state, and a non-violent stance to international events were but a few of the binding characteristics of this predominantly left-wing movement.

What began as a hopeful, healthy and exciting foundation slowly disintegrated into a failure of the disarmament movement, massive drug usage and a violent opposition to the police as representatives of the state. This writer fails to see much of enduring value in the rise of these moral vocal segments of youth culture.

A more recent report, B. Lewis, et.al. (1974), concerned with youngsters "who drift away from their homes and backgrounds" looks at the problem from a radically different perspective. The authors, who were commissioned by the Roundtree Memorial Trust, say that, "we shall comment on the vitality and resilience of unattached youth in the face of ever increasing pressures for conformity . . . And we shall argue that, amongst all the turmoil and confusion that passes under the name of hippiedom there is a point of view . . . which persists because it has a great deal of validity." The authors suggest that anyone not looking at events in this way are lacking in sympathy. It is, in the opinion of the Brighton Archways staff, an alien perspective. We found very few youngsters possessing the "vitality and resilience" that Lewis et. al. met with in their study. Their book settled on the term "unattached" in contradistinction to the individual histories which demonstrate a considerable degree of "attachment" to a wide variety of institutions.

Before we move on to discuss the target group in this study a few words about the drug culture in Britain are in order. I am indebted to Leech (1973) for the ideas contained in this concluding section. They are most relevant to our discussion in later sections, of the group of youngsters we call beats.

The development of the British drug scene has been rather different from the American experience. There have been three principal streams of illicit drug abuse among young people. First, the use of psychedelic drugs, including powerful chemicals such as LSD, and mild psychedelic intoxicants such as cannabis. Secondly, the use of oral amphetamines, legal in origin, by young delinquents within the world of discotheques, coffeeclubs and cafes. Thirdly, the use of opiates and other injectible substances. The years since the mid '60s have seen significant changes in the social patterns of drug abuse. First, the use of cannabis, and to a lesser degree LSD, has spread from

44

the early underground drug culture to a much wider section of youth, dispersed geographically and covering a wide socio-economic spectrum. Secondly, high-dose amphetamine abuse has remained the problem of a geographically concentrated minority of very disturbed "pillheads" in districts like Soho in London, while nationally abuse of amphetamines among young experimenters has declined. Thirdly, there has been a significant movement from oral to intravenous drug use, not simply heroin and cocaine, but methadone, barbituates and other injectible products. The spread of the process of injection, has made the British drug scene more needle-prone, more destructive and damaging. All the aforementioned trends were vividly observed in the Brighton Archways project.

Chapter 3
Research Methodology Of The Selected Problem

General

Findings are the result of methods of inquiry and thus must be prefaced by a discussion of the methods of study. This discussion is not overly concerned with the correctness of technique nor the notion that the right methodology assures scientific progress; these are epistemological issues. The question addressed is "Not the question of whether everybody's doing it, but the very different question whether anything gets done by it (Kaplan, 1964:25)." The aim is to discuss the process of inquiry used, its limits and its resources.

In this study several factors figure prominently in the choice of methods. The first is the fact that the subject are a group of young people requiring service, oft times intervention in their lives. Secondly, the persons doing the study would need to be delivering this service or directly involved in the administration of the services. Thus, being a detached observer was impossible. Thirdly, the subjects are a little-studied group and service to them was an unknown realm of practice. Those collecting the data also had a desire to improve their skills and service to such youth and recognized a need to expand the knowledge base on this group of youngsters. Therefore, the method of necessity and of choice was a method of action research, that of participant-observer.

Participant observation has a long history in the social sciences, especially with regards to social outsiders (Goffman, 1961; Henry, 1965; Thrasher, 1927). Such a method typically produces a general survey of the context and case histories of specific individuals. Participant observation lends itself to detailed inquiry of individuals (and their group), and to studying the intricacies of social interaction. It is limited by the presence of the observer, who acts and whose actions alter the situation. In addition the presuppositions of the observer(s) are unavoidable. However, the test of "intersubjectivity" (Kaplan, 1964), whether others see those subjects as we did, will remain for later observers and to the readers.

The founders of the Brighton project were initially driven to provide much needed services to the large numbers of young people visiting seaside holiday resorts. It became apparent that some research into this complex social phenomenon was necessary. The group decided to utilize the well tried methods of action research projects, particularly those methods used to research violent gangs, street corner boys, and other problematical, fluid, unstable and uncooperative groups.

At the inception of the project (1965) evaluation of social-youth work practices in Britain was an alien concept. There were few research-oriented social workers or youth workers that could be consulted as to the best approach. Based on collective experience it was decided to use a nonstatistical model. We also decided that limiting our sample and comparing with a control group would not answer the special circumstances and problems that we had observed. A more informal, flexible approach is necessary if a predesignated hypothesis is to be tested. The researcher has to, first of all, be intimately involved with those whom he wishes to study. As Merton (1957), says:

> . . . any theorist who is remote from all research, of which he learned only by hearsay as it were, incurs the risk of being insulated from the very experience most likely to turn his attention in fruitful directions. (p. 12)

Merton advocates a "post-factum sociological interpretation." This research method lends itself well to the conditions encountered in Brighton.

Yablonsky (1967) also believes in the validity of this method. He says:

A model for current gang research might very well be the anthropological field study approach generally reserved for more exotic cultures. The researcher literally moving into the neighborhood and experiencing the various social forces operating, would be in the most ideal position for gathering a wide range of data . . . (p. 179)

Yablonsky's methodological approach in his classic study of violent gangs serves as the model for this author's study of itinerant youth. The use of case materials, interviews and observations remains the most valid method of study for this target group, from the days of the Chicago School in the late '20s to the present day.

Although the Chicago School was primarily concerned with violent gang research, similar and additional problems are found in work with itinerant youth. For example, suspiciousness born of deviance is common to both, but the mobility of the itinerants creates a massive problem for the formally oriented researcher. In fact, the more formally oriented researcher who attempts to utilize questionnaires, and the like, usually meets with considerable ethical obstacles.

The brief review of the background to the project as described in Chapter 2, provides a cultural and sociological context for an understanding of methodology. The manner in which the organizers were drawn to each other is relevant to the whole question of social work and social work research. We described the way in which, in the early stages, the provision of services dominated the meetings between the principals. Gradually, a team evolved with diverse interests and, as is so often the case, a period of time was necessary to allow the strongest voices to bring into being a project which allowed for a happy coordination of research and service. From the foregoing it is clear that we did not see how we could manage to study the problem in any depth without providing rudimentary services.

We, therefore make no apologies for the broad wide ranging methodological approach, in fact, we feel given the state of the art, it was the best approach. As Cohen says regarding difficulties with methodolgy in his study of mods and rockers, "In an explanatory study of this nature there are few guidelines on which method to use for collecting data. In the event almost all possible methods were tried." (Cohen, 1971:228) We believe that our chosen method as participant observers allowed us to do, to observe, to record, and to interpret; these we did as honestly and assiduously as possible. It was agreed that the in-depth selected case history approach would be of great value. Also an account of the functioning of the groups who would be attracted to the archways was considered necessary. Finally, it was agreed that a compilation of basic data on numbers, ages, sex and point of departure were most essential. We opted for what Yablonsky would call a "field study of an exotic culture."

Further clarification as to methodology is provided by our attempts to define the target group. The concluding section describes these efforts and the relevance to our special methods of action research.

Defining The Target Group

The problem of finding a suitable term for our chosen group of youngsters was compounded by the plethora of terms in general usage and in academic use. We tended to avoid the issue during the early stages of the project by speaking in somewhat vague generalized terms, referring to the group as kids.

We had all used at certain times terms such as runaway, tramps, vagrants, homeless, vagabonds, beats, beatniks, hippies, and drifters. We settled on **itinerant** because it conveyed **less** condescension, and was not associated with the notion of violation of the law. For example, Runaway is defined by the Shorter Oxford English Dictionary as "Fugitive, Deserter, and Renegade." Vagabond is defined as "leading an unsettled, irregular, or disreputable life not subject to control or restraint." We anticipated from our past experience with youth that in our catchment group we would undoubtedly encounter individuals who tended to display undesirable characteristics. We did not, however, feel justified in prematurely consigning wandering youngsters to a quasi-criminal category.

Some terms previously mentioned evoke notions of healthy non-pathological adventure while other terms orient one's thoughts to a problem group of people, people who have problems or people who cause problems. For example, the term "beat" alludes to the dual concept of beaten down and of beatific, supreme happiness, of being blessed. Hence, subsequent terms beatnik and beachnik which were coined by a reporter on a San Francisco newspaper. Most beats tend to be itinerants but by no means are most itinerants beat. Both itinerant and beat groups contain many young men and women running away from the law, from parents, from the armed forces, from husbands and wives, and a more generalized inability to cope with life.

The issue of homelessness is a recent public concern and raises major social dilemmas not easily handled by statutory social service institutions. In Britain, the National Health Services are designed for geographically stable populations who rent or purchase a home. Without a home one cannot register with a general practitioner. Thus this simple deviance from the norm makes the itinerant unavailable to the institutions which are there to serve them. Although we do not speak from a depth of experience, we feel there is no great distinction to be made at this point between the attitude of the public and social institutions to adult itinerants and the attitude of the same people to young itinerants. When itinerants do reach the institutions they are generally not wanted and their needs are actively avoided.

Being unable to cope with the demands of conformity, itinerants arouse fear and hatred. The reaction of many people, not least of whom may be in positions of authority, is one of disavowal. Even social workers who wish to be of service to this clientele have difficulty coping with their own disavowals. Public repudiation strengthens precisely those regions in the worker's minds with which they have not yet come to terms: partly they feel that the persecution is justified.

In Britain during the '60s, young people who were not members of a youth club were termed "unclubbable," often implying some inherent weakness or sickness. Later the same group were more benignly labelled "unnattached." Belatedly it was realized that unclubbable is a relative term. The only aspect that all such youngsters had in common was their rejection of the youth service, either statutory or voluntary.

This attempt by practitioners and researchers in the youth work field to treat awkward groups as monolithic entities unified by overt symptomatology has not yet disappeared. Witness the widespread use of the term drop-out. The same criticism can be levelled at the use of the term runaway as it is conceptualized in the United States of America. Recently, the National Statistical Survey of the U.S.A. (1976) has outlined the current demographic characteristics of runaways. What follows are some facts and figures which might be helpful in giving some idea of the prevalence of running away as well as the general composition of the many adolescents who are now on the run. Operationally defined, runways are "youth aged 10-17 who absented themselves from home without parental permission at least overnight." It is estimated that 733,000 adolescents run away annually. Obviously, the term runaway is inappropriate for the target group in our British study. However it is interesting to note additional factors concerning the majority of runaways as they relate to the Archways project. The runaway population in America is about equally divided between males (53 percent) and females (47 percent). The largest proportion were 15.6-16 years of age. Although runaways are most likely to come from low-income families (the annual rate is about 40 percent higher than average for these families), the lowest rate does not come from the highest income families, but rather from those in the middle income range. Family composition and household size are also a factor. Lower rates of running away exist for 2-parent, 2-child households while those households with 2 people, that is, one parent and one child have a much higher rate. The highest rate of all is for households with 8 or more persons. It seems likely that these rates are not due to family size alone; single-parent and very large families tend to have lower incomes as well.

There are three prevailing schools of thought regarding the etiology of runaway episodes. (The fact that it is regarded as more of an episode in the U.S.A. rather than a style of life seems to be the fundamental difference between the two terms runaway and itinerant.) The same schools of thought can be legitimately applied to British itinerants since they represent long established psycho-sociological ways of categorizing deviant group phenomena.

The first view treats the runaway as a rite of passage. This social problem model cites the lack of definition of clear cut rites of passage as a motivating factor for the runaway episode (Skinner, 1949; Walker, 1974; Dean, 1973; Shellow, 1976).

The second view sees running away as evidence of individual pathology. This model minimizes the effect of environmental and social factors and lays stress on the youngsters pathological personality and impulsive behavior (Leventhal, 1963; Lerkiss, 1971; Bartollas, 1975).

The third model posits the locus of the problem within the family. The runaway is adaptively responding to marital problems with the parents or the parents pathology. The parents may be overcontrolling or hostile, rejecting or overly protective (Bosley, 1963; Goldmeier and Dean, 1972; Stienlin, 1973, 1974).

All three models and the now suggested high incidence of sexual assault by family, friend or relative are some of the major causes for running away. However, we have to recognize that runaways and the more limited group of British itinerants also include those youngsters raised in orphanages, foster homes, and other social institutions.

We can make some important distinctions between runaways and itinerants. To run away to the home of relatives or family friends is one thing, but to run away and not to be heard

52

of again is a highly unusual and deeply disturbing matter. It speaks to the possibility of trauma, or lack of family and community ties, and the disinterest in using others to mediate in the struggle between parent and adolescent. From our collective experience of working with young people in a variety of experimental youth work settings we anticipated that we would be in contact with a more pathological group of youngsters whose contact with home was minimal or non-existent.

The literature on adolescent runaways or itinerants in Britain did not exist at the time the project was set up. The studies concerning crisis centers, runaway shelters, and street clinics all post date the Brighton project (English, 1971; Epps, 1976; Moriaty, 1974; Wollen and Brandon, 1977). The studies which were of most help to us were classic reports of experimental legal-correctional-educational facilities (Aichhorn, 1936; Wills, 1960; Makarenko, 1951; Neill, 1926; Miller, 1964; Whyte, 1943; Becker, 1930; Gosling, 1962).

If we were to encapsulate and summarize the methodology, underlying philosophy and orientation to subject pool we could do no better than refer the reader to Aichhorn and Neill. Therefore, in all the above mentioned patterns it has to be recognized that any study will come up with a very mixed bag. Being itinerant can be a matter of choice or an inevitable tragic link in a long chain of events leading to even greater personal tragedies.

To be itinerant can be a cry for help or a defiant act of noncomformity. It can be an uncontrollable unconscious need to master a traumatic past or identification with a parent through death, imprisonment, desertion, schizophrenia, or alcoholism. The youth may run to avoid being left. It may be sexually based in reality, a survivally directed act to avoid physical injury, or it can be delusionally based. The latter youngsters believe they will find an entirely new life and identity. Many go a long way in acquiring the behavioral trappings but have little ability to see that the intrapsychic state of affairs remains unchanged.

The foregoing makes clear the development of ideas and techniques culminating in the adoption of the action research model and participant observer model of study.

Chapter 4
Results Of The Study

Four Typical Itinerants

John

John was 22 years old. He came from a Leeds slum and was the eldest boy in a family which consisted of a sister, and two stepbrothers. His own father was killed in the war when John was two years old, and his mother remarried an old friend from down the road when John was eight. John never felt accepted by his stepfather, he said he felt "accepted at home but not wanted." At school he teamed up with a gang of three "tearaways" with the result that John was always fighting, playing truant and being disobedient. At the age of ten years, he was taken into the care of the local authority for three years. Just after he came out of care, he was involved in offenses of larceny and grievous bodily harm for which he was sent to an approved school for two years. This he hated, and according to him, "while I was at this particular place I got my grudge against society." He managed to escape, and was free for six weeks.

Academically, he showed promise when he was at his secondary school, but when he was transferred to another school in order to take his "O" levels, he did not work well as he missed his old school pals. Later he developed an interest in joinery and succeeded in passing many examinations. He claims he was talked into going to technical college where he had a girlfriend. He married his girl, who gave up college and split with her parents over the wedding. Unfortunately, the marriage did not last as John left his wife for a 15-year-old girl. About this time he served a period of detention center training, and two rehabilitation sentences. His rehabilitation training was officially described as long and difficult, with a minimum of cooperation from John. He was reported to be making an effort 'towards the end of his sentence' to come to terms with his problems and his future. Each time on his release, he returned home to his parents, (with whom he never felt easy) and was supervised by the probation officer. He never worked for more than a few days, preferring to live rough, or subsist on Ministry of Social Security money. His girlfriend was apparently killed violently, although he has given several versions of how this happened. After that he took to wandering the country as a beatnik. He described himself as a drug addict, but gave up drugs after cold turkey in prison. Eventually he drifted to London and then to Brighton in June 1968.

John was first noticed as a quiet boy who sat on the beach with the others. He usually had a girl with him, but otherwise he spent his time writing poetry which nobody ever read. Finally he gained enough confidence to show a few poems, and received such an enthusiastic response from students that he began to have ideas of selling it. He was helped to get it duplicated, and sold two collections of his own poetry for 30 cents each. He was extremely shy, often irritable and he took things very seriously. He discussed his ideas for setting up a beat community, although the problem of the lack of money bothered him. He identified very much with the arch, and began to feel that the beach boys themselves could do something to help. As the drug scene was getting worse, he decided he could use his experience as an ex-addict to warn others off drugs. He maintained a happy mixture of both users and nonusers amongst his friends, although he tended to idolize a 36-year-old-man who he described as "the biggest junkie out." His first move in his plan was to call together a meeting of all interested parties — consisting of Brighton Archways staff, beats, drug clinic social workers, voluntary social workers, and a clergyman — to discuss his plans to form a musical group which would tour the country reading poetry and warning young people of the dangers of drugs. The coup de grace would be a demonstration of Isaiah "fixing" in front of them; this was calculated to shock people enough to be put off for life. He intended to focus on school children and people who were not yet on the drug scene, so that they would never progress that far. After thinking about this for a while, and having talked to one headmaster about it, he changed his plans and decided that the group could start at home. He wanted to set up his own slightly more formalized help and information bureau in the archway image, and employing a team of workers from the beach. John received encouragement from some outside people and asked if they could start in two days' time, using the archway premises. We were unprepared for this but decided that if they were to learn any form of responsibility they would have to manage the premises themselves under certain conditions. John accepted, and took over the leadership of his team of workers. He found it difficult to hold a position of authority at the best of times, and reflected his ambivalence by sometimes interpreting the conditions liberally, and sometimes enforcing them strictly. Since he had difficulty in rejecting people the B.A.V. workers placed demands on him which he found very difficult to implement and he sometimes telephoned the worker to question him. All worked well until his team began to split up over his tendency to keep things to himself. His leadership challenged, John abdicated from the responsibility but continued to make his own plans. One of these involved putting on a successful concert performance as a fund-raising activity, which unfortunately did not make the money he had naively expected. The archway workers found that they were unable to help him when they stood in a direct authority relationship with him. He tended to use women as emotional supports during his spell of leadership. He fully admitted that he did not have a business brain and felt that it was unfair that one had to work to keep the group solvent instead of getting on with the job of helping people. He would dicuss his feelings of over-responsibility, fears of suicide, his conviction that it was his duty to help people, his girlfriends, past life, and prison. Little by little he unfolded some of his life story, but he always preferred to remain a mystery. Even now, some of the facts do not fit.

After the concert, John walked out without a word. He felt that the concert had been a failure as it had not raised any money and had left them in debt. He, therefore, resolved to save the situation by getting some. Unfortunately, he did not tell the group what he was up to, and they felt deserted by him. John was unable to see that this could happen, and the worker was able to explain this to him by telephone when he rang us from Scotland. He came back in haste and was welcomed back by the group, but by now his interest had gone and the project died a natural death. Instead he focused his attention on a one-sided love affair, and when this fell through he made the dramatic step of giving himself up at Brighton police station for crimes committed in London, Leeds and Brighton. This was the first hint anyone in Brighton had had of his past record, and we were forced to see him with new eyes when his old probation officer described him as a violent criminal, name of John Sutherland. The police in Leeds considered John and his friends to be responsible for most of the city's crime (or so he had said) and on a subsequent occasion one of his friends had 1,505 charges (sic), to be taken into consideration.

John was pleading guilty to two charges of housebreaking. The archway workers felt that he had tried to make a go of things in Brighton, and although he had not perhaps been able to avoid breaking the law, John Art of Brighton was very different from the John Sutherland of Leeds. John said he gave himself up as he wanted to clear his plate but after a spell in prison, he wrote "I've realized that John Sutherland and John Art are two entirely different people and I've come to the conclusion that John Art isn't dead as I originally thought."

The workers felt that it was important they should send a report on John Art to his probation officer, who turned out to be very disbelieving, as he had written John off a long time ago. One worker had a long telephone conversation with him, in which the worker tried to establish that perhaps John showed different responses to different environments. The probation officer was unconvinced, and stated that he would be sending in a negative report recommending Borstal training. As John had spent most of his teenage years in penal institutions, the archway workers decided that it was important to travel to Leeds to speak for John in court, backed by a couple of references from respectable people in Brighton who knew him.

In court, the police, probation officer and solicitor all expected John to go to prison for a long time. The archway worker was treated as someone who could only see the white side of him, as they could only see the black. The court appearance resulted in a suspended sentence, and John stepped out of the door only to be picked up by the police again. He was wanted for questioning, for something which had happened the night before! In such an atmosphere he was not given a minute to relax, yet John still returned to Leeds.

When he came back to Brighton, he was unable to settle with nothing to occupy his time and returned home and got a job. He had only worked for a couple of days before he was picked up again by the enthusiastic local police force and remained in custody for a total of three months, still protesting his innocence. The trial was delayed so long that eventually John was released on bail — perhaps the worst thing that could have happened to him at that point in time. The police were still on to him and the worker received the following letter a few days later:

> *"As you can see I'm back in prison. This time I can't explain because I am here on two other charges, entirely different to the others and whereas I didn't commit those, I did commit these. Why? Spite, I reckon, because I was locked up for three months for something I didn't do. I think I would have made it at first when I got bail because I was determined when I walked out of court, then all of a sudden it was the sessions all over again. The CID arrested me outside court and said I had hit a guy over*

the head with a bottle the night before I was arrested in March. They said they had four witnesses to prove it too, and would pick me on an identification parade . . . all four people failed to pick me out. The inspector didn't like that and before he let me go he said he'd do his best to bust me and he did, 24 hours after, but at least it was for something I did this time. Honest, I must have been mad. I was dead beat after being up about three nights and I broke into his house. I found a bottle of mandrax and I took two there and then with the whiskey and I must have fallen asleep because this guy caught me in his house. He said I had robbed his meters but I couldn't have done it because I only had two bob in my pocket when the police arrested me. They started asking me questions about a shirt I was wearing and found out it was one stolen from another house so I told them it was me."

Together with the suspended sentence, he got three years' imprisonment. The first eight months were spent as an A class prisoner because he had tried to escape and "I started digging through the wall." At his request he was moved South when he came off the A list but was sent to a maximum security prison.

During his spell in prison, he had been fairly active. He started divorcing his wife, who had had a baby by another man who also deserted her. John says he feels rather mean about it and blames himself for leaving her, but on the other hand he is not ready for the responsibilities of marriage. He comments "I have started divorce proceedings against my wife and this time when I get out after this lot will be the first time I've been absolutely free with no ties like probation, fines, or welfare officers. Maybe the whole answer is total freedom."

The worker asked him for a definition of the word "beat." "One of your questions really sets me back, can I think of a better word than 'beat?' No, I don't think so, I think it is ideal. Take it simply as a word in everyday life. If you beat an egg correctly, you achieve something edible. If not, ugh. If you beat a drum you create a sound. If it's a good sound, it's music, otherwise it's just noise. If you compete in a race the object is to beat the rest, so 'beat' is a form of individual expression which leads either to a total achievement or utter disaster, which all 'beats' are prepared to accept. It's either win or lose, hence their fatalistic attitude.''

John's parents had by now given him up, and he settled down to writing poetry again, taking part in a poetry competition, debating, reading, and keeping himself active. He is an intelligent young man but lacks the discipline to study. How he lived when he came out of prison in 1971 (he was then 25 years old) is hard to judge. He has had little chance to learn to cope with life outside an institution during the most formative years of his life. We were thankful that the arch was able to provide him with some opportunity for learning responsibility, short though that time was. It had also been a confusing time for him when he was caught in an identity crisis of swinging between John Sutherland and John Art. He has still to discover where the real John lies, and during this time the role of worker is primarily that of providing support, contact, and clarification.

A Sample Of John's Poetry

Inside the Gates of Heaven

They're gonna build me a jail
Inside the gates of heaven
And I'll be there with all my friends
From Brighton.

There'll be John Jones
Serving 75 years
And ravers watching Isaac fix
As the angels stand shedding tears.

There's Pudding doing 50
Yet he doesn't care,
Even Beelzebub is happy
Serving out his thousand year.

60

Joe Thompson plays the blues
National Guitar across his knee
Great artists of the past stand
In awe as the genius plays for free.

Mike Steen reads the Bible,
Sue recites the Lord's commands
While hippies listen in silence
Joints in their hands.

Wullie stands too tall
Looking very wild
But really very pleased
For Barbara expects yet another child.

The poet Jock is writing
Poems by the score,
As Girl Joy slowly understands
He doesn't love her anymore.

Irish Dan upon his rostrum
Telling friends a whopper,
There goes ancient cursing
He can't find his topper.

Jasmine is quietly humming,
Stroking her pet cat,
There's Cathy Massion laughing
Because I said she's fat.

There's Eve who's very sweet
Nursing Michael who needs a jack
And Texan shouts he's leaving,
A doss-bag on his back.

Arthur's stitching up his pockets
With all his bread inside
Christine and Nick are coming
Taking ravers for a ride.

Sean is playing the guitar
While Paddy just sits around
And the Fuzzman is smoking
All the pot he's found.

Mrs. Manes keeps shouting
The revival's nearly here
As McGregory comes in laughing
He's been rolled by a queer.

Alf and Paddy and Grew
Are turning on the Vicar,
Pil Drake shouts at Sunshine Sue
'Cause she's drunken all his liquor.

The feud at last has ended
Between Barbara and Jane
They sit holding hands
As Yogi plays the harmonica.

It seems so hard to understand
That Pan no longer wants to roam,
And even the strange Hiawatha
Regards this place as home.

Susie Tree and Sandra
Begging straights by the scores
While the sweet little Di
Is still as shy as she was before.

Even the lonely Gina
Who is so hard to please,
Sits and paints those fingernails
That grow from all her trees.

There's people standing at the door,
Making fun of us inside
But it's us who have the laugh
For this is paradise.

God bless Nick and Leo
They've reopened up the arch
They've had to move from Brighton
Due to Mayor's anti-beatnik march.

We must admit the council won,
There's no more beats in Brighton
They're all in jail with me,
Inside the gates of heaven.

John Art

62

Introduction To The Word

I'm just a poet with no bread,
And nowhere soft to lay my head,
Day by day I push my pen
Then tear it up and start again.
I go to the toilets to take a fix
Try again to do my tricks
Finally, after a dozen times
I find the phrasing rhymes.
What led me to this life of sin?
My girlfriend packed me in
She wouldn't like my kind of life
And wouldn't be my wife,
So sleeping bag and I did go
To places I did not know.
Finally to Brighton town,
After roaming round and round,
Morning, noon and night,
I settle down to write
Of love and hate and war and peace,
It seems I'll never cease.
So in this book there's just a few,
And some from Christine too.
It starts with War and Roses
and ends a tribute to Isaiah.

John Art

The Questionnaire

Is there really a God above?
Who cares for me with all his love?
Is there someone in the sky?
To love me when I die?
Will this guy to me be kind?
And help me find some peace of mind?
If I offer out my hands?
Will he show his promised land?
I believe that he is there,

Yet inside I've got this fear
If this step I decide to take,
Will I find it all a fake?
Will he get me off the road?
And help me bear my load?
Will he take my hand and lead?
To a place where I'll be freed?
And cleanse my mind of sin and pain
Help me start my life again.
If he will, then this I know,
Jesus Christ with you I'll go.

John Art

Amy, Age 17 Years

Amy's parents had recently moved to Brighton from London suburbia. She came from a family of five children, of which she was the middle one. Her elder brother and sister were both married with children so she was effectively the eldest child at home, and the only girl.

She saw herself as very different from her sister, who was "nice and normal, the spitting image of her parents," and therefore "boring." Where her sister was conventional, Amy wanted to be unconventional, so that she could lead a more exciting life and become a more interesting person. Although she was receiving psychiatric treatment, she felt she had so much more to offer than her sister had.

Amy did not get on with her parents, whom she claimed did not understand her. Her best friend was her younger brother, whom she tended to mother and teach about life, i.e. play the role she felt her parents should play.

However, the relationship with her parents was complicated and doomed by the fact that she had had a long history of an incestuous relationship with her father. She thought her mother was jealous when she seemed suspicious of any sign of affection between father and daughter. Certainly Amy declared her love for her father with the passion of a lover and talked about the difficulty of living with her mother. When

64

Amy was 13, she had an affair with a married man, who was eventually prosecuted for having intercourse with a girl under age. Amy spent some time in a remand home, where she was a ringleader in smuggling boys in at night for intercourse, and she was eventually transferred to a mental hospital where she became engaged to a fellow patient. After her discharge, she commenced treatment at the local day hospital, where she formed a strong attachment to a woman doctor, and then transferred down to a day hospital in Brighton. Amy's engagement had been on the rebound from her love of her first boyfriend. She occasionally saw him, although an association had been forbidden, and she announced her intention of having his baby. In fact she had a phantom pregnancy.

Relationships with her parents had been very strained. Her father had visited her in the hospital, and, according to Amy, had felt guilty for leading her into trouble. Her mother did not want much to do with her, and expressed strong disapproval and disappointment in the way Amy had turned out. Amy knew that her elder sister had been conceived illegitimately, so she read her mother's attitude as echoing a bit of her mother's past life. She could not communicate at all to either parent about her psychiatric problems, so they took the attitude that she was lazy. Why couldn't she get a job, settle down and be a nice girl? The thing which had hurt Amy most in her relationship with her parents had been their getting rid of her adored pet Alsation dog when she was in the hospital. She never knew what had happened to it and had never been able to ask them.

Amy had run away from home a couple of times, but always she was found and returned to her parents. In fact it cost her a great effort to be out on her own, as she felt so unsure of herself. Her lack of self-confidence had led her into sexual relationships as it was the only arena in which she was not shy.

Amy was introduced to the arch by a boyfriend who lived in Brighton and occasionally visited. He explained to the worker that his girl was very shy and would not come far into the arch, so he had to make her coffee for her. Amy had a guitar which she had brought with her by way of introduction. Within minutes she had treated the archway to a beautiful singing voice. She sang folk songs and soon she was coming to the arch on her own.

The first person she began to relate to was the worker. She approved of the worker's combination of informality with a professional relationship, and, thus, reassured she began to talk a lot about herself. She talked about her family and her feelings about them, the day hospital and her treatment, her feelings about sex and having a baby, and her guilt and anxiety that she was infertile. With the worker, she explored such topics as the possibility of a generation gap affecting the lack of communication between herself and her parents, her desire for a baby and the possibility of this being a search for affection, the use of baby substitutes in the form of another dog, her need for adventure and new experience conflicting with excessive shyness, her use of singing for emotional expression, the responsibility one has for leading one's own life, the use of other people for one's needs, and the problem of loneliness. Amy was able to talk freely and constructively but she was extremely reticent about showing emotion. She talked with the worker about her wish to be seen as a nice person who never lost her temper, and her feeling that she was three different people; one at home, where she tried to communicate, one at the hospital where she said she tried to impress, and one in the archway where she was straightforward and nearer her true self. She had many strong feelings to contain, and she sometimes came to the arch very tensed up. She provoked people when she felt it would help to release the tension. Amy began to test out the worker (making suicide attempts in the arch, asking the worker to rescue her from her home situation by taking her to the worker's home or getting her into a hospital) to which the worker responded by being sympathetic but unimpressed, and by clarifying her fears or rejection with her.

Eventually she settled down to use the arch therapeutically; she painted, sang, wrote messages on the walls, lent her guitar and demanded it back again, smashed cups in the kitchen area, helped in sweeping up and generally made herself at home. The worker thought that Amy was frequently bringing tensions with her from her day at the hospital, and wanted to make contact with her doctor to see how the archway was complementing the treatment. Amy took this move as a great threat, and seemed to think that the doctor would forbid her using the arch. It took her several weeks to allow the meeting to be arranged, but unfortunately, it was unable to take place until after the arch had closed.

Amy had received psychiatric treatment for so long that she used very sophisticated language. However, emotionally, she still needed to be a baby. Her problem was that of not being able to relax sufficiently to enjoy herself. Instead, she presented a serious, sincere, problem oriented front to the world, combined with a keen insight, through which she was trying to work out where she stood with other people. Many figures were used by her as mother-figures, including the female worker. She wrote, "I'm writing to you (the worker) because I would find it very difficult to put into words what I want to say. I said tonight that I did not know how to cope with some of the feelings I have. Mostly they are about you and the arch. I am very worried because I feel I am demanding far too much of your attention but the problem is I get depressed when I don't get it, I can't understand why. I don't look on you as Eve anymore. I look on you as something else. You are a mother figure, and that can't be very nice for you either. I really don't know how to explain how I feel, but I think why I get depressed is that I know you aren't my mother and you can't be. Also I find it very hard to realize you are human . . . please try and understand although how you can when I don't even understand myself I don't know."

In this instance the worker chose not to be understanding but to reverse roles as she felt Amy had too many understanding people helping her and now was the time to face her as a person. Amy found herself in the position of having to cope with the worker who was offended at not being seen as a real person. It was a stretching point for Amy, and initiated a discussion of the ways in which people use others to help their development. Amy got the point and just as some of her testing-out behavior ceased once she felt sure of the worker, so she began to drop some of her psychoanalytic talk in favor of seeing other people's individuality. After this she volunteered to help at a Bank Holiday weekend, and enjoyed herself thoroughly. Not only did she show herself to be perceptive and reliable, but she also managed to take on some responsibility for making the work in the sleeping center a success. She also contributed to the weekend with some songs from her guitar, and became relaxed enough to forget her shyness, in order to talk to the young visitors.

Amy had periods in which she was confident of herself, and spells when everything became too much for her. She needed prolonged emotional support during the ups and downs of her unusual life. During the time when she was known to the worker she left home to sleep in a derelict house with the beats, and was returned by the police. She decided that home was too stressful for her and went into a psychiatric hospital. The worker visited her regularly in the hospital, and frequently walked down to the beach with her to talk in more congenial surroundings. Amy had made friends with one of the older beats, Pan, soon after she began visiting the arch. Pan was age 30 years and is more organized than most of the beats. He carries a tent in a rucksack on his back. Every summer he travels to Cornwall, and returns to Brighton in the winter. He was one of the earliest archway contacts, and was notorious for his inability to find a girlfriend because of his fussiness, and insistence on playing "little boy." This latter side of him appealed to Amy, and she took him under her wing; she demanded that he do the same for her when she felt small. Pan could hardly believe his luck, and responded well. He was particularly vulnerable to Amy's manipulative games. Eventually the two became lovers.

Amy returned home to her parents and for the first time in her life she got on well with them. Her friendship with Cathy also blossomed at this time so much so that Cathy moved in with Amy's family (Cathy had no family of her own). Amy had acquired an Alsation dog from a patient at the day hospital. The worker was used by Amy as a constant support during the minor traumas of living with a dog and girlfriend. This was the case long after the arch had closed. The two girls made plans to go abroad together, and Amy left the hospital and took a job which lasted only four weeks. Factory life turned out to be too boring for her, and she returned to the day hospital. She was still getting on well with her parents and discussed with them the question of leaving home to live with Pan. To her surprise they agreed. She keeps almost daily contact with her mother — the same mother whom she could hardly speak to one year ago. Amy still has a lot of developing to do, but now she acts more like a teenager than before when she seemed overburdened with the problems of life.

The arch was a placc in which Amy could begin to discover something of herself in interaction with other people, and in which she could learn to play. She needed friends whom she could rely on for company, instead of finding lovers in one-sided affairs and she fortunately met many people through the arch. The role of the worker has been that of giving long-term emotional support, which has been necessarily more active at some stages than at others. The worker has had to play the role of coping with many crises, giving constant attention discussing hopes and fears, pointing out the psychodynamics of situations which Amy got herself into, and manipulating these on occasions. For example, Amy once slashed her wrists in the arch, came up to the workers and said "Sorry," and walked away. The worker got to the point that Amy was trying to get her (the worker) to reject her, like everyone else. She followed Amy and found her huddled up in a corner of the arch, crying. The worker checked that she had slashed her wrists only superficially, so it had not been a suicide attempt but a gesture. With a bit of coaxing Amy began to talk. She admitted that she expected the worker to be hurt at her action. And with pressure from the worker Amy figured out that it was her own feelings of being rejected that made her set the scene. A suicide gesture for her was really a bid for freedom from her worries, and it was aimed at people about whom she was worrying. The arch was, therefore, able to give her scope for acting-out, clarification, and relaxation in a secure setting.

A Sample Of Amy's Poetry

The Want Of The Unwanted

All my life I have been searching,
Combing the unconscious mind
Wanting to be wanted
Someone to pour my troubles to
Someone who will be there to dry my tears
When I go to bed.
I needed someone to tuck me up
So that I go to bed feeling secure
This person who will help me
With the different frustrations
Churning my body.
This somebody who will sort me out
But I fear for me it is too late
I have wandered from the straight and narrow
Only because I lacked the guidance and love
And understanding that only
One person can give —
The one person whom I could give
My frustrated love to.
This person is wrapped up in one
Small word "Mother."
But I must make myself content
With any substitute I can find
And be grateful I am wanted
By some no more than strangers
But show me the love I have lacked for so long.
                                          Amy Day

Depression

Depression is a state of mind
People become unkind
Loneliness and sadness surround you
Hardly letting you breathe.

People become objects to hate
For the barrier is being put up
Nobody can try to enter
For you are within yourself, alone.

Thoughts fly through your head
Why can't I die or be left
Then all that is left is muddle
Your heart inside is like lead.

You try to find the way out
But it surrounds like a thick cloak
You cry for the light to come
But darkness is all you see.

It enfolds as if it is night
Going on you think endlessly
Until suddenly it begins to unfold
The hour is passed, and again it is light.

Amy Day

Sunset

The sun glides across the sky
Casting its golden rays
The clouds drift slowly by
Then the sun is so high.

Evening comes so soon
And the sun slowly glides down
It wasn't long ago it was noon
But the sun sinks, casting its golden gown.

Sunset is so beautiful
When the sun is one golden ball
Pink, Mauves, Oranges and Reds,
Such wonderful colors are so plentiful.

71

I stop and stare at such a wonder
But other people hurry by
And then I stop and ponder
Why they take such beauty for granted.

Amy Day

Amy said, "As you can see from the poem above, I love anything that is beautiful. Sunsets are one of the most natural beauties there are. Yet a lot of people take this wonderful thing for granted. They would be the first to complain if it suddenly stopped. Sunsets are wonderful because you never see two the same. I hope I shall enjoy them for the rest of my life."

Jamie — Aged 17 (Pauline)

Pauline was born in Glasgow, when for some reason her mother remained in the hospital for five years. Her father left the home when Pauline was two years old, and Pauline moved in with close friends of the father.

When Pauline's mother came out of the hospital, Pauline was returned to her but the mother apparently had difficulties in coping. She would often move house and live with various men whom Pauline was encouraged to call "uncles." It seems that Pauline would often be returned to the friends when the mother moved house, or found Pauline too much to cope with. Pauline's mother often gave her sleeping tablets to keep her quiet. She was six.

Her mother encouraged Pauline to trust the "uncles," and one whom Pauline remembers as her favorite promised her a horse and a sewing machine. This promise came to nothing and she began to mistrust these uncles. Other stories which she has recounted point to a build-up of sexual mistrust of any man with whom she was in contact, and her behavior when in the archway showed that she had eventually grown to mistrust everybody.

She tells us various stories of horrible incidents which occurred to her as a child, and which have affected her life since.

They bear remarkable similarities to each other and yet she remembers them all as very separate events.

She tells of how she was walking back from school across an open stretch of ground with some friends from school when she was eight years old. A man joined them and asked if he could walk with them. Her friends thought that it would be all right, but Pauline had misgivings. She says that she was assaulted by this man and although she could not tell the police about it tests proved that she had been raped.

She was with some of her friends in a park playing on the swings, again when she was eight years old. She adds that she remembers wearing her bracelet. There was a man sitting on a bench nearby watching them, and he asked each of the girls in turn to go over to him. None of the others did, but somehow she did, and the man exposed himself to her. She was shocked and ran away.

Again when she was eight, and yet again in the park, a man was giving the group of girls piggy-backs. One of the girls told Pauline that the man had been putting his hand up the girl's skirts. The man then grabbed Pauline and "did something to her."

Once she was on the coast and a man invited her to walk along the beach with him. Once there he exposed himself to her.

When she was nine, and staying with her father's friends, she was left alone with the husband who put his hand up her skirt.

It is not surprising that she ran away several times from home, once she says, managing to travel as far south as Carlisle when she was eight in a nightdress.

When nine years old, she was sent to her father in Devon. If any of her past involvements with strange men were at all connected with an unconscious search for father, then her arrival in Devon and the discovery that her real father had already started a family with another woman, must have again upset her greatly.

She had apparently been sent to Devon because her mother was having a child, and when the child died Pauline returned to Glasgow.

She sat her examination in Glasgow, and passed. Later she was sent to a secondary modern school in Devon. It seems that she was transferred backward and forward between mother and father from the time she was 12 until she was 14, when she remained in Devon with her father's family.

When she was 15, she left her father's house and took a flat with another girl in a nearby town. She took several jobs but managed to get behind with the rent and recounts how she went on the streets to find the rent money. Intensely disliking this step she had taken, Pauline ran away to Brighton with no money and with nowhere to stay. She began to sleep rough, and in time began to make use of Arch 141. This was in September 1967.

When she first appeared in the arch, she was a nuisance to the beats using the place because she would rather shout at them, or tread on them, than be quiet and gentle as was their habit. Her only apparent way of making contact with others was in this off-putting aggressive manner. She called herself "Jamie" and refused to tell people her real name.

One of the workers felt that Jamie needed to make some different kind of contact with people and decided to attempt to build a relationship with her. The worker said nothing to her but Jamie soon recognized that the worker was interested in her. She classified the worker as a social worker and, therefore, resented his intrusion and so, combined with what is now known of her basic mistrust of men, she felt the need to test out the worker's sincerity.

From about Christmas until March 1968, the worker allowed Jamie to swear at him, punch him, throw ashtrays at him, empty rubbish over him and threaten him, always careful not to rise to this continued provocation. It was obvious to the archway team that Jamie wanted to make use of this worker, who also knew that for her to feel secure with him she must test him out first.

The testing out progressed in a step-by-step manner for the three months until one evening Jamie repeated all the steps one after another. The worker then said that he had had enough. The provocations and punchings ceased immediately.

74

Jamie was now much more certain of the worker. She knew what annoyed him and also knew of his stamina in dealing with awkward people and situations. She also knew, and this sometimes distressed her, that the worker was interested in her in a professional manner, however unorthodox this may have appeared, and not because he was in love with her. The worker realized that they were building a deep and complex relationship, and he needed to be sure that no false assumptions were being made about each other.

Jamie was then able to talk to the worker sometimes deeply and always very guardedly. They would talk about her past, although she was mostly reluctant to mention this; and about its considerable influence on her present life about her increasing use of drugs; about her relationship with others; about their own relationship; about her wanting people to trust her, and so on. She began to rely on the worker and would often discuss decisions which she had made, or things that she had done, though almost always in retrospect. The worker understood her well enough to be cautious when advising her because she had the habit of doing the opposite of what people had recommended. Her life became more difficult mainly because of her increasing misuse of drugs, and because of the rows which she had with people.

A local man had felt sorry for Jamie and very soon after she appeared "on the scene" offered the use of a room in his house. Since she refused to sleep in the open in the winter, or in a derelict house, she found that she had to accept this offer. She was thankful for it in that it kept her dry and out of the way of the police, but she resented the control that this man now could hold over her. She broke out of this for a short spell and moved in with a prostitute who was registered on morphine. She hated this and for once, after a conversation with the worker, moved out and eventually moved back into the local man's house.

Whilst under the influence of a considerable number of sleeping pills, another drug addict injected her intravenously with nembutal. Jamie has hated this man ever since, because this action accelerated her slide into drug addiction and she was soon fixing huge quantities of methedrine.

She was arrested in Brighton for being disorderly whilst drunk in April 1968 and remanded for three weeks for psychiatric and medical reports in Holloway prison. She was conditionally discharged. Only three weeks later she was again in court on a charge of being disorderly and fighting with a barman. She told the court that she was unemployed and was fined $10 which she was allowed to pay under a probation order. She found the $10 very quickly, considering that she was not working. It was likely that she started to traffic drugs or again went on the streets to find the money. She would not tell the worker where she had got the money.

During the autumn of 1968, she became more and more involved in drugs and began to make trips to London to buy the stuff. By December 1968 she was regularly using eight ampoules of methedrine daily as well as several sleeping tablets.

Her desire to remain independent of people meant that she was reluctant to become registered at the local drug clinic, although she ran the risk of being arrested for being unlawfully in possession of drugs. She felt that to be registered as an addict would be an irreversible step for her. Eventually she registered at the clinic in December 1968, but felt so ashamed of this step that she kept it from people in the archway for several days.

At this time she appeared to undergo a change of personality. This seemed to be due to her registration as an addict. She became even more assertive and moody, and would take issue on almost any point mentioned. She seemed to revert to the way she behaved when she first arrived in Arch 141.

She moved into an apartment with a male addict. Since she was now registered, she was able to draw sick pay, and she could become more independent. She despised her flatmate and plagued the man, who had become very fond of her. She would pick at the sores on her mouth so that he could not kiss her, and one night she attacked him with a carving knife. She also threatened to leave him, and blackmailed him into buying her a coach ticket to Glasgow so that she could visit her mother at Christmas.

The relationship with the worker appeared to weaken during this period, and the worker often felt that he had little to offer Jamie. However, one night at midnight, Jamie rang the worker in obvious distress. She screamed that she was feeling suicidal and needed to talk with the worker. As she calmed, Jamie kept asking, "What ever happened to that sweet kid T _____." She often referred to her real name as if it belonged to a different person. After a long conversation and agonies of tears, the worker was able to take Jamie home again. The worker was convinced that she had been sufficiently upset to be careless about her next fix which could have killed her.

As part of being registered as a drug addict, each person was expected to "take a cure." No one seemed to expect these cures to work, but they did have the lifesaving effect of feeding up the addict again and making him physically more healthy. Jamie felt she was conned into entering a mental hospital in January 1969, but remained there for almost two months. The worker was able to visit her regularly and she began to build a useful relationship with a psychiatrist.

She appeared in court again in March 1969, accused of harboring a fugitive. One of her friends had run away from a remand home and Jamie had given her a cup of tea at the local man's home. She was again conditionally discharged.

Following her spell in the hospital, she contracted jaundice and was removed to an isolation hospital. A restriction was made about her visitors because the hospital was worried about drugs being smuggled into her. This was a very real worry in Jamie's case. Once she had recovered she began to argue with the staff, and one evening was forcibly removed to a restricted ward in a different hospital, where she spent the night in a padded cell.

Since her discharge from the hospital, she has remained out of serious trouble. She is still registered at the clinic and is still supplementing her dose from the black market. She has begun to grow independent from the worker. The worker knows that should Jamie really be in a tight situation then she will contact him. This is the type of situation which Jamie has wanted — a person whom she knows will trust her. On the occasion, the only one, that Jamie phoned the worker for 30 cents, the worker knew that she was desperate. He found her ill and wanting the bus fare to return to the local man's house. She also needed to buy dog food for her pet.

She will become more deeply involved with the drug scene, and will eventually be arrested for a drug offense, that is if she does not accidentally take an overdose one day. The only hope, because these situations do not remain static, is that the police will pick her up before she kills herself.

Cathy

Cathy told us that her father was a Black American serviceman and that her stepfather was a retired policeman. Her white mother, with whom she lived for only five months, placed her in a Church of England children's home. She lived in four different homes. The longest period was spent in a seaside town on the south coast. At 15½, she came to live in a home for boys and girls in Brighton. In 1968 Cathy was 18 years old, when she came into the Archway. She is of slim build, medium height, with a light brown skin, slighty negroid features, and short black curly hair. She dressed consistently in jeans, flat shoes, blouses, often under a V-necked pullover: the predominant color was dark blue. This style of dress made her look rather tomboyish. She tended to move in a rather gangly way. She spoke loudly and acted as she felt with little awareness of how she came across. She was the mother of one son, born when she was 16. She had not seen the father again. She worked on an assembly line making electronic equipment, a job at which she excelled, regularly receiving high pay for exceeding her output norms. However, even frequent shifts to different parts of the line did not reduce the ultimate tedium for her. She was prevented by her youth and brashness from being promoted. As she grew more confident, she relieved her boredom by taking an occasional day off.

Cathy first visited Arch 167 in the January of 1968, within three days of her move from the church home to a boarding house. The house-parents, known to her and the other children as aunt and uncle, had moved to another town at the same time. Cathy was introduced into the archway by her friend Millie, another girl of West Indian background. Millie knew some of the beats and the older, criminal-fringe Celts who frequented the beach and were coming to both Archways at that time.

Cathy was taking drugs, mostly dexedrine, to keep her awake and able to enjoy the all-night activities. She confined her drug-taking to Friday and Saturday nights as she said she needed her sleep on the other nights so she could go to work regularly. She also acted as a source of information for others who wanted drugs.

She was well liked because of her friendly and cheeky manner. She helped her friends if they were heavily drugged and always helped to take them somewhere to sleep it off when the archway closed. She also helped to hide her friend Millie who was on the run from the authorities. Millie was very much a "yo-yo absconder." She kept leaving and being returned to hostels and remand homes, and to our knowledge was picked up four times by Brighton police to be returned to her legally prescribed home. Millie always wanted Cathy to allow her to sleep in Cathy's room, but Cathy knew that this would get her thrown out of her lodgings, so she refused.

The first contact with Cathy was when one of the church hostel workers came to enquire about Millie's disappearance. The worker stood nearby as she spoke to Cathy, since we didn't want any unnecessary pressure put on her. This was the first of several such incidents when we observed Cathy acting as social worker. She telephoned the children's home to make excuses for Millie's absence, saying Millie was going to a friend's for the night; she helped soothe Innes one night when he was causing a commotion; another night she took the police, who had been sent for by the hostel matron on a tour of the town looking for Millie, though Millie was in fact in the Archway; on another night Cathy phoned the police because of a fight in the Archway between Hughie and Alan.

Looking back over Cathy's time with us in the Archway, it is possible to see a pattern of mutual relationships which are strikingly similar to the patterns of her behavior before we knew her. During the first weeks of her appearance in the archway, we knew her only as Cathy, the black girl, who wanted to put her handbag and coat in our storeroom to prevent them from being stolen. At first we unlocked the storeroom on each occasion. Before long, we trusted her and gave her the key whenever she needed it. The next step was to give her the key when she told us that we needed more coffee or sugar for the coffee-counter. However, one evening we discovered that she had abused this trust and was using the storeroom as a place to hide drugs. In the next few weeks she did this on several occasions, and each time we had a long discussion about our policy of not having drugs in the Archway and the uses and abuses of trust. Because we believe that accidents are caused rather than merely "happening," we thought that our discovery of Cathy's deviousness was intended by her. By letting us discover her hiding the drugs, she was, it seemed, asking for help.

From a position of initial trust between us, Cathy had tested us by her deviousness, through which we worked together to develop a deeper trust. This was confirmed to her because we did not ban her from the Archway, and continued to give her the keys. The worker also spent considerable time telling her of our disapproval of drugs in the Archway and making it clear to her that only her decisions could help her out of this dilemma. She was in a spiral situation from which she could see no exit. She said she took the drugs because she was scared, and that she was scared because the drug-pushers scared her. They scared her into buying drugs for their own profit, and because she then used the drugs, she felt guilty and more scared. It appeared to us that the only way she could break out of this trap was to learn to say no.

Many months later when we closed the project down, Cathy wrote a 27-page life history. This account shows that her devious behavior was well established during her childhood. She used deviousness as a testing out mechanism in the Archway because it was the only mechanism she had. Her account tends to highlight incidents of past deviousness, rather than feature exciting or happy adventures. She described incidents which seemed to us to have elicited unnecessarily unsympathetic responses from house parents. On one occasion, she went window-shopping rather than to go to church. But she was discovered by the house father, whom she thought had been following her (which was supported in her mind because he was an ex-policeman). He insisted on taking her into church for the last five minutes. On another occasion, she decided to keep ten shillings which had been given to her to place in her post office savings account. Though she copied a signature into the book, it was not stamped, and this misdemeanor was also discovered by the house father:

> *"He hit me around my ear hard and pulled me in his office by my ear and said 'This is a very serious thing you've done; do you realize you could go to prison for it?' I didn't know. He asked for the ten shillings back but I'd spent it on soap and toilet stuff. Then I was sent to bed. Uncle said this man who came to see me about this bank book was a C.I.D."*

Her misdemeanors were short-term responses to the apparently impersonal atmosphere of the home. She describes another incident:

> *"I remember I lost my temper over a boy because I wanted to do a puzzle by myself and he kept putting bits in.*

81

I was sent to bed because I threw all the pieces on the floor."

She was about 12 years of age at the time. She seemed to have developed an impulsive pattern of just doing the things she felt like doing at the time. The home's response to this was to punish her. She remembers being threatened with loss of pocket money when she refused to eat fat meat at the age of five — when in fact she did not even know what pocket money was. Her life story seems to illustrate that as long as she acquiesced to the home's demands and regulations she was accepted; it appears that no attempt was made to help her understand or to learn to be autonomous. This careful, well-regulated home life in no way equipped her to make choices. A tragic example of this was that she was unable to prevent herself repeating her own history by having an illegitimate child.

One area in which she did, in fact, gain from the home was her attitude in maintaining a stable job. She realized that in order to have a secure supply of money to enable her to retain her lodgings, buy cosmetics, clothes and cigarettes, and have money for entertainment, she needed to keep her job. She was quite emphatic about not taking drugs during the week, because they might stop her from getting up on time and going to work regularly.

Immediately after the testing out period Cathy began to tell us about people who were trying to push drugs in the archway. We talked about the possibility of her confronting these people herself and telling them she did not want them in the archway.

At this time we also talked about her potential to effect a change and make the archway a more fulfilling place. Though she was not willing to take on such arduous work as confronting people, which the workers themselves were only learning about, she did find a way to be positively helpful. She decided quite spontaneously and on her own accord to collect and wash the cups at closing time and to sweep and mop the kitchen area. At times she shared this task with Jamie and one or two other girls she knew, but generally she thought of it as her responsibility. Because she was helpful in this way the workers decided that we would offer her more interesting tasks, and invited her to be responsible for collecting all the newspaper reports about the project and any of the people connected with it. She would come along to our office on her afternoon off and work her way conscientiously through piles of newspapers. On many occasions when we met for this purpose, the discussions with the workers would be chatty and gossipy. However, as we got to know each other better, we all felt more able to talk about personal matters. Cathy had initially been reluctant to do this. She did, however want to talk about sex. Her first experiences of sex, resulting in the birth of her son, seemed to have left her feeling, if not guilty, certainly hard done by; "I fell for a baby," and "the boy always gets off free." It seemed for her sex was not related to feelings. Cathy's feeling was that this experience was an event which happened to her: she still had to learn the delicate and tender responses necessary to sustain a loving relationship. Like all teenagers, she was interested in finding out about sex and relationships. She often talked with the workers, seeking information and understanding about sexual relationships, though her inquisitiveness was at first considerably hampered by her use of innuendo and euphemisms. On and off for some months, we discussed her anxieties about the future of her son. Mostly this was about her concern as to whether or not she should allow the foster-parents to adopt the boy. In fact, she has never been able to make up her mind. Though she realizes he has a good home she is unwilling to give up the only family she has.

Also during this time, Cathy's femininity began to blossom. Though she retained her jeans and jersey for Archway use, when she came to the office or visited our homes, she wore skirts, long socks and skinny bumpers, which were currently fashionable among working girls.

We also spent a lot of time talking about her use of drugs and the need for her to choose whether to buy and take them or to say no. She took a considerable step when she finally decided to inform the police about a pusher, one of the "Celtic fringe," who in the past had taken a lot of her money for drugs and who now wanted her to take a forged prescription to be made up. This was a significant positive decision, in which she was able to say "no" to someone else and "yes" for herself.

During this time, Cathy, through her knowledge and friendships with the workers had been able to build a kind of extended family for herself. On different occasions she confided in each of us.

When the Archway went into its closing down period, we were very careful to explain to Cathy that eventually we would also have to close the office, and that we would need to make other arrangements to see each other. For a few months after the project closed we saw her intermittently, and then during most of 1970 we only saw her by chance when out shopping, and she only came round once. This was a marked contrast to the considerable amount of time she had previously spent with us in the Archway, office and our homes. We presumed that she now had a life of her own, and this was confirmed by occasional comments from other people. It may be that she stayed away from us to prove that she could do without us. Whatever her reasons, she had built a life of her own.

Early in 1971 she telephoned and Jago asked her to lunch. On this occasion we were able to catch up with a great deal of news about each other. She told him about leaving her old job and trying several different ones — she was about to start another new one. She has had a steady boyfriend for almost a year and she experiences sex as a natural part of this happy relationship, rather than thinking of it as something done to her. She was much freer in talking about her feelings and used far fewer euphemisms in discussing their domestic arrangements. She also took great pride in telling us that she had not taken any drugs for more than a year. She had also saved up enough money to be able to go for a day trip to Belgium with her workmates. She now has a bed sitting room of her own after a period spent living with a family. She also reminded us that it would soon be her 21st birthday. When Jago visited her to take a birthday present, Cathy told him that she had been made a charge hand at her new job and that she felt appreciated because this was a recognition of her skill and responsibility.

Over the three years we knew her, Cathy had gone through many of the normal stages of growing up. She has tested out her own autonomy against other people in many different situations: several factories, a boarding house, and the Archway. Like many young people she has passed through a period of experimenting with drugs and sex and is now testing herself in more stable relationships. Her own disadvantages: being at the mercy of a rather impersonal system, the lack of any deep family ties, and having a child at an early age, have not prevented her from becoming a reasonably normal, happy, young woman.

The Young People

Some 20,000 young people used the Archway scheme during nine Bank Holiday weekends in which it was in operation. The moods, fashion sense and values of the young people changed considerably during those three years from Whitsun 1966 to Easter 1969, and obviously one group differs considerably from another.

An attempt has been made to describe some of the groups of young people who were in evidence, and this has been related to the year in which they appeared. For instance, the hippies appeared only during 1967, and there were only a few rockers in the archway during 1967 and 1968. The categories used in this chapter are somewhat ephemeral. They are only of importance in describing some general aspects of the youth scene. For this purpose, therefore, we distinguish:

A	Scooter Boys	G	Beats
B	Hard Mods	H	Girls
C	Younger Boys	I	Students
D	Smooth Mods	J	Youth Hostellers and Campers
E	Rockers	K	Couples
F	Hippies	L	Older People

The types of young people mentioned in this list have existed at different times throughout the three year period from Whitsun 1966 until Easter 1969. At the early Bank Holiday weekends in 1966, the scooter boys, the hard mods and the rockers were very much in evidence. However, by 1968, the scooter boys had disappeared and a better dressed and more sophisticated young man was in evidence. During the summer of 1967, the psychedelic year, the hippies arrived wearing fantastic clothes and bells around their necks.

Although the terms mods and rockers, which appear in the list, are in general use, they are confusing since the young people making up these groups have changed so considerably during the years, that the classification ceases to have any concise meaning. For instance, the term mod has been used by the press when referring to any one of our categories of the scooter boys, the hard mods, the younger boys, the smooth mods, the girls and some of the couples. The hard mods remained apparently unchanged in dress and mannerisms throughout the three years, except that they also wore bells around their necks during the early summer of 1967. There were always a number of young boys, who were learning how to behave from the older boys. The girls tended not be to distinguished on their own account, but rather by which group of boys they were with. Several youth hostellers or campers appeared each weekend unable to get into either the youth hostel or the campsite. Students tended to crowd out the archway during the early Bank Holidays but they were around less by the later weekends. A variety of couples have made use of the scheme. It seems that it is useful to distinguish the couples from the others because the other groups were mainly male, and a couple involved with one of the groups tended to be perceived as separate by the group. The rockers have been in existence in Brighton throughout the three years, but they have not used the archway consistently during that time. Their habits appear to have changed, although their dress has remained unaltered. The last group listed, which caused the archway helpers more headaches than any other, are also called the older ones. These tougher more criminal men often tried to convince the helpers that they were under 25, when it was obvious that they were not. This was the group of people to whom it was necessary to deny entry to the archway.

The beats will be mentioned only briefly and are discussed in greater detail in a separate section.

A — The Scooter Boys

As the name suggests, these young men were very much involved with scooters. They were very similar to the idea that police and press had of the mods of 1964/65. They dressed smartly, yet casually in trousers and pullovers at the Bank Holiday weekends, and wore long anoraks when riding the scooters. These anoraks were often trimmed with fur at the collars, cuffs and hoods. Many were only half prepared for the night, they would produce just a blanket or a sleeping bag in the sleeping centers. They had come expecting to sleep on the beach, although having a means of transporting luggage on the rack of their scooters, they had not prepared themselves for a rough night. They seemed to move about in convoys of about 8-10 scooters during 1966/67 (though this number is reported in the press to have been as large as 25-30 machines in 1964 or 1965). By the August of 1967, very few scooter boys were seen.

Most seemed to be within the 17-20 age range, and none appeared to be under 16. This may have been because these younger ones could not have been legally entitled to drive a scooter. Helpers found that it was easy to hold a conversation with this group, and, generally, they were responsive to the helpers' requirements. They seemed gentle, and seemed able to understand that people different from them had a different view of them. They appeared uninterested in the violence that had occurred and their only mishaps seemed to be with the letter of the law. These were usually concerned with speeding, driving without lights, driving with a pillion passenger without a full driving license or driving without a license at all. They talked about their encounters with the police in a nonaggressive way.

They appeared to be permanently employed. It seems that they were used to spending quite a considerable sum of money when they went out for a weekend. It was interesting that the groups seemed to be made up of young men with very different incomes. One group, for instance was talking about how they afforded to make so many trips around the country. One boy talked of most of them being in sufficiently well-paid jobs for them to be able to save up for a fortnight's holiday in a matter of a few weeks, whereas some of their number, who had opted for apprenticeships, had to save up for most of the year for their holiday. The difference in the income was considerable. The apprentice would earn about $12 per week and another one, who was working as a waiter, could earn $38 or $40 per week. It was interesting that adolescents with such very different incomes could co-exist happily in the same group.

There is no record of where these young people lived, though it was listed that many of them came from the East end of London. Many seemed discontented with their jobs, and used the Bank Holiday weekends as a means of compensating for their discontentment. They talked of dressing up and taking their "birds" to dances at home. Certainly, they had come to Brighton looking for some excitement, including finding new girls, and they seemed unprepared to involve themselves in any bother. It might be supposed that they were able to channel much of their exuberance into their scooter rides.

Before 1966, a lot of the trouble that occurred in Brighton is said to have been caused by the scooter boys. It can only

88

be assumed that the groups had altered by 1966/67, or that the scooter boys of 1965 became the smooth mods of 1966. Also scooters were the first cheap form of private transport for the non rockers in the 1950s. It could be that with more money available to this group a wider range of vehicles were being used.

B — The Hard Mods

One kind of gear seemed almost a uniform for the three years in which the project had operated with the hard mods. In the day, these young men would appear in heavy shoes or boots (sometimes with steel caps for protection) jeans supported by braces, open neck shirts or a round necked pullover, and their hair was always cut very short (early skin heads and the origins of punk). Most also carried a dark colored wind cheater for extra warmth at night. It was unusual to see any of these carrying anything burdensome. Their necks were always free of any restriction like collars or cravats.

They moved around in very large groups. In the streets of Brighton, the group could, on rare occasions, be as large as 200 and yet, as they arrived to sleep at the sleeping centers the groups were never greater than 30. They gave many helpers the impression of being jumpy and unsure of themselves (and they were easily recognized at any Bank Holiday weekend because they moved around in these very large groups for their own safety). They tended to be self-absorbed and it was difficult for the helpers to make jokes with them, because the mods appeared unsure of whether to join in the laughter or not. It would take several hours of severe testing out before the helpers became accepted by any of these groups.

"The boys from Hounslow and Southend — about 30 in number — got involved in a fight with some local boys in Ship Street outside a pub. One of them, and six of the local boys went to Sussex County Hospital for minor

89

repairs, stitches and bandages. Our boys (those from Hounslow and Southend) were expecting revenge all night and waited in the hall with chairs and bottles, ready for trouble. Any slight disturbance outside and they all ran into Air Street, but everyone else in Brighton had gone to bed. After about eight false alarms, everybody settled down to sleep around 3 a.m. Then a West Indian boy called Sambo, and his rather high mates crept around the back of the hall into the girls' room, from which they were ejected quickly. They came back into the boy's hall, which was then a total darkness, shouting, running and jumping. Panic. Half the hall sprang to attack the invaders for a short time. Chairs and fists were flying wildly until the lights were put on and everybody gradually calmed down. By about 4 a.m. everyone was back to sleep.''

Recorded conversation shows that they appeared to talk a lot about their parents having a control over them, and it became apparent to the helpers that they needed to prove to the helpers that figures of authority, such as their parents or the police, and also other groups of young people, had little effect on their existence. It was obvious, both in the way they talked and in the way that they behaved in Brighton, that the group identities became the support for the sum of individuals who were so unsure of themselves. It seemed that the group could partially substitute for parental support. Their strength lay in the size of the group, and their individual prowess seemed to be related to their status within the group, and to the incidents that the group became involved in. The group support was a protection for the individual, but the protection extended to seemingly protecting the individual from reality. For instance, the group support and protection at times enabled individuals to stab other young people, or boot them in the face, which they would most probably not have done if on their own.

They were full of stories of dare-devil escapades, and of fights with other young people, and of brutal encounters with the police. Some of these stories were obviously fictitious but an incident in the Top Rank Suite at the Whitsun 1968 Bank Holiday weekend showed at least one of these groups was capable of being involved in particularly unpleasant situations.

On this occasion, the boys were in the dance suite in a body of about 35 people. They were obviously creating a disturbance because a bouncer told one of the group to leave. The boy obviously took exception to being singled out and so pulled a gun from out of his pocket and threatened the bouncer with it. Apparently, the bouncer had said "Go on then, pull the trigger," to which the youth had replied "I haven't any bullets." The gun was a toy capgun. The youth was then in the position of having had his bluff called, and he was defenseless. Obviously, loss of face was involved in this as well. His friends realized this and created a tremendous uproar in the dance suite to make sure that they did keep the upper hand. There was a bloody fight and the police and the ambulance were called. Many of the boys had to visit the hospital for first aid.

Members of the group were arriving all night at one of the sleeping centers where they were staying. From their conversation with helpers, it appeared that these young people had come to Brighton with the intention of enjoying themselves. Their habit seemed to be to look for excitement, and if it did not appear, then the group was prepared to create the excitement themselves. The excitement could become violent and, on occasions, they seemed content even to fight amongst themselves. They were recognized by the helpers as being the likely provocateurs in any incident in which they were involved.

On their own, the members of the group appeared very different. They knew that their strength was with the group, and they had obvious fears about being separated from the others. This is borne out by the concern that the members of the group were showing, after the incident in the Top Rank Suite, about the individuals who were either alone in hospital or in the police station. Some even seemed scared that their friends might have been detained by the police. The relief shown by those waiting for their mates, as each member of the group appeared, was quite startling to the helpers.

Another incident, which is quite different, shows this in another way. One youth had become separated from his friends. It appeared that they had gone home, leaving him on his own in Brighton. He arrived at one of the sleeping centers with blood all over his face, moaning that he had been hurt really bad. He refused to be looked at, but eventually one of the helpers persuaded him that it would be advisable to clean up his face. The youth had been muttering stories of knives and chains and to look at his face, it appeared that there were several razor slashes across his face. It soon became obvious why he had been reluctant to have his face cleaned. The blood had been wiped away, there were no marks at all on his face. He had no more than a nose-bleed, and it was likely that he had not even been involved in a fight. With the fantasy gone he went into the hall and woke up all those sleeping, behaving like a child in a tantrum. The youth was conscious that he was on his own, he had got drunk, and had got a nose bleed. This made him appear fearsome.

The helpers found that it was quite easy to cope with this type of youngster if they heeded the values and motivations of the group.

Each group appeared to have a leader or a pair of leaders. The leader, or leaders, would make the group decisions. In the sleeping centers, these would be things like deciding at what time they would wake up in the morning; whether or not they should "play up" the helpers in the sleeping centers; what time they should leave the centers; whether or not they would fold up their blankets, etc. Once the decision had been made, the others followed it, often immediately. This meant that once the leader or leaders had recognized that the helpers were okay then all was plain sailing in the sleeping centers. The members of the group could be relaxed without each person having to be on the defensive.

There was usually a clown or a chatter-box (often, and probably mistakenly, called the "brains") who was able to dispel or create tension within the group easily. This joker was able to save situations by making the others laugh, and conversely, he also liked to create tension simply for the sake of a laugh. One of the best examples of this occurred in one of the very early weekends, when the joker found a hammer in another boy's rucksack. Halfway through the night, he had gone around to each person sleeping in one of the rooms, had thrust the hammer under their nose, waking them up and asked each one "Is this yours, mate?" In an atmosphere of potential violence this had an electric effect on the sleepers as they were woken up. There was no disputing that the incident was sadistically humorous.

These groups were obviously self-sufficient within their own sub-culture which meant that few external trends had an effect on them. For instance, their dress has remained unaltered for the whole of the three years of the project, whereas other groups have changed considerably. There was one incident which did appear to be out of character for this type of young person. During 1967, the hippies, who are described later, had started to wear small high-pitched bells around their necks. Surprisingly, this caught on with the mods, and for one weekend, Whitsun 1967, they wore bells around their necks like the majority of young people in Brighton. It lasted only for that one weekend. This was one of the few occasions that they had taken up anything that originated from outside the group.

The records show that the majority of the young people in this group were between 16 and 19 years old, and most came from the North or the West of London. During the later Bank Holiday weekends, when helpers were asked to find out where the young people came from, the towns mentioned most often, with reference to this group, were Ealing, Acton, Chiswick, Wembley, Harrow, Richmond, Hammersmith, and also further out of the center of London, Staines, Uxbridge, Watford, Luton, Barnet and Enfield. It was interesting that as this group emerged as being most common in Brighton, the number of young people from the East end of London dropped. At the Easter 1968 Bank Holiday weekend, of the total of 380 young people who told us where they lived, there were none recorded as having come from the East end of London. It was obvious during that weekend that there were no scooters around either. A simple deduction could be made that those with scooters appear to come from the East end of London, and those without, from the other parts of London.

They were usually reasonably well off, though there were occasions when individuals would ask their friends to lend them the fare home. Most managed to bring enough money to last out for the whole of the three days of the Bank Holiday.

They had little contact with girls, though occasionally a couple would attach themselves to a large group of this nature. There were never any free-floating girls within the group. The boys' dress and behavior was not such to attract the girls and this was probably another way in which the group protected its members from outside influences.

This group differed considerably from the scooter boys. It has already been suggested that the scooter boys were able to channel their exuberance into riding their scooters, and perhaps the behavior of these mods is an indication of what happens if there is no suitable provision for coping with the excitement and exuberance of adolescence. With a means of transport, the scooter boys were encouraged to be independent and go places, and this either made or attracted outward-looking young people. On the other hand, the scooterless boys did not travel, except to the seaside, and they were definitely an inward-looking group.

By a simple comparison of these two groups, it would seem sensible to encourage mobility in the young. It was not possible to explore this idea in any detail, but it was obvious that the hard mods were less socially adaptable than were the scooter boys.

The hard mods have appeared at all Bank Holiday weekends between Whitsun 1966, and Easter 1969. There is evidence that they were also involved in the disturbances of 1964.

C — The Younger Boys

There were always several boys of less than sixteen involved with the older boys. There were also sixteen-year-olds who were unable to get involved in any group, and would be left on their own. These boys, who were on their own, could see the excitement and safety offered by larger groups, and seemed to be trying to get themselves accepted by them. The groups, which the younger ones were trying to get into, were most often those described as the hard mods. There is an obvious link between the insecurity of the younger boys, probably because of their lack of years, and the insecurity of the larger groups.

Those who were on their own but drifted together in their twos and threes, were the ones that the helpers noticed most. There was one possible exception at the Easter 1969 weekend, when a group of eight, all under 16, had come to Brighton together from Victoria. They were very tired by the time they arrived at the sleeping center, yet they were determined to keep awake for as long as they could. Part of the thrill and exploration in coming to Brighton was to stay awake for the whole night. The older ones could manage this with little fuss, but the younger ones had to get very lively to stop themselves from falling asleep, and this tended to keep the remainder awake.

On the whole, the younger boys appeared to respond well to the helpers, though often in a playful way. On occasions, it was possible for a helper to say to them that it was probably time they got some sleep, and they would go to sleep.

Many of the helpers were concerned about the younger ones, because they were so young and made efforts to ensure that they were as comfortable as possible. One helper wrote in the log about the group that came from Victoria:

> ". . . One in particular is very restive, he looks worn out and overtired and keeps moving from spot to spot. This group has enough blankets between them to keep the rest of the sleepers warm; we feel that if they get as comfortable as possible, they'll drop off to sleep."

Many helpers expressed the idea that it was more than fortunate that the Bank Holiday accomodation scheme was in operation as far as the younger boys were concerned. Several helpers appeared thankful each time a young one appeared in the safety of a sleeping center, because they were still only children trying out the "bright lights of Brighton." Two boys of 12 and 13 were given a lift home to Streatham during the Whitsun 1966 weekend. Their father wrote a letter of thanks to the scheme.

D — The Smooth Mods

Whereas the types of young people already mentioned tended to wear casual and work clothes, there were a number of young men who came to Brighton dressed very smartly. Most of these seemed intent on "looking for a bird," but there were a few others who came to Brighton as leaders of a group of younger men. These better dressed young men were mainly aged between 17 and 22, i.e. they were older than those already mentioned. It is easier to deal with each of these separately.

These young men seemed to have a very clear idea of how they were going to enjoy themselves in Brighton during the Bank Holiday weekends. They were expecting to make use of the Top Rank Dance Suite, probably with the intention of pairing up with a girl, either for the evening or for the weekend. From their somewhat limited conversations with the helpers, they gave the impression that they were hoping to spend the night with a girl, the helpers felt that this was mainly big talk.

Some came to Brighton with their girlfriends (these are dealt with in section k — couples) but often their mates would be on their own, and those without girls were the ones who appeared to be most uncomfortable.

Probably one disadvantage of setting out with clear ideas of how the weekend will progress was that the plans did not always come to fruition and many of these better dressed young men were very disappointed. The major drawback was that there were not enough girls to go around. In one group, which is mentioned later in this section, five boys managed to "pick up" two girls. The tension that was created within the group appears clearly in the difficulty that the helpers had with them in a sleeping center. With there being so few girls around, most sleeping centers at any weekend had two or three well-dressed young men sitting in the entrance of the hall, on the off-chance that a suitable partner would appear.

It was not surprising that most of these appeared sullen and non-communicative in the sleeping centers. It was not possible for the helpers to get any clear idea where the individuals came from. In this way, this group appeared to disturb the helpers more than other groups because they would make use of all the facilities grudgingly, and without any show of gratitude. This may have been because the young men needed to be independent of anybody in case they found a girl. In addition, during 1967, which was when this group was most conspicuous they seemed to be taking pep pills in the evenings to keep them going. By the time they arrived at the sleeping centers, the effects of the pills were beginning to wear off, leaving many of them in a depressed state. This made it hard for the helpers to feel at ease with these young men.

They were affluent compared with the other young people, though it was not possible to decide whether this was because they saved up for the weekend or because they had well-paying jobs. Being prepared to support a girl for the weekend, in such places as the Top Rank Suite and the 101 club, meant bringing a considerable sum of money to Brighton.

Although this group of young people had come to Brighton knowing what they intended to do, they appeared to have no real idea of how to carry this out. Much of their conversation, which was limited, revolved about events of the minute. Few were able to see what they intended to do in the following hours, and remarks made by one group in the sleeping center were usually of the type "What's happening now?" One boy in this group, who was getting upset about being left out of the fun that his two mates were having with the two girls, was all ready to start something. However, he did not say "When they come in . . .," he said "If they come in **now** . . .,"

This continual hopping from one mood to another created a feeling of mistrust, and tended to increase the difficulties of talking with them.

During 1967, more young people started coming to Brighton in cars than on two wheels. There were some groups who acquired a large van, filling it with anybody who wanted to go to Brighton. It may have been that each person going on the ride shared some of the cost of the van, but this is not known for certain. The drivers tended to be older and much smarter dressed than the others in the group. He would be between 17 and 22, and the others between 16 and 18/19. The younger ones in this group seemed to be the link between the younger boys and the scooterless boys, as already described in the text. They had used an older person or persons to get them to Brighton and yet they would be on their own once in Brighton. The van would take them home again.

It is easier to describe two groups of this nature, who joined together after apparently passing each other many times on the journey to Brighton. The leader of one group, who was about 23, was dressed casually though smartly, and was obviously the driver of the dormobile; he had brought about five others with him who were about 16 or 17 years old. They were dressed very much in the way that the hard mods dressed except that the uniform was not complete. They gave the impression that they were a young group trying to copy the others. The other group had a leader and deputy. Both were dressed in expensively cut navy-blue suits and were very smart. They were about 19 or 20, compared with the other four boys who were again about 16 or 17 years old. These four were dressed very similarly to the younger ones in the first group.

From the way that they dressed, and from the way that they behaved with the girl helpers, it was supposed that the suited young men were hoping that they would pick up a girl for the weekend, or for the day, although this was never declared as openly as by those already described in the first part of this section. It seemed that the leaders of both groups were more than ready to drop the younger ones, and move around the town on their own. This was not always easy because the younger ones were taking their lead from the leaders. Paradoxically, the leaders seemed content to let them build on this dependence. There was one incident which illustrates this well. One of the suited men pulled out a packet of cigarettes from his pocket; there were five in it. He gave one to his deputy and one to the other 23-year-old leader of the other group and said to the other nine younger ones "Catch!" He then threw the two remaining cigarettes into the air, and watched as the nine boys clamored for them.

E — The Rockers

During the 1950s, considerable national publicity was given to several large groups of motorcyclists, who were considered delinquent and hazardous to motorists particularly on the North Circular Road, London.

The groups were recognized as being aggressive and violent from their daredevil escapades; from the speed at which they rode (each young person within the group needed to have ridden faster than 100 mph — i.e. 'done the Ton'); from their apparent indifference to death or accident; from their black leathers, the size of their groups and their high powered motor bikes.

Various terms, often of a derogatory nature, were used to describe them. "Ton-up boys" and "Leather boys," as used in the 1950s have been superseded by rockers and greasers and hell's angels. The term rockers is used in this report for convenience and because it appears to be the least offensive.

The term, rocker, was used as long ago as 1964 to describe one section of the young people involved in the mod and rocker riots. The type of young person may not have changed, we have no check on this, but certainly those in 1964 all appeared to have motorcycles, whereas this was not true for those in Brighton during Easter 1969. The term, greaser, was the favorite name used by the beats. It is spoken and understood as a term of abuse. Rockers are easily recognized by their dress, leather jerkin, leather trousers or jeans, calf-length boots, neckerchief and crash helmet. Many had long greasy hair, so that it appeared well below the mandatory crash helmet.

The rockers rarely used the archway. There seemed to be nothing in Brighton to attract them. However, a motorcycle exhibition was staged in Brighton at the Metropole Exhibition Hall at the Easter Bank Holiday weekend of 1969, and thousands of motorcycling enthusiasts were attracted to the town. Most of these were young people who could not be categorized as rockers in the way we define the group.

Several of the helpers were apprehensive about working with these young people in the Archway. Those helpers who had been working on the scheme before knew that these were new, and no one was certain how they would react. In fact, they were found to be the most cooperative group of people who used the Archway and sleeping centers.

It was hardly surprising that some of the helpers felt apprehensive about them because they appeared most formidable. They moved about in very large groups, at times up to 80 strong. Words and phrases, often painted on their clothing, were preoccupied with death. At Easter 1969 weekend, these were recorded as being the most common: Hell's Angels; Red Hawks; White Hawks; Death Squad. Two very popular signs were swastiksas and skulls and crossbones.

An unusual feature was that they seemed unconcerned about giving passersby information about themselves. Much was communicated on their jackets. Some had the name of the town from which they came, many had the name of the gang to which they belonged, such as Red Hawks; some even painted their name on their jackets, Pete or Mitch. Several sported "59-Club" badges and many had the make of their motorcycles appearing somewhere on their effects. This brazenness about themselves was worrying too many people. They appeared self-assured in their groups, which was not the impression one got from many of the other groups.

The helpers eventually found the rockers easy to cope with as they responded much more quickly than did many other young people. On many occasions, as a group of boys in leathers arrived at a sleeping center, all talking and shouting at once, if a helper asked that they should be quiet because there were others asleep, invariably they would go silent. And they seemed happy to do so. Helpers also recorded that boys in leathers would fold their blankets in the mornings at the sleeping centers, and make a point of thanking the helpers for the night's accomodation. This was unusual as the majority of other young people tended to be grudgingly courteous rather then distinctly polite. Another incident in the archway illustrates their reasonable attitudes. A large group of boys in leather had brought in some bottles of cider with them, and began drinking. The terms of the lease forbade the use of alcohol. A helper explained the situation and without any fuss they went outside, finished their drink and came back in.

This group contrasted very well with those young men, described as smooth mods, who were shifty, unresponsive and sufficiently unsure of themselves with other people. This self-assurance, and lack of tension within the groups, suggested an absence of overt aggression and many helpers thought that they would not be the aggressors in a fight. Their clothing, however, was somewhat aggressive.

Records show that these leather boys came from all over the country; there seemed no distinct area from which they came. At Easter 1969, no less than 10 percent of those young people, who gave information about their home town, came from further north than the Midlands. Two came from the Northest of England. There were some from the London suburbs, but no detailed recording was possible.

One of the most fascinating discoveries about this group of young people was that only about half of them owned or even rode a motorcycle. Those without bikes travelled to

Brighton by train in their gear, and joined in with those with bikes once in Brighton. There seemed to be no particular concern within these amalgamated groups about these differences. This is illustrated by an incident when a group of about 20 boys dressed in leather were informed of a sleeping center two miles out of Brighton, they were able to say without any obvious embarrassment that only half of them had bikes. Much of this self-assurance could have been because they were quite an old group. Their ages ranged from about 17 to 25. And there were one or two people older than that. Very few girls were associated with this group and no couples were recorded.

There was one rather humorous event, which involved these boys dressed in their leather clothing. A helper was driving a group of these boys in a van up to one of the sleeping centers. Each time he turned a corner, he could hear a strange staccato sound coming from the back of the van, which could be heard distinctly through the chatter of the travellers. The helper found it a bit disconcerting at first, until he discovered that as he turned a corner many of the boys shoulders banged against the side of the van, and the staccato sound was a result of the many hundreds of studs in their jackets coming into contact with the van.

F — The Hippies

Hippies have been in Brighton for some considerable time, but their numbers suddenly increased at Whitsun 1967. At this weekend, there were about 200 using the archway as a social center. Most were between 17 and 25, though there were a few a little older. There were about as many boys as there were girls, a different picture from other groups of young people.

They were easily recognizable by their dress, which was extremely unconventional by the students of 1967. Both boys and girls wore ill-fitting clothes, such as wide bell-bottomed trousers, loose jackets, floppy pullovers, cloaks, kaftans, bedspreads, anything colorful. One local man possessed two suits; one was colored bright orange and splashed with scarlet and the other was red and white in harlequin style. Almost everyone wore high pitched bells around their necks. They tended to wear their hair long, sometimes fluffed out in the style of Jimi Hendrix. The girls dressed very similarly though their hair tended to be shorter than that of many boys! Those who called themselves hippies ranged, in our categorization, from the regular beats to young people with steady jobs, who dressed oddly at weekends. As is implied by those becoming hippy for the weekend, those in regular employment did find that their jobs were the least interesting part of their lives. There were many others who were not at all interested in work. Some, who were close to the beats, were unable to hold down regular employment, either because they found the type of jobs they could do completely boring, or because they were unable to accept the routine of a job. There were a few who felt that work was a symptom of the values of present day society and that it should, therefore, be avoided, and there were others who used this argument as a rationalization for not working.

Many seemed preoccupied with searching out new experiences. Many talked in terms of the present day living as being lifeless and meaningless. They would say "Who is living today? Most are just existing." They felt that the values of society were all wrong for them. Those who were able to articulate the need for experimentation said that this could only occur with a new set of values. They felt that our present vocabulary was insufficient to describe the new experience. One of the ways in which they did practice this need for expansion of experiences was by taking the hallucinogen LSD. They talked mainly of having "fantastic trips" and explained the wonderful experience in terms of colors and shapes. This is disconcerting to people who are not familiar with the drug because colors and shapes are not the most important things in life. And yet these people had found a set of values in the immediate sensory experience in which these were important. Few were involved in the hard drug circles in Brighton.

They also aimed to create an unusual atmosphere about themselves, such as burning joss-sticks or blowing soap bubbles while walking along the seafront or sitting in the archway. Many also painted their feet, faces and clothes with designs which were basically stylized flower designs. This was the year in which the word "psychedelic" was introduced into our vocabulary from drug use. Its meaning then was not very clear, but it was associated very closely with the way in which the hippies wanted to experience life.

An interesting side issue was that when Archway 167 was first used at the Ester 1967 weekend, two volunteers had painted many stylized colored flowers and leaves on the outside doors of the archway. This had happened before the hippies had appeared and it seemed as if it meant we had anticipated the mood of the year. At the Whitsun 1967 weekend, the workers were concerned that the flowers on the door might have too great a hippie feeling about the Arch, which would discourage other young people from using the archway.

Many of the conversations that helpers held with the hippies were concerned with rejection of contemporary values. Some of these conversations became very depressing. For instance, one boy spent a long time trying to convince a helper that there was no point in living. Many were certain that there was no point in working for the benefit of other people, and most said that there was no point in being respectable, for instance, in their dressing habits because there was no point in conforming to standards.

The main characteristic of this group was their gentleness. Very few seemed prepared to show their anger, or even to raise their voices. There was one incident which illustrates this well. A group of hippies had been obstructing the lower promenade and a policeman started to get cross with them, and started to push a few of them in their backs quite violently. This would have provoked any of the other groups, already mentioned, into some retaliatory action, but all that happened was that one of those being pushed carefully presented the policeman with a chrysanthemum.

An issue with this group was their effect on the passerby, who were more provoked by the hippies than by any of the other more active groups of young people. There were many scenes of fascinated passersby accumulating to watch a group of hippies. There was one crowd of 100 people leaning over the upper balustrade watching a girl paint her feet. The comments revealed a mixture of wonder and horror: "Look! They're painting their feet;" "Isn't it disgusting?"

The behavior of this group seemed to make people's minds run riot. People saw these strange things happening which they seemed unable to understand and, for some reason, they assumed that all the nasty things that they imagined also happened with this group. This appears in more detail in the section on the beats. A simple illustration of this is seen in the complaints that were made to the town corporation about the hippies. The complainants said that they had seen these people making love on the beach. This group became a mirror of the "respectable" people's imagination, and it was startling what so-called respectable people could imagine!

Generally it would appear that the hippie movement in Brighton followed a similar movement in the U.S.A., so that when the hippie life ended in San Francisco in the spring of 1968, hippies ceased to exist in Brighton as well.

G — The Beats

Many young people came to Brighton during the summer months with the intention of going beat. This was often a consequence of wanting to avoid responsibilities associated with parents, wives, examinations, the police and so on. Some stayed for years, others were not seen again after the August Bank Holiday. Some beats have reputedly always been around Brighton.

They move around Brighton in ones or twos and, when they meet, it is in a manner which does not interfere with other people. They are a passive group and when people are abusive to them, they mostly walk away from the unpleasant situation rather than stay to defend themselves. Two incidents are recorded when the beats were attacked by passersby. A waste bin was emptied over one group of beats, and another group had stones thrown at them by some holidaymakers. In both cases, the beats did nothing but walk away.

They dress oddly, often copying the style of dress of the hippies. The sad point is that some are still wearing the very same clothes that they were wearing two years previously. Their long hair, dirty appearance and their tendency to be rude in conversation, makes them unattractice to others. Many people find them so repulsive that they talk of terrible ways of getting rid of them. One group of people in Brighton even wanted to train fire hoses on them.

There is a fascination about beats which is felt by many people. Several well-dressed young girls come to Brighton to meet the beats, and there is always a crowd of people leaning over the balustrade at the bottom of West Street, looking at a group of beats on the beach. The beats are able to make use of this ambivalent attitude that people have about them; repulsion on the one hand and fascination on the other. They con money, cigarettes, cups of tea, out of the Brighton holiday-makers.

H — The Girls

The girls at the weekends were mostly between 15 and 19. Very few above that age came into the archway or the sleeping centers. It could be that these older ones are more certain of having a boyfriend steady enough to bring them to Brighton. These girls, unattached to any single boy, seemed to be anxious to keep on the fringe of a group of boys. Experience shows that all male groups, with the exception of the younger boys, would have a few girls on the fringe. They seemed ready to be picked up by a boy, though they tended to be choosey,

106

in the hope that he would offer them some protection. It was interesting to watch the girls push their boys into the archway to find out what was being offered, and the way they hung back in a conversation, if a helper tried to chat to them directly. They were suspicious of everybody.

These girls were mostly completely unprepared for a night in Brighton. They were often dressed very fashionably, often without even a coat, and many felt the disadvantage of a miniskirt, when stranded on the seafront at 2 a.m. and with nowhere to sleep. They often had small amounts of money, which would cover their fare home, and possibly pay for a few meals. But since their intention was obviously to be treated, there seemed little point in bringing any large sums with them.

There is only one recorded case of a girl being in the archway entirely on her own. An extremely distressed girl found her way into the archway at its busiest time at about midnight. She had come from London to Brighton with two girls whom she did not know very well. When they decided to go on the pier, which she did not want to do, they had split up and she had been left on her own. She had been very worried and frightened about where she was going to spend the night, and so had plucked up courage to go into the archway, but once there, the noise and bustle had frightened her even further. A helper saw the state she was in, and took her immediately to one of the sleeping centers where she spent the night. She talked for a long time about how dreadful she found the archway.

There were other cases of girls coming to Brighton looking for some fun, and being unable to cope with the situations that developed. One example of this concerned two girls who had come to Brighton for the weekend together, and had not made any arrangements where to sleep for the night. They had been picked up by a couple of boys and had enjoyed the mutual chatting up. When the boys suggested a walk, they agreed but, once out of the archway, the boys stole one of the girls' purses. She was terribly frightened by this and took some time to calm down.

Many girls came to Brighton with the intention of mixing with the beats. They dressed up in the hippie/beat type of gear for the weekend, and then returned home after the weekend. Many of the girls who were spoken to had respectable homes and jobs. There was one such girl who said that she had a boring job in a factory in Bingley, Yorkshire and that she came to Brighton at Bank Holidays to mix with real life. She was attracted to the beats and considered them as the real life. Two other girls came down with the express intention of being picked up by a beat. They were very heavily made-up with false eyelashes, and wore smart mini dresses, and slept every night in a sleeping center without apparently once removing their make-up.

A few groups of two or three girls, aged 18 or 19, came into the archway during the day, dressed in trousers. They had come prepared to stay in Brighton overnight but did not appear in the sleeping centers. It must be assumed that they were some of the few young people who were able to find bed and breakfast accomodations in the town.

The group that the police showed most concern about were the girls who were underage. Often the police visited the archway to see if there were any girls there who were 16 or less. Although the police often liked to know of any girl who was under 17, they would definitely remove one from the archway if she was under 16. The helpers also showed concern about the young girls, in the same way that they were concerned about the young boys and it was obvious from the way they were looked after in the sleeping centers, that the helpers were offering them all the protection that they could muster.

The girls were segregated from the boys in the sleeping centers. The segregation was received by the girls in two very different ways. Some were thankful, in that they could escape their partner for a time. Often this appeared to release them from any implicit sexual obligation that may have been made as a result of a pairing up. (This is dealt with in more detail in the section on couples.) When attached to a group, there may have been a feeling amongst the boys that the girl was a plaything for the whole group, and the girl would have been anxious to avoid that type of situation. On the other hand, if the girls were feeling in the least apprehensive about the scheme itself, then for the helpers to separate them from the boys whom they saw as their support, would have added to their misgivings. This produced situations where the girls would adamantly refuse to be separated from the boys. Often such couples or groups would stay chatting in the office area of the sleeping center, until the need for sleep finally made the girls accept the separate accomodation.

I — The Students

There were a large number of students in Brighton from the several institutions of Further Education: The University of Sussex, the College of Education, the Art College, the College of Advanced Technology, and several language schools for foreign students and the Technical College. Most of the students who used the archway were from the University or the Art College. A smaller number were from the College of Education.

Students were usually more aware of the value of conversation than were other young people. They were also able to articulate their reasons for being attracted to the project. The student knew, and could explain, that he wanted to have an interesting conversation with someone very different from himself if he went to the archway. Other young people used the archway for essentially the same reason, though they were not able to articulate this as well.

There appeared to be six fairly distinct reasons why students were attracted to the project. With one exception, these reasons would equally apply to any other young person:

1. To look at this social phenomena.
2. To mix with these rather way-out people.
3. To enjoy the atmosphere of the archway.

4. To use their enjoyment of the atmosphere in such a way as to contribute to the atmosphere.

5. To help because it appears to be the thing to do, or it might help them as students — particularly social studies students.

6. To help, in the hope that they will enjoy the work.

Since students are more articulate than other people, they made good helpers. Some of those responsible for the weekends often resented the students who were not helping in the archway. For some reason, none of the students were expected to behave as clients. There was an inability to understand that the student was as likely to want to use the archway in the same way as any other person. One worker remembers being angry when a student sat on some blankets which he was trying to stack and another worker threw out 20 students from the archway at Easter 1967 because they were being disruptive.

Those students who behaved like visitors were resented less than those who went in for high-pitched academic arguments. It was as if the students were seen as people not in need. To be in the arch, they could either be as the other young people, i.e. mods, rockers, beats — or they could help. In many ways, this has been disturbing to those responsible for the scheme. The fear was that all students were likely to be seen as helpers, because of their distinctive middle class background and behavior, and this would easily be resented.

By August 1967, the reports about the students being a nuisance in the centers stopped. The workers had initiated formal meetings in their colleges to explain what it was we hoped for in the archways.

J — Young Hostellers And Campers

At Bank Holiday weekends, many young people come to Brighton intending to stay in the Youth Hostel or camp on the Municipal Camping Site. Unfortunately, the Youth Hostel becomes full at Bank Holiday weekends. The YHA does recommend that hostellers book in advance if they are intending to stay in a popular hostel like the one in Brighton. The campers who are unable to use the Municipal Camping site often feel worse about the situation than do the hostellers. It is local policy to reufse accomodation to young people and people without transport. Youngsters would find that after they had walked the three miles out of Brighton to get to the site, they were turned away because of their age, or because they had no car. In our experience, we found that the prospective campers and hostellers were respectable, lower middle class young people. Many of them were from London and tended to be clerks or secretaries. They seemed to come to Brighton very much for the same reason as any other holiday maker but they were more ready to have a quieter time than many of the other youngsters. They usually moved around in pairs, the most common being two boys. The boy-girl pair tended to be wanting to use the youth hostel, though there were a few cases of couples who said they were married, who wanted to use the camping site. There were several groups of girls who were in this category. Many were in pairs, but there were several instances of larger groups of girls ready to use the youth hostel. We also found that the young people affected were of a placid nature, and so were unwilling to let their resentment carry them any further than having a moan with the helpers about the unreasonableness of the youth hostel association.

These people were grateful for our limited facilities, and were able to adjust easily to the nature of the accomodation we could offer. They were well prepared for the night with sleeping bags, etc. They tended to keep very much in the background at the sleeping centers, probably because they wanted to avoid all the excitement that the others were trying to create in the halls. Few helpers can remember having had any long conversations with anybody of this type. However, this group did show their gratitude on several occasions by helping clear up the hall in the mornings. This may have been an extension of the routine expected of youth hostellers after a night in the hostel.

K — The Couples

It is worth drawing attention to the boy-girl couples who did appear at the Bank Holiday weekends because there were so few compared with the numbers of other young people. For instance, at the Whitsun 1968 weekend, out of a sample of 277 young people, only 20 were grouped in a boy-girl couple.

Those in Brighton were mainly of the camping or youth hostel type or smooth mods. This latter sub group would have come to Brighton ready to enjoy the Top Rank Suite together.

There were a few young people who could be described as couples attached to a larger group of boys. This was more obvious in some of the groups of hard mods. On occasions a couple would be seen in the background of the group. The dynamics of this seemed quite complex, and there are two possible explanations for the arrangement. The first is that the girl felt the need for protection, and associated herself with a large group of boys. She might then have needed protection from the group of boys itself, so may have taken up with one of them. The second suggestion is that the couple already formed before coming to Brighton had felt that need of old friends to offer them support and security whilst they were in Brighton.

Rocker couples were more common than any others, and they seemed more self-sufficient even than the campers.

Few couples were married, and records from the sleeping centers show that helpers viewed those who announced they were married with considerable scepticism. It can be supposed that many of the couples were not in fact married. Many of the helpers found considerable difficulty in separating these, and would often find that the couples were prepared to sit awake all night, rather than be separated from each other. As was mentioned in the section on the girls, it might have been wrong in many cases to try to force the pairs apart.

The beatnik couples are described in greater detail elsewhere. The relationships that they built between them seemed different in many ways.

The ages of the couples ranged from about 18 years old up to 25. There were older couples using, or trying to use, the Archway and these are dealt with in the next section.

L — The Older Visitors

These do not come strictly into the category of young people using the scheme, but a considerable amount of time was spent by helpers trying to keep them out of the archway and they need to be mentioned.

At the beginning of the project, it was clear that this was a project primarily designed to provide a service to young people. This made it important that there were helpers on the door of the archway each Bank Holiday weekend, keeping out those people who were older than "young." By Easter 1968, it was found essential to make it a rule that people over the age of 25 should be kept out.

Many of those who did try to get into the archway were about 30 to 40 years old. They had invariably been drinking all evening. Being drunk in many cases, and belligerent, the people on the door had considerable difficulty in saying to these men "You are too old." They were mostly dressed respectably in dark suits, white shirts, dark ties and highly polished shoes. Their dress suggested a well-behaved person, whereas the helpers found that these were the most unsavory and potentially violent people to work with over the weekend.

It is obvious that these older men could not be allowed to mix with the younger ones. They managed to upset the atmosphere very quickly. A good example of the way in which a group of these older people were able to upset the atmosphere happened at the Whitsun 1968 weekend. At 1 a.m. on the Sunday morning, a crowd of about a dozen men blundered into the back of the archway. They were so drunk and aggressive that there was little point in trying to stop them at the door. However, one of the helpers stayed with the group all the time that they were in the archway. A very drunk man had previously bought three sticks of Brighton rock and in dancing to an imaginary beat, he lost one of the sticks of rock. He immediately set on one of his mates for pinching the rock. Two others in the group tried to separate the first two, and found themselves fighting as well. The others then tried to stop the fight and got involved themselves so that, in a matter of about ten seconds, most of the group were fighting each other. The fight stopped as suddenly as it had begun. The more sober men hustled the others out of the archway apologizing for the scene.

The Beatniks — Introduction

The beach at Brighton and Hove is a straight single beach. The beats tend to hang around one particular area of the beach which they have adopted and which seems to have remained constant in recent years. Two years ago one of the beats showed me how the group moved down from the Palace Pier in the morning to the present site in the evening, supposedly following the sun. The present site is right in the center of the activity. The beats sit in front of the seafront traders, photographers, deck chair attendants, and are not far from cafes, ice cream vendors, public bar, public conveniences, first aid center, children's paddling pool or fishing boats. There is also a subway to take pedestrians from the beach to the other side of King's Road, and the beat group is usually found on the beach just at the entrance to the subway. Most people walking along the popular part of the front cannot, therefore, fail to come across them. When it rains, the beats, like everyone else, move into the only shelter of the subway, where the beats line themselves along the walls to make room for other people to move in and out.

On the beach they tend to gather in one large group near the lower promenade, or else scatter themselves in small groups amongst the holiday-makers. The beach can get very crowded in the summer with family groups in deck chairs interspersed

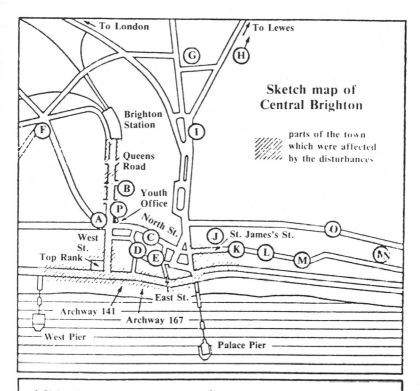

Sketch map of Central Brighton

parts of the town which were affected by the disturbances

A Union Congregtional
B Presbyterian
C Countess of Huntingdon Hall
D Elim Church
E Friends Centre
F Dials Congregational
G Salvation Army
H St. George's, Moulsecoomb
I Lismore Hotel
J Dorset Gardens Methodist
K St. Mary's
L St. John's
M St. Anne's
N St. George's
O Brighton College } helpers
P Young Adults Centre } only

with clumps of young people. The beats are readily distinguishable from the normal population by their scruffy appearance, long hair, old clothes, decorations of trinkets, scarves, sheepskins, and by the presence of rolled sleeping bags (doss bags). They spend the whole day on the beach only occasionally walking around the town visiting pubs or coffee bars. As much of their activity concerns drug abuse, the focus of attention is frequently on the toilets. In the evening they are the only people left on the beach when everyone else has gone home. Some of them sleep at the same spot. Others move under the pier to sleep, crawl into boats or search for a derelict house to break into. Thus, as a group, they may look suntanned and healthy, but are living close to starvation and are usually looking to see what they can con off the people in the way of food, money, or cigarettes.

They are noticeable by their numbers, (maybe 60-100 in mid-summer), high spirits, and by their bizarre appearance. People who cannot stand the sight of long hair, scruffiness, laziness or blatent sexuality find their existence offensive. Many of the complaints which were levelled at the archway were really objections to the presence of the beats in town. One of the complaints made to Brighton Archways Ventures was that the beats made love on the beach. This story was parallelled in St. Ives, Cornwall in July 1969. Judith Cook in the Guardian of 12th July 1969 reported that the crowd at St. Ives claimed that the beatniks spent all their time having sexual intercourse on the beaches in front of the children. "I saw you," said one young woman with a child in a pushchair, "and someone was playing a guitar while you did it. And I saw you too," she shouted at a fair-haired youth, "and it wasn't even with a girl . . ." Promiscuity seems to be the main course of objections to the beatniks though there is little actual evidence of it. However, people's investment in an odd phenomenon is strong enough to draw a curious crowd to the railings at the top promenade to look down at the beats. Passersby stop and stare as if at a zoo, and in the words of one of the beats "look you up and down." Some of the beats become very sensitive to being stared at, although others either enjoy it or ignore it.

Other groups which are attracted to the beats include English and foreign girls on holiday who befriend them. Girls are always a good con for food and money for few girls will let their boyfriends go hungry. The beats have the romantic appeal of the hobo, the Bohemian living close to nature and free of social demands. They also exhibit a little boy quality. One of the beats stood in front of the worker and asked appealingly "Will you take me in, give me some food and clothes, and look after me?"

However, the newcomer is soon aware of the way in which the beats look after each other with warmth and care. Each newcomer is taken into the fold, and everything is shared with him. Usually, one is struck by the way in which the beats have blatantly rebelled against those aspects of society which they do not like. They do not work, and many do not even claim social security. They wear what they like, look how they like and do what they like. They spend their time sitting, talking, or singing to a guitar into the night. They have time on their hands, and they have no ties except perhaps that of the absence of money, which is suitably nicknamed "bread." What they have got is a background philosophy of allowing individual freedom and looking after each other. Sometimes this is translated into a demand for society to look after them entirely, but when questioned more closely they seem to have an ideal of being given a place in which they can just be themselves. Maybe this is a reaction against the pressurized pitch of free enterprise culture where people have no time to find out about themselves and each other as people. The beats have a word for people who work, conform unthinkingly, and are content to be lost into the stereotyped mass of society as "plastic people."

Many of the beats express the conventional desires of marrying, having children, or running their own businesses. This can be taken to mean that they are conventional at heart, despite their contradictory appearance, and maybe they go beat in order to confirm where their real values lie. Certainly, it is found that many of the beats view themselves through conventional judgment, so that they see themselves as grots, not worth bothering about, lowest of the low, nothing, no good. On the other hand, the expressed desire to marry may be a way of saying that if they had someone behind them, who gave them something to live for, then life would be different. Similarly, the desire to marry may just be an expression of the orientation towards people as people; the beats do not like a society which erects artificial social barriers between people, even when they subscribe to this themselves. Characteristic of the beat group is their interest in one another. Many of them say that they went beat in order to see life, meet people, or find out what it was like. The beat way of life has, therefore, provided some kind of challenge which has to be met by one's own resources. Although young people generally find ways of asserting themselves and testing themselves, most would not have the courage to face the extreme deprivations of the beat way of life. For whatever reason, the beats have travelled far away from the pattern of life into which they were born; and many have reached the point of no return. Many of them have no families, or have left them, and others keep contact to a minimum. They cannot see themselves fitting into any part of society, and this gets confirmed every time a magistrate calls any of them a nuisance to society. Some see themselves as having been pushed out of society, and others as having chosen to drop out. Unfortunately, beatdom can become a rut if the persons drifts too far. Many learn to occupy themselves with everyday concerns, or join a movement to save them from stagnating. Stagnating would mean that they would have to face their problems when they are not yet ready to do so. Many of the beats who express discontent with their lot are in fact not yet ready emotionally to make the effort to get out of it. It is hard enough for anyone to change their way of life, let alone sacrifice their adopted family and friends in the process. Some do manage to change their circumstances, e.g. a drug addict undergoing a cure, but subsequently find that the price of leaving the emotionally protective environment of their friends results in an isolation which they cannot

118

bear, and so they return to the old scene. Our beats mixed with the beat group in every town they visited for (like everyone else) they need to find people who are like them as their emotional prop. Only a few individuals have enough self-sufficiency to go a long way on their own away from the group. Sometimes, a relationship with a girlfriend will help to make the break easier, or friendships with a new group of people. Brighton Archways Ventures aimed to provide a worker who would primarily stand in a supportive capacity so that the individual would have some prop, even though a professional role can only provide a very limited involvement.

However, there are occasions when a professional role can, in fact, be a positive support; people often need someone to say something for them in court, or refer them to hospital. Sometimes they need to be escorted to appointments to overcome their fear of meeting new people, helped to see a landlady's point of view or to have someone to whom they can refer their worried parents. More frequently they are faced with a decision to make, e.g. whether to turn up in court when they are certain to receive a prison sentence, whether to get registered or not when they do not really need to, how to get money to pay for a fine which they do not feel they owe, what to do about a pusher who keeps pestering and blackmailing and so on. In these discussions, which may be brought up by the young person or the worker, the worker's role is to enable the young person to see his position and choices open to him more clearly. We saw this clarification as being one of the most important aspects of the archway work. After all, these kinds of decisions determine the amount of control a person takes over his own life. Many people, beats included, make painstaking efforts to avoid making a decision and use other people (who are often only too willing) to tell them what to do. The consequences of these actions are not accepted as their responsibility since they only did what was advised. More seriously, some people are not able to say no to others who push them into situations. The role of clarification can sound harsh — "what would happen if you asked him to go away?" — but it seems necessary if the person is to sort out his confusion, and gain any concept of taking control of his life.

Similarly, since much of the beats thinking is taken up with fantasy, and one can never be sure what is real and what is fiction, it is necessary to try to sort out the confusion. The archway workers seldom acted, despite pressure from the young people, until they had established a clear picture of the situation. The beats tend to like involving other people in their fantasies so it is often worth the time to sort out all issues first. This becomes especially important where the person has picked up from the worker, either consciously or unconsciously, what the worker wants to hear; this situation can become doubly confusing if the worker is not aware of his or her own biases. For example, a worker who is interested in drugs may suddenly discover that she has talked of little else with the beats, who have been quick to spot her interest. In these ways, the worker in an unstructured situation faces far more personal exposure than in any other setting. The obvious way to avoid this would perhaps seem to be the approach of nonresponsiveness, and waiting to see what the other person wants to talk about. But for a worker who is actively interested in young people, this would be even more difficult, and would raise suspicions. There is no escape for the worker but to face him or herself. To help the archway workers with this, they were supervised by a psychiatric social worker once a week, and were able to explore their work problems in terms of their own motivations. As problems became clearer, so they became easier to handle.

In the following section the work with the beats is described. The indivisibility of work and workers personality is detailed and clarified.

Unstructured Social Work With The Beatniks

Arch 141, September-December, 1967. Phase I

Arch 141 is a small arch consisting of two rooms on two floors, both about 15 feet square. The beach in front of it was a favorite spot for the beats. Even now it is difficult to say why we were convinced that the beats needed a woman worker, though we have not changed our opinion. We were after nothing so intrusive as motherliness or sex appeal. Partly we felt that the beats, many of whom we suspected had had very disturbed lives, needed someone around who was most of the time passively and unobtrusively caring, a role which comes more easily for a woman in our culture. Partly, we also felt that a sexually nondemanding, unthreatening, unexploitative woman could help to do away with unvoiced worries about sexual matters. It is relevant to note that we thought we could also use a team of Franciscan friars. The reason we did not have them was that we could not get them — we could see nothing against it in principle. We did not fully understand our opinion in this matter.

On the Friday of the August Bank Holiday 1967, all the external relations problems we were to encounter had already made their appearance. We had been storing the 1,200 blankets, which we used at Bank Holidays, in 141 during the summer. Volunteers helped to get them out and into the various sleeping centers. The van came and went at intervals during the day. Then some of the beats we knew came to help clear the place and sweep up. In the late afternoon, they were sweeping out the top floor, whose double french windows overlooked the lower promenade. The dust upset a neighboring trader who had been using the place in front of 141 for his ice cream counter. He is a quick tempered man, and came out shouting his protest, while a wet mop was being swung out of the top floor. He thought it was being swung at him. For the next two days, it proved impossible to pacify him; many attempts were made, but he was full of hatred for the beats, and piled grievance upon grievance. In the interest of peace, it was decided, from that Friday night, to open 141 only when the neighboring archways were closed. Nevertheless, the traders continued to complain that they were losing trade.

At the same weekend, two people had volunteered to paint the front door — a weird, rather gloomy, psychedelic design, which aroused a lot of interest in the passersby. To this, too, the traders took exception, though the Archway team always suspected that the striking design led the passersby to turn their eyes on the adjacent ice cream and candy floss stall. The traders' hostility never abated.

During that weekend, there were many more beats than had been anticipated — their numbers had grown since the previous summer, which had provided the evidence on which the application for a grant from the Department of Education and Science had been made. Many of them were highly gifted, not only in painting but in music, and Arch 167 ran a spontaneous cabaret every night in which people sang, played the guitar, recited, and made impromptu speeches. It was rowdy and cheerful in 167, while 141 was quiet and intimate — people moved from one to the other as they needed a change of mood.

The beats had performed a very important function that weekend, in both archways, but we were committed to using 167 for the young townspeople and 141 for the beats. The beats, however, were happy with their two archways. The next week, they were in both again, and the next. Looking back, we feel we made a mistake, based on a prior mistake. The mistake was that we attempted to enforce our original intention; the prior mistake was that we had committed ourselves — in the application for the grant and in the leases — to particular uses of the two archways. We now feel that even such generously wide terms of reference, as those on which we were given the grant, were too narrow, so that we were inflexible at the wrong moment and unable to exploit the situations which actually arose to the best advantage for all.

About this, at least, our views are now clear. If you trust your workers, you must give them money and an entirely free hand. In fact, by all existing standards, the Department of Education and Science were outstanding in the trust they placed in Biven and Klein. But existing standards are unrealistic in experimental work in rapidly changing social situations.

We found a beat worker, a warm, cheerful, pretty girl, and put her through our usual procedure — interviewed by a psychiatrist and by a socially and psychologically sophisticated teacher of social work — and she had proved acceptable. During September, she worked as a volunteer, as she was still employed elsewhere. Like 167, 141 opened on Thursday nights and Saturday nights in September, and she was regularly there. There were always two or three other volunteers in 141 at the time, including Klein, who was hoping to help the new worker get used to the demands of her job.

During September, Biven and Klein came to the conclusion that a determined effort must be made to free 167 for its purpose — a place for young townspeople, and the beats to be centered on 141 and kept out of 167.

The beats naturally resented being kept to 141, and the beat worker also felt, though mistakenly, that she was being relegated to the smaller and tattier arch. This split between the beat worker and the others hindered the growth of trust, which turned out to be very unfortunate, though it strengthened the bond between the worker and the beats. The beats and their worker protested in words and action against their rejection. They decided that if they were not allowed in 167, they would exclude those they saw as non-beats from 141.

At this time there were also three special visitors worth mentioning. Mrs. A., a resident in the town, had been in contact with beats longer than any of us. Over the years, she had come to realize that they needed somewhere to live, protected from society, to sort themselves out without the constant need to make a living, and to come to see some assurance that they could belong to a worthwhile community. She had discussed all this with her beat friends on many occasions: how this place should be run, who should be included, whether they should keep pigs as well as poultry, and so on. At this time, she found the ideal place, and she often dropped into 141 to see her friends and to make plans. (Nothing, alas, came of all this, but she continues with her friendliness, wisdom and affection, with very little real support from anyone.) The Hall was much talked of in 141 — the archway workers tended to keep rather aloof and neutral on this, on the principle of not counting one's chickens before they are hatched.

Through her, a Franciscan friar came to Brighton to see if his community could help. Again, nothing came of this in the end, but Brother Peter was a valuable visitor. His dress was a clear signal for people who wanted to talk about religion, which many did, but he was also a pleasant man, happy to chat about anything. He stayed till Easter 1968.

One night in October, a new face appeared in 141. A depressed-looking man in his mid-20s, who looked older, in the tatty clothes of the wayfarer, with an old Air Force over-coat, he sat against the wall of his mattress, speaking to no one. After a couple of evenings like this, one of the volunteers, also very quiet in demeanor when working, got slowly into conversation with him. He liked 141, and expressed his appreciation of the nonauthoritarian atmosphere. A conversation ensued about the good society, and the ills of the present. He had come from a Simon Community and had intended to go to another. On his way through, he had come to Brighton, liked the archway and was beginning to see opportunities there for his main concern: the homeless traveler and older dosser. So we got to know Bic who, with Michael Naylor, was later to start the Brighton Hostel Project. He was very valuable to us. A very pleasant man to be with, a brilliant observer, he worked (though he might not call it that) most nights in the archways, and reflected on his experience there. He stayed for a while with Jago, and his insights were of great use to him. On the other hand, Archways gave him friendship, helped him clarify his ideas, gave him local information, and for a while, paid for him to be formally supervised, in the same way as our own workers were.

In all these three instances, we could have been of more use, if we had had more time and more money. Here again, the need for flexibility may be noted.

However, the split between the beat worker and the others was a burning issue, as basic differences were left unquestioned and were often not recognized.

Our beat worker began to feel depressed. Her cheer and bustle had been welcome and valuable. But beats, maybe more than many others, are very depressed people. This depression had been covered by elation in the previous two months, but this emotional situation could not be sustained for long. The worker had been used to evading depression and became worried at her clients' feelings and her own. Moreover, she had lived a conventional life, where sexuality was kept within strict, almost ritual bounds. Some of the people in 141 were obsessively promiscuous and frank as well, and this was disturbing to her. Some, sensing this, teased her and played on her hopes and fears. She could not digest this, nor even talk about it. The conversations she had with the other workers, who were trying to help her, frightened her too. Communications were not so good anyway, because of the 141/167 issue. Gradually 141 became a depressing and frightening place to her, often unbearably so.

She had been working very hard. The weather was not good, and she had tended to open 141 during the day as well, to give the beats a warm and dry place. This doubled her working hours.

On November 2nd, she arrived to find the Archway a foot under water. A storm had driven the sea in. It was an unfortunate happening to her in her mood, though it delayed a full consciousness of her distress as, once again, there would be a bustle, drying things out, and getting everything ship-shape again. Yet during this time, the beats left 141 for 167 which, being higher up, had not been damaged by the flood, so that she felt deserted. She, too, took to going to 167 or elsewhere, leaving 141 with no one in charge.

From her records, 4th November:

"At 8 p.m. I returned to 167 but everything was damp and miserable. Canterbury John and Mike were high on hash. I had a splitting headache and, therefore, was rather uncommunicative. The beats moved to 167 as soon as it was opened, leaving 141 with a brief passing clientele.

At 1 a.m. 141 was empty and with the help of Phil, I cleared up, closed and trotted along to 167. This Arch was full, but Peter Jackson didn't want the beats at the sleeping center as they wouldn't sleep, and Leo didn't want charge of the beats. Great chats went on about this, it was all a blur to me as my head was thumping and I had double vision. Eventually, I reopened 141, but then Leo said it was pointless going back on my word — agreed — but everything was getting rather disagreeable and I was in no fit state to think properly. Having already worked 11½ hours I was tired and so burst into tears. Phil took me to my car and I went home about 3 a.m. No helpers at 141 tonight — must do something about this position as I can't cope single-handed all the time. Remembered to put mattresses upstairs in case of another high tide, once bitten — twice shy."

On 23rd November:

"Arrived at 141 at 3 p.m. to find Sancho and Jed having their tea break. However, there was ample evidence they had been working extremely hard upstairs. The ceiling and top half of the walls were beautifully painted. Others were sitting by the fire, quietly enjoying coffee. I stayed for a couple of hours . . ."

The three workers were to spend some days in Leicester at the National College for the Training of Youth Leaders, to get a rest, and evaluate, away from the stresses of the work. During that time, a rota of volunteers looked after the archways. At this time, the weather was bitterly cold and wet in the November gales. The Mermaid Hotel, where many of the 141 beats lived, had just evicted them on the advice of the police. The police had also secured with locks and bolts the derelict buildings where homeless beats went to sleep. This meant, that instead of merely trespassing, they could be charged with breaking and entering if found on the premises, an offense which carries much heavier penalties.

There were large numbers of homeless and distressed people at a loss how to survive. They had stayed together as a group right into the autumn, instead of dispersing as often happens at the end of summer, because something good was happening and they knew it. It was tragic that the police were, at that time, still carrying on their old repressive and harrassing tactics, as with Gypsies, just at the time when, in spite of moans and grumbles, this group of people was achieving a certain amount of stability.

At this time, a sense of community feeling was building, to which a sizeable minority of the beats, as well as Nic, Pete and Mac, were emerging from the beat life. Certainly these latter three could reliably be in charge of 141 and ensure that no offenses were committed on the premises, and cope with police and other visitors. There were also Brother Peter, and Mrs. A. There was also Mrs. S. and Kate, the beat workers' friend and constant volunteer helper.

The beat worker had been tending to open 141 for the day whenever she happened to be in the area, often leaving it rather casually in charge of reliable and, at a pinch, less reliable people while she went off again, not wishing to spend her time there and not wishing to throw everyone out when she felt she had to leave. Moreover, as the weather deteriorated, in spite of the repeated carpentry, we were beginning to have trouble with some of our clients who would break into the top window for a kip or a party after closing time, thus committing at one go both the offenses for which the lease could be withdrawn.

In this emergency, Klein decided to regularize the situation for a while and move to a 12-hour-a-day service, mid-day to midnight, with a rota of volunteers in charge. During these last few days of November, there were constant discussions, as to how the few still available derelict houses could be distributed with justice and discretion among those who needed them to sleep in, and where 141 would fit into this scheme, since we could not stay open forever. It was, however, a crushing blow for the beat worker to find all these changes going on in her archway on her return from five days at Leicester. From her records on 30th November:

"Arrived back from Leicester and got to 141 at 8 p.m. Jo had kindly opened up and all was in full swing by the time I got there. There was little time to take everything in, except that there were lots of new faces, before the Telegraph photographer arrived. Mrs. S. objected violently about his presence, and Ireland was rude to him, accusing him of having come to make trouble for the beats. I said anyone who didn't want to appear in the photos should go upstairs. Many photos were then taken. The photographer, myself, Nick and Leo then went along to 167 for more shots. Miriam and Mrs. A. arrived but were soon busy talking to people. It was a brief hello — goodbye. Mr. Axford, the Probation Officer arrived, accompanied by Jo Callaghan the lady P.O. who had written to us. We had long chats about her and about the Arch in general. We have different approaches to things, but now we also have a good sound base for communication. Mr. Axford is bringing a settee for 141 on Tuesday. Perhaps furnishings aren't going to cost as much as I thought. Free again, I returned to 141 just in time for the start of a meeting held by Jo re: the sleeping problem. I was too tired to take much in or be very responsible, but I don't altogether agree with some suggestions on the grounds that they are a little ambitious . . ."

In the next month, Klein worked more and more in 141. Her intention, beside her pleasure in the work and the fact that she was a regular part of the rota, was to take the load off the beat worker a little, but the latter's spirit was breaking, and little useful interchange took place between them, though a lot of talk. At the time she did not realize what a major influence, for good or ill, her presence was. Maybe there were better ways of coping, but the succession of emergencies (including our troubles with the Council) kept us too busy to stop and evaluate.

At about this time, several of the beats acquired dogs. They were a bit of a nuisance in the arch at times, when they fought and when they kept chewing up the paper coffee cups, but it was good to see people love them and look after them when they seemed off-color. The pets were used as all lonely people use pets, safe objects for affection. The dogs were also useful in a material way for those who slept rough — they were warm in a sleeping bag.

On 8th December, a blizzard hit Brighton, which was blanketed with snow for over a week.

The more common variety of blankets were also causing trouble at this time, due to the need to clean them frequently. The arrangements with the Sanitation department were more than satisfactory but there were some people in the town who thought we might promote an epidemic of some kind. We were just as keen to avoid this possibility and also felt that it would be to our advantage to have a Doctor call in at the archway from time to time. There was additionally another matter which promoted Jo to write to the Medical Officer of Health.

The Medical Officer of Health   7th December, 1967
Brighton Corporation

Dear Dr. Parker.

I was sorry to miss Tuesday's meeting because I had hoped to have a word with you about the work in the Archway 141, with which I am associated.

We are under heavy pressure at the moment. The allegations made against the work are by and large untrue, but underneath there is a more general mistrust, which I associate with the common man's mistrust of mental illness. I write to you to clarify some aspects of what we are doing, in the hope of your informal support, in confidence because it is not in the best interests of our "patients" that these aspects should be publicly discussed.

There are, of course, a considerable number of relatively stable people who frequent arch 141, but there is also a proportion of confused people, in casual work or unemployable, now in the R.G.'s Social Class V, though they came from a variety of social backgrounds. It seems that we are, in a sense, a reception area for the "schizophrenic drift." The theory, as you know, is that "schizophrenics" of all social classes tend to end up at the bottom of the social hierarchy.

After two months of more frequent contact, we are beginning to understand something of their situation. Maladjusted and disturbed when they first leave their home-environment, they try on a variety of "personalities" in order to fit in as they drift from scene to scene. In this way, they discover something of their potentialities, but in an unconscious and confused way, and they remain unsatisfied with themselves and directionless. Fashions of behavior in 141 also change, but in a vague sort of way their personalities of yesterday are remembered — sometimes too much, sometimes too little, but sometimes providing about the right amount of continuity of identity.

The arch provides rest, few demands, some opportunity for clarification of the direction in which one might go, and some help in seeing the steps on the path to going anywhere. With some, the assurance that it is possible to get somewhere is important.

As you see, I have been leading up to my view that we are running a day hospital for the mentally disturbed, and you will also see why it is not a view we would wish to air publicly. But some understanding of this point of view by people in important positions could help to take pressure off us, in that the present climate of opinion is including the police to see it as their function to scatter, to other parts of the country, the people we are working with, and this perpetuates the problems we are trying to solve.

(Signed) Jo Klein

Dr. Parker wrote in reply, inviting Biven and Klein to meet him. A good discussion followed, and relations with his office continued to improve.

The letter sets out what was good and hopeful about 141. Besides individual counselling, the place gave a good opportunity for group work. For a newcomer, a typical sequence of events, when not brought by a friend, would be that he would walk rather assertively through the door of 141, his defensiveness showing characteristically in his obvious readiness to take on all comers for a fight. No one would take him up on this, as they had already sufficient security of status in the archway not to feel put down by refusing a challenge. This in a way was the newcomer's first disconcerting experience, because outside the arch the rituals are clearly established. He would see people sitting talking, just sitting or walking to and from the coffee area with cups. He would sometimes be offered coffee, or sometimes, having quickly taken in the scene and being at a loss, he would walk firmly to the kettle and make himself coffee like the others. Either way, the coffee-making led to interaction with others. The newcomer would reel off a lot of places that he had been to, which could sound very impressive, except in this setting, where most others had been equally on the drift. A second attempt at achieving conventional status had thus been defeated. If he could, he might also reel off his list of approved schools and Borstal but this, too, was nothing special in this group. Seeing no need for his habitual mask, the newcomer woud sit on a mattress and pass the time of day like everyone else, soon establishing common ground. The loss of the mask was progress, but painful progress. At last, no longer needing energy to keep his end up, there was time to rest and reflect, so that depression, long held back, came through. It must be remembered that many of our clients had a dreadful past of rejection and degradation. For days or weeks, they would just sit and suffer, alleviated only by the need to get money and buy drugs. Some eventually took the next step which was to get bored — the springs of action were beginning to stir at last. Tragically, at this point, there is a discontinuity to what might have been a natural developmental sequence. What was there to do? Work on a building site or as a kitchen porter? Whereas most young men accept the necessity of dreary daily work when they are fond enough of a girl to marry her and start a family, the beats were not ready for this. Nor were they the stuff of which revolutions are made.

At this point, another tragedy became relevant. Mario had been friendly with the workers for some months and a frequent, somewhat detached, visitor to the archways. He was somewhat remote from most of the beats, from whose way of life he was beginning to emerge. He was paying off a fine for a drug offense.

Mario had a good idea for the beats and for the town. He hoped that a number of beats, who were interested in making things and in painting, could find a market for their products and thus avoid the depressing round of sponging.

His idea was to find an old shop or garage and provide tools and materials for the beat artisits. These he hoped he could scrounge from factories in the vicinity. He had sufficient knowledge of tenancies to know that the tenant of such a shop would have to provide convincing evidence of their ability to meet all the conditions. And he knew that he would be unable to do this. He imagined that the archway workers would take on a lease and pay the rent for an indefinite time until the team were self-supporting.

His scheme met with excitement and renewed interest in staying in Brighton. There had been other ideas and schemes which had fallen by the wayside but this seemed more realizable than most and was taken up by those with some talent. There was, not unnaturally, pressure from the artists to get on with the scheme. The beats had most of the day and evenings to devote time and thought to the scheme, while the workers were only able to give an hour or a few minutes each day. Mario hoped that he could speed things up and find premises by involving the workers in 141 in the scheme. He thought that the worker could be responsible for the administrative side of the scheme while he attended to the more mundane job (as he saw it) of ordering and finding materials and a market for the finished product.

At the same time, Mario formed a friendship with Barrie and Barrie felt confident enough with Mario to allow him the free run of some business premises which needed decorating. Mario said that he had been a decorator and a window dresser for Bewlays at one time. They worked intermittently on the decorating together over a period of weeks, and during this time, Barrie came to understand more about Mario and what it was he wanted for himself.

It was harder to understand why Mario was not able to work towards a home, like most other people. He considered that the normal route was agonizingly slow. He had more talent than many and could easily have commanded a high salary. He also smoked marijuana, experimented with LSD and (unverified) injected heroine. He was quietly spoken, sensitive to others and spent a great deal of time washing and combing his dyed hair. He was confident in an unassuming way and was a good person for the beats to regard as an organizer. It was because of these factors that the archway workers and Barrie felt that at least one of the beat schemes would come to fruition. But the workers were equally determined not to be seduced into playing a leading part in the preparations and finding that they had become committed to a level of involvement from which it would be difficult to withdraw. This scheme had to be run by the beats and they had to take responsibility for it. They did not want it any other way and yet responsibility was the one thing they all disliked. It was the one common bond among them.

As much as Barrie liked Mario, he felt it was essential to work him. That is to say, he considered that with this scheme, he had to help Mario see all the problems and pitfalls. He also tried to help Mario see why the archway could not take on the responsibility of yet another lease. Barrie thought that Mario understood this very well but somehow Mario thought that all these difficulties might be solved by someone.

Mario relied more and more on the beat worker for guidance and action, when it became clear that Barrie was not able to help in the way he had envisaged. The beat worker, at this time, was having her own problems in the archway and was not in a good position to make an objective assessment. Possibly the scheme was another escape for the beat worker from the arch which caused her so much difficulty. She took the scheme to heart and tramped the streets of Brighton looking for a garage or derelict building. She phoned council officials and estate agents and in spite of some pressure from her colleagues, became totally identified with the aims of the scheme. Temporarily, she became a beat and was not able to take part in the weekly workers' discussions. She attended as a beat, not a worker and it became impossible for the workers to discuss the work as a team.

Mario became more depressed and disillusioned with the archway and the weekly repayments for a loan from the archway project gradually tailed off. (The question of loans will be discussed elsewhere but in retrospect the workers are still prepared to defend the principle but are unsure about the wisdom of this particular loan.)

The relationship between Barrie and Mario became cool and this break was reinforced by the beat worker, who saw Barrie as a destructive person, cold and unwilling to offer assistance even when more than capable of doing so.

It became obvious that Mario saw Brighton and, more particularly, the archway project as an obstacle to his ideals. They were also a source of embarrassment and worry. The police drug squad shadowed Mario most days and he had to report to the probation officer at regular intervals. Although he considered full time work, and tried it on a number of occasions, he could never maintain the morning routine of arriving at a specific time. It was not made easier by sleeping in derelict houses without a clock. It was just all too much for him. The tragedy was that the people with the greatest potential to help had failed him. He had to leave Brighton to maintain his self-respect and anyway, the people there no longer meant much to him. There is always the chance that Mario will make it on his own, without youth workers, evangelists, or the efforts of the tireless drug squads.

Thus ended the first phase of beat work and the development of the project to date. A new beat worker was found from among the more seasoned volunteers, Eve Ross, a recent graduate from the University of Sussex.

February 1968-April 1969. Phase II

Several people have asked us to justify the setting up of the archway (usually students and social workers) talking in terms of success — whatever that may mean in the field of human relations. Since we had no particular goal, for example, to cure people of something, any measurement of success, therefore, is quite arbitrary. We preferred to adopt the approach that if the arch was used, and considered to be a good thing by the people using it, then it was successful. On humanitarian grounds, we felt that if two people had been helped over a period of years, then we felt fully justified in setting it up, whether or not we could see the effect on all those hundreds of others who used the arch for some small part of their lives. Since we were concerned with the development of adolescents, we also saw it as a measure of success when people grew out of their need of the arch, and moved on to other things.

Use of the arch can be measured by number — 500 to 1,000 over a Bank Holiday, 100 known people passing through the arch in an autumn period of nine weeks, 300 case history sheets of people known to us — or else by the type of use which was made of the arch.

We hoped that our clientele would come to realize that they themselves had a large part to play in the running of the archway and in making it the kind of place where they wanted to be. We envisaged that ideally the arch should be a place of fairly uninhibited interaction, and that people could meet others in an atmosphere of free communication. Thus we expected the mood to be constantly changing, and that it would enable people to make up their own minds about things. Adolescence can often be a period of searching and self-discovery — and a no man's land — for which the young person needs to be allowed to experiment with values in his own time. How people explore life is up to each individual, but it seemed to us that the archway had an important function in providing a holding situation. Thus people who were just drifting could be given the chance to stop and think, and have somewhere diffferent to go that was restful. Ideally, a bank clerk, monk, beatnik, university lecturer, and a man just out of prison could find something common to talk about in an archway-type set-up and become aware of other people's points of view. We felt it important that the arch should be in a position to bridge the gap between society and its outsiders. If this was to be possible, we could not afford to condone one way of thinking more than another lest we take advantage of a young person's state of indecision in order to get a conversation to a particular point of view. It seemed essential to keep an open mind on things in a working situation.

We tended to assume that people had reasons for being what they were, and doing what they did, and that they alone were the authors of behavior. We saw our jobs as endeavoring to pick up the communication, and to check it out to see if we were right. We were then able to use this information as a basis from which to work. We felt that it was better that someone should talk about his wish to go around hitting people than to actually do so, and hoped perhaps a compromise could be reached (like splashing paint on the wall). Because we demanded that our visitors take on a lot of responsibility for their own actions, we hoped that this would avoid making the arch into an authoritarian set up, in which we told them what they could or could not do. By throwing back the responsibility the young person has to make a decision about what he is going to do. This approach frightens outside people who imagine all sorts of horrors going on in places where young people make decisions about their own behavior. The main concerns for those people outside the arch were sex and drugs. It is perhaps worth noting that nobody tried to have sexual intercourse in the arch, and that most of the sex-play was on a healthy level. Violence was contained in a few brief fights which were often provoked by visitors to the arch. The actual amount of trouble seemed to be out of all proportion to the fears expressed.

On the practical level, however, there were several areas in which we did act as an authority. For instance, when the arch was open we always had a worker present who could deal with any situation which arose. Since the premises were leased to us, we could not afford to be as tolerant as much as we would have liked. We were all very conscious of the amount of bad publicity (mostly unfounded) which the arch had received, and so we were very anxious to keep our noses clean. We enforced the conditions of the lease all the time, even when it would have been kinder to our visitors not to. This meant that there was no sleeping on the premises, no cooking or preparation of food, and no music audible on the seafront outside. In addition, we were dealing with a group of drug-takers, so we tended to get anxious about the police, even though we were never raided and never accused of harboring people on the run. We did not always succeed in our efforts with the beat group, but we could generally appeal for their cooperation and the spirit was always willing even if they had little persistence. There were also human limits as to how far the worker was prepared to act as detective.

137

The workers always took it upon themselves to "vet" outside people who were visiting the arch. There was always the possibility that they were disguised policemen, reporters, prostitutes, homosexuals, etc. We felt strongly that the arch should be primarily a place of rest for young people away from such pressures, and we were usually able to explain to outsiders that it was a place for young people only.

The Day To Day Work In The Archway

The beats gravitated towards the small back room where they set to with the crayons we had provided for art, and covered the walls with slogans, graffitti, and cartoons. Some of the slogans were apt, "When reason fails, stagnate;" "Owing to apathy, tomorrow has been cancelled;" "Den of Iniquity." One of the most artistic beats drew portraits of them all so the room began to take on the semblance of a rogue's gallery, especially when the odd name was scrawled between them. There were the expected odes to loved ones, their own poems copied out, and tributes to speed, hash and the syringe, interspersed with the warnings that speed kills. It was interesting to note that the real graffitti was confined to the toilet, along with the love messages, and the standard work in the back room at this stage was generally kept much higher. The back room went through many phases, but it was never as decorative as it was in those first few weeks. We encouraged the use of those walls, as they seemed to provide an eternal source of entertainment, which we saw as an important function of the archway. It seemed to us that the beats express themselves quite rigidly in their set way of life and yet seem to have a need of further self-expression. Only the odd one is talented enough to turn this to clowning, guitar playing, painting or writing poetry. The rest do nothing. One may speculate that because of their enormous need to play, they have not had the opportunities as children and, therefore, need to discover themselves by regressing to a former stage of development. Or else the

138

beat has enormous difficulties in coping with the demands of the external world and instead of living in total isolation benefits from the chance to relax in a social group. Whatever the reasons behind it, we were happy to provide an environment in which they could safely meet this need. Some of the beats expressed appreciation of the atmosphere in the back room, but a surprising number said "they wouldn't allow it" and "it was grotty." A couple of these took it upon themselves to paint out all their friends' hard work, but gave it up when they discovered they were fighting a losing battle. So we had a spell of half finished iron grey and vivid green walls which were already daubed with names, phrases, and cartoons. Later on, we went through a violent spell which was reflected by the holes in the walls where people had put their fists, and by the trails of paint which had just been flung out of the pots on to the walls. Not even the boxes and floors escaped the artists' attention, and eventually the decor spread into the main hall and into the kitchen area. We had phases when red was the predominant color, focusing on a large red eagle of the fuzz bird, where even the light was painted red; black phases when the light was made completely useless by being painted over, and gruesome dark faces peered out from the gloom. A number of personal grouses were enacted on the walls, when Robbie daubed paint over Speedy's portrait, and Speedy lovingly washed off the offending marks. Because we kept it more or less confined to this area, and because it is more in the nature of the beat to write on walls than on paper so they can see themselves, we did not feel it to be harmful. The walls could always be painted over again, and in the meantime, people had a lot of enjoyment. Some of the beats got very worried by what they saw as destruction of the walls, but our view was that walls are repairable. Time and again we were struck by the thought that we were a playgroup for deprived children. There was the same restlessness, jealousies, need for attention; the same over-exertion, destructiveness and need to shock, the same spontaneous game of "killing" each other or tying each other up, the same inability to concentrate for long, the same failure to understand things which were not immediately pleasant to them, and the same need to take something which had been made by someone else. Fortunately for the nerves of the workers, the beats also had quieter moods when they just needed to rest, talk, or just be, and although the calls on the worker may be just as demanding, at least the tempo was less hectic.

The policy was to let things run as they wanted, not to organize people unless they wanted to organize themselves, and just to provide some materials by way of hints. Few people came up to ask what they could do, and most of them just copied each other until they got an inspiration of their own. Cathy once said she was bored, so we suggested she write a story. Her story was all about a little boy who grew up and got married. She then wanted to know what else she could do. The worker suggested she write one about a little boy who did not get married. This got her to thinking and she told the tale of the young boy who was too shy to go out with girls, even though he wanted to, and ended up by taking drugs to bolster his self-confidence. Then he discovered that he could only be sociable while under the influence so he took more and more until he eventually forgot all about girls and just lived on drugs. Jamie was fascinated by this and wrote her own story about a little girl who had lost her parents, and one day went to London where the drug circles accepted her and looked after her. Again this girl became so hooked that "all she could think of was the next fix . . . fix . . . fix . . ." Jamie showed this story to Ross and then tore it up. Maybe it was autobiographical. Ross thought we were on to a good thing with story writing, but it did not last long — perhaps because it was really too revealing.

Scraps of material from a tie-making industry were another source of fun as people decked themselves out as gaudy pirates, or tied each other on to chairs. Sometimes there were puzzles to do, balloons, or an extra bouncy ball to play with, and other amusements. But they got just as much fun out of smashing pieces of wood or tea chests to see who was the strongest, cutting holes in blankets so that they could play highwaymen and wear them as a cloak against the cold, stitching tassels on to their jeans to make them look more decorative, frizzing out each others' hair, wrestling or tumbling on the carpet. John had organized the selling of some poetry by this time, and now wanted to have a couple of poetry reading sessions. He got the boxes together to form a platform, and we all sat around to listen to several people reading their poems. We finished with more than we had bargained for — a platform dialogue between two people about the use of violence, and a gory story about a man who murdered his wife, which entertained the sadistic side of the beats.

Besides being a playroom, full use was made of the arch as a place which provided facilities. Most of the beats live out, so they do not often have a proper wash. The sink was in constant use as people washed themselves, and their clothes (which could be dried on the heaters) and occasionally, we could not go anywhere near someone's bath until they had mopped up. The toilet held an unfortunate attraction for the junkies, some of whom would store their drugs in the cracks in the walls. There were always calls for needles and thread, and first aid for blisters, cuts, abscesses, headaches or sanitary towels. Letters were written and received, (as often the beats who were sleeping out had no other address to give,) from which they could keep in touch with their families and friends. The coin telephone was well used, and we felt it was important that people who have normally rejected all their contacts should have a base from which to keep in touch. Later on, Ross provided some magazines which were read, and then cut up for various collages. She also started a library, which did not function as a library after they had read a book it was easier to sell it than return it. But people were enthusiastic about reading and we had some very quiet evenings as they all settled into a living room atmosphere.

It was perhaps more in this kind of atmosphere — of people reading, painting or just sitting — that the small group discussions, which were to prove one of the essential aspects of the archway, developed. We had originally conceived of the idea of the arch as a meeting place, and in its best moments it was just that. Helpers met the beats (and vice versa) and the beats were provided with a warm place where they could be with each other, away from the discomforts of a derelict house or the beach subway. The odd visitor was sometimes detained in discussion. For example, a London policeman (of high rank) wandered in in plain clothes trying hard not to look like a policeman. After Ross had talked to him for a short time and satisfied herself that his intention to be treated like anyone else was genuine, they were joined by a group of three or four beats who engaged him in a discussion on poetry and religion. There were many other discussions: one where people lamented on the deterioration of the scene to a stage where they no longer trusted one another, and related this to the increase in hard drug-taking; one where two people discussed their theories of personality and ideas of a state of heaven with the worker; one on the pros and cons of corporal punishment for children.

On many occasions the worker would be engaged in discussions when someone was trying to make up their minds about something or were puzzling over a problem, or needed help in coming to terms with their feelings over something. Some people would announce that they had made a decision, for example, to get registered and gave their reasons for doing so. Although they presented a fait accompli to the worker, they had done a lot of thinking to reach that decision (whether or not it had been provoked by the threat of police) and implicit in it is the way in which they saw their lives. One girl wanted to talk about her feelings about death, as she had been working as a wardmaid on a hospital ward where a young child had just died; this also reminded her of her father's death. A boy asked what was wrong with him and wondered why he was always the one before the boy his girlfriends really fell in love with. Many others talked about their relationships with their boy or girlfriends, other people in the arch, relationships with the workers. Since we always let the young people pick their topic for conversation, the workers would always play these conversations by ear. Many of the beats just needed someone to take an interest in them, and used the worker as a daily diary, in which they saw the worker every day and chatted on about everything which had happened since the last time they met.

Many tense dramas between lovers were worked out in the semi-privacy of the back room, and many individuals would seek a corner of that room just to be alone or to think about things. Sometimes, it was to have a good cry, or to smash the walls or cups and saucers, and one girl slashed her wrists (very superficially). Sometimes the worker was able to be there to sympathize and talk things over, and sometimes this was done by their friends. We were able to tolerate a lot of acting-out as the beat group is normally very sympathetic to other people's problems. This quality makes the beat group a refuge for many misfits who need company, but who cannot be tolerated by normal society.

Sometimes the arch was used to work out personal problems. Often these would be private ones, but sometimes people made an effort to involve everyone else. Speedy furnished an example of this when he made out a petition to exclude Cathy, the black girl, from the Arch. Some people refused to sign it, and others made an effort to change the wording so that it was more generalizable.

Sometimes use was made of the worker in the straight education sense. A small number of people could not write, and needed to get other people to write their letters for them. Apart from that, the educational ignorance was appalling. One boy assumed he was the father of a baby who was born one month after his arrival in Brighton; another girl thought babies came out of your belly-button. One boy thought the pill was taken to increase fertility. Many did not know what was happening in the world as they seldom saw a newspaper. The level of literacy varied over a wide range; some appeared to be so limited in understanding as to perhaps be mentally defective, while others spent their days in the library and were very up to date (usually on psychological or religious thinking.) When we started the library in the arch we deliberately chose to buy a wide range of so-called good books. Frequently people would read comics and magazines, but we wanted to see what the reception would be for more demanding literature. It was extremely good — all the books were seized and read immediately, and there was a demand for more. The only unpopular one was *The Bafut Beagles* by Gerald Durrell; the others disappeared like magic, whether they be *Nausea* by Sartre, *The Adventures of Don Camillo* by Giovanni Guareschi; *The Castle* by Kafka, *Huckleberry Finn* by Mark Twain, *Loneliness of the Long Distance Runner* by Sillitoe, *Saturday Night and Sunday Morning* by Sillitoe, *Freedom, the Individual and the Law*, by H. Brown, *Sons and Lovers* and *Rainbow* by D.H. Lawrence, *Games People Play* by E. Berne. Educational magazines, such as *Life*, *Book of Life*, and *Animal Life* were also well received.

At one point, Ross took some agar plates down to get samples of the air in the toilet (where they fixed their drugs), and on the seafront but people did not really appreciate what she was trying to do, especially as the seafront air turned out to be more polluted than the toilet air! (Ross had asked one boy to give her a sample of a dirty needle after use, but he lost the plate. Losing things was typical of this group who had no property that they can call their own.)

Certainly there seemed to be plenty of room for gentle informal teaching, and had we had more helpers maybe this could have been developed. Perhaps it should be mentioned in this section that the beats have an inclination for religious thought (although they do not often subscribe to orthodox religion). It may be part of their search for values, but many seem to follow the Eastern religions with enthusiasm, and others are attracted to the cults of scientology, spiritualism, meditation and yoga, and black magic seemed to hold a special attraction with its ritualism.

144

Ross encouraged any time filling activity which could help that individual in his discovery of himself, since the beats are one section of society who have plenty of time and usually "waste it" (in the words of Ginger Paddy). Their situation is ripe for fantasy, thinking, writing poetry, painting, planning. Four poetry books were printed and one cartoon manuscript. One Bank Holiday the helpers became very suspicious of a sudden passion for eating chocolate which developed among the beats, who would troop out to the chocolate machine again and again. What could they be getting out of chocolate? Did they want the silver paper for something else like LSD or hashish? Of course, the beats were happy to play this along saying things like, "it goes better with chocolate," but apparently there had been nothing more to it than a mass craze for chocolate! As drug-taking was accompanied by similar frenzy, we often felt tempted to hand out Smarties at the door!

What drug was taken varied with its availability on the market, the amount of money individuals had to buy it, and whether anybody had got themselves sufficiently organized to be receiving a regular supply. Individual beats were always travelling up to London and back with their supplies of drugs, which they could then sell to others in Brighton. Traffic in cannabis resin was forever popular, and there seemed to be no shortage of it. Almost all the beats had smoked at one time or another, and some of the beats said that "shit" came before everything. Some beats made sure that they were never to be found carrying the stuff on them, but more often than not they would forget the danger of being picked up for the sake of their enjoyment.

There was less of a cult than might have been expected built around the use of LSD during this period. Eventually, people would take their first 'trip' and often find it disappointing. Normally, the acid users were very little trouble in the arch as they would be found just sitting quietly staring into space, and would make little or no response to conversation. One of our objections to drug-takers in the arch, was that one expected to be able to talk to them and it was annoying to be continually frustrated by blank stares!

When the arch closed, one boy came into his own as an acid-head and would lead groups of "trippers" in his flat. His feeling was that he wanted to "turn the whole town on" as it was so "fantastic and relaxing." Apparently the beats revered his superior knowledge on acid, and were willing to take everything he said as true.

The dominant aspect of drug-taking was the sleeping pill phase. It lasted about two months, when a number of individuals took it upon themselves to con doctors into giving them large quantities for their nerves. (Most of the beats are sensitive and nervous anyway, so a doctor may be forgiven for prescribing an aid to sleep.) Mandrax was the most popular for its effect of sending one to sleep could be delayed. This power of fighting the drug off could be intensified by taking a shot of methedrine as well. People would come into the arch staggering, pull themselves together, talk non-stop for a few minutes, and then pass out. Mandrax by itself seemed to make people randy, and they would go around the arch declaring their love for us all, kissing anyone they could, and then collapse in a heap on the floor. Obviously, this was great fun, as the victims would never remember what they had done or said under the influence, and everyone else would respond to them by gently guiding them to a place where they could sleep when they threatened to flake out. Everybody loved a druggie, so Ross used this feeling in trying to get the more responsible ones to take people home before they collapsed. Unfortunately, not many of them had homes to go to and it then became a question of begging someone's hospitality. There was a side aspect of this phase; because Mandrax made people feel so loving, they decorated themselves with flowing scarves around their heads and knees, and liked to play with decorating each other. For example, when Johnnie collapsed on his back, spreadeagled as if he was crucified, people reverently laid joss-sticks on his stomach!

Although Ross was appreciative of the fact that most of the drugs had been taken outside the arch, nevertheless, she was annoyed that they expected her to cope with the bodies.

Jago had held a meeting with the beats to discuss the problem when his archway was going through a similar phase, but Ross found it far simpler to make the saner people of the group responsible for looking after the others. During the period from November to December, there was a strong group feeling originating from the Action group that they could and should look after themselves. Of course, people were only too happy to oblige, since all parties thoroughly enjoyed the game. One night when there were about a dozen bodies asleep, Ross yelled to the Action group to "get the druggies out of here." They responded with remarkable alacrity. There was not a druggie in sight! Astonished, she went out for a breath of fresh air, only to discover that the group had propped up all the bodies outside along the wall of the ramp! Ross consistently took the line of getting the group to cope with its victims, and would close the arch an hour early as a token of her inability to work with unconscious people. Perhaps it should be noted in passing that the beats take drugs like this for kicks as they enjoy the effects, and they think that it enhances their appreciation of the world (even when they cannot remember it afterwards). One evening, when there were no drugs going round, we were treated to a sound and light show which had provoked a genuine "high" feeling in the arch. The beats misheard that the showman was coming back the next day, so in anticipation of this event they all got "stoned" in order to appreciate it better. Of course, most of them spent the second evening peacefully sleeping it off, and Ross closed the arch early yet again.

Being a trained nurse, Ross first of all worried when people collapsed, and she eventually learned that people did not hurt themselves when they fell. Some of the more hardened drug-takers would knock themselves out for 3-4 days.

The battle against people fixing in the arch was a losing one so long as we continued to have a toilet in which people had some privacy. We would catch people washing out their syringes, and would ask them again not to use the arch for fixing, but the evidence of discarded needles, syringes, swabs, and ampoules told their own story. Some individuals would get others to fix them, perhaps trying to share something, and then two unrepentant faces would emerge from the toilet. Short of searching people, the only technique that we could think of was to pin a notice up in the toilet which would niggle. It read "Owing to the fact that we cannot provide hygienic facilities for fixing, we must ask you to take all drugs outside. Thank you." This notice was painted over, had needles stuck in it, and was removed nearly every day. It became a matter of routine to replace the notice each time that the arch opened, so that there was no peace of mind for the people fixing in the toilet.

Many drug-takers and addicts are exhibitionists at heart. Ross was adamant that fixing was a private affair and the arch was a public place. She would not tolerate syringes being handed round or addicts fixing themselves out in the open for an audience. Always they would protest that they were all right because they were registered. Ross made it equally clear that whether they were registered or not, they were taking a dangerous stance in flaunting their addiction before a group of people who were hysterical about drug-taking and well prepared to be party to their exhibitionism. They would attempt to engage her in the classic arguments about drug-taking — do you smoke — thinking that she disapproved of drug-taking. Fortunately, Ross never witnessed such an alarming scene as Ashwell did in 141 when a girl drank a syringeful of her own blood. Ross took it upon herself to speak to all addicts personally to ask them to keep all drugs out of the archway when fixing was most prevalent in January. Ross must have shattered a few individuals by finding and destroying their secret stores in the cracks of the walls!

Brighton Archways Ventures did not have a very good liaison with a clinic, but this did not seem to matter as our roles were so different. They were concerned with treating serious addicts medically, and we were concerned with young people (some of whom were addicts) who wished to talk out their decisions. We soon realized that clinics had a policy of gradually cutting down people's drugs. This first of all made addicts very angry, until they found Dr. Z., who would freely prescribe narcotics to them (despite frequent requests from the drug clinic not to). So addicts would go to Dr. Z. to get drugs, and when they either felt ill or ready for a cure, they would get registered with the clinic. A couple of the more frantic addicts would go to both sources, but the surprising thing was in the new acceptability which the clinic had for junkies who had become scared of the hold that drugs were gaining over them. The clinic also had the means for getting people into hospital if they had septicaemia or jaundice, and a few individuals gained from a spell in the hospital. Under these conditions, going into hospital for a cure became less threatening and more acceptable. Many of the beats resented the lack of contact they were allowed with their drug friends outside, and others tried to get them to smuggle stuff into them. The relapse rate for people coming back on to the scene was, of course, very high, but at least they had the experience of being without drugs for a while. One of the most disappointing things for the most hardened addicts on going into hospital for a cure was the bitter realization that they could not live without their hopes and fears. The symbol of death for addicts lay in the death of Curly Dave who had died of an overdose the year before. When people talked about Dave they were usually trying to talk about death from addiction.

Since drug-taking endangered our position, we were faced with the arch being used by people who had nowhere else to go and was safe for them in their condition. Some individuals managed to keep their drug-taking right away from the arch (when they had flats to go to), so as they moved further on to the drug scene, we lost contact with them. One boy explained that his flat was so important to him as a place of his own that he endeavored to keep it clean of drugs. This, of course, meant that he used the arch instead! Other people seemed to seek the sanctuary of the arch when they were high as being the only place which was warm and safe. When people were in a state of complete oblivion, (as one boy was when he walked out in front of a bus and never knew how it had to brake to avoid killing him) was it not better that they should be in a relatively protected environment with other people around?

One important aspect of drug-taking seems to be the desire to turn someone on, i.e. give them their first drug. Sometimes this is for the financial gain of a pusher only, but more usually the beats make it a compliment to someone with whom they would like to share the good things of their life.

This then was the typical working situation in the Archway for day after day, week after week, month after month. It was a most gruelling time for the staff with little community support.

Streetwork

In the original Department of Education and Science application, it was planned that cafe and street work would be the task of the person whose major responsibility was for liaison with the town authorities and keeping the project records. In the event, Ashwell found that it was not possible to include the cafe and street work, and for the first year of the project we made no contact with the townspeople in these places. At the end of the summer project 1968, it was decided that Ashwell would take on the work with the local townspeople. It was expected that he would be able to use different cafes and entertainment centers (such as amusement arcades or the Top Rank dance hall, bowling alley and skating rink) as places where he could meet and work with young people.

Ashwell visited a number of cafes which did attract young people, but for various reasons did not consider them suitable. In several the clientele formed enclosed groups, exclusively ethnic in character; another attracted university students and this was ruled out because the University had an excellent health service for advice and consultation. One other was discounted because while it attracted young people, they were attached to an adult group.

150

The cafes which were considered all attracted young people to a leisurely atmosphere. They were all located on the fringe of the town's commercial and entertainments center. These cafes were a kind of halfway stage between the young people's homes and the commercial entertainments. The young people used the central entertainment facilities (cinemas, dance halls, discotheques, amusement arcades) but considered the cafes their home base. Ashwell did visit the dance hall, bowling alley and amusement arcades, all of which were considered unsuitable because they were incredibly noisy, very joyless, and were also used mostly by visitors. There were three cafes which were considered suitable work venues. One of them, used by a nucleus of boys who had visited the Archway, closed down before Ashwell had a chance to get to work. Eventually he concentrated on a second cafe and, because of this, did not again visit the third.

The chosen cafe was situated beside a small park which included a hard surfaced, floodlight football pitch. Apart from its day time clientele of market stallholders and shoppers, the cafe was used by a teenage group who were spectators at the football pitch and who occasionally used it themselves when it was unwanted by the club. As in all other cafes visited, Ashwell went as a customer, buying a meal or a cup of coffee depending upon the time of his visit. He read a copy of the local newspaper to make the whole procedure last longer. He found that the paper was often borrowed by the young people, and this was one way to start a conversation. He also took any available opportunities to comment on the weather, or any local incident which was in the news. This cafe's layout was surprisingly like the other home bases: there was a restaurant area with tables and chairs (all of which were movable), a small back room kitchen and a tiny basement containing football machines and pintables. The proprietors of this cafe had a policy of permitting the use of the basement only to the older boys: they never let any young girls or schoolboys go down there.

By the sixth visit Ashwell knew about a dozen people by sight and knew that all the young people referred to the middle-aged woman proprietor as "Mum." On the next visit some of the younger girls and Ashwell enjoyed themselves when they decided to flirt with him.

He was not at home in this cafe as it was not the kind of place he would use by preference. Unlike the young people, he was a stranger. He did not live in the area and the stable people they focused on were the cafe proprietors, which is clearly evidenced by "Mum's" affectionate nickname.

Visiting these cafes confirmed our view that the work in the cafes in Brighton was not possible unless one was the owner-manager. In this case, the proprietors set the conventions of behavior — there were specific rules about the use of the basement, which had originated when boys and girls were found kissing, which the proprietor thought would get the place a bad reputation; no dancing to the juke box was allowed; and one of the girls had been banned on her parents' request in their attempt to keep her away from that group of teenagers. These rules seemed acceptable to the young people, but they obviously restricted the clientele to those who were prepared to accept them. In a situation like this when the worker is a customer at the cafe, it would not be possible to build up a clientele beyond a number of people that the proprietors felt able to cope with. We estimated that this would be no more than 30 young people regularly using the cafe.

On reflection after this foray into the hinterland, we decided that our limited resources were best spent with the large numbers of youngsters attracted to the archways. We therefore abandoned streetwork.

Summary

Trying to find a definition of a beat is an academic question since the beat group tend to define themselves by sticking together. We asked one of the more articulate beats, who was in prison at the time, if he could suggest a better expression. His reply was as follows:

"I think it is ideal. Take it simply as a word in everyday life. If you beat an egg correctly you achieve something edible. If not, ugh. If you beat a drum you create a sound. If you compete in a race the object is to beat the rest, so "beat" is a form of individual expression which leads either to total achievement or utter disaster, which all "beats" are prepared to accept. It's either win or lose, hence their fatalistic attitude. They are prepared for either."

Of course, many of the beats, in common with other people, are sensitive about being classed as a group. They assert their individuality by announcing that they are a person, individual, human, me, and will also go to great pains to point out how different they are. For the purpose of working with young people, it matters little whether a person is technically a beat or not if he wants help.

The beats referred to in this report are taken to be the colorful characters who are on the road, and who tend to congregate on Brighton beach. They are a restless changing group of young people with no permanent employment, no address, no permanent identity, and often caught up in the drug fringe of London and Brighton. (This does not mean to say that some do not hold flats, for example, or cultivate their individuality, but these remarks are intended to serve only as a general guide.) Dress is frequently bizarre, and sometimes they go out of their way to alienate the rest of society; Isaiah is tall, had long hair trailing off after him, he walks with large strides, his nose is squashed, and he has a cleft palate which makes him impossible to understand; Pudding hides behind dark glasses and wraps himself up in a belted sheepskin; Ancient wears a worn-out top hat, tails and decorates his clothes with scraps of red taselses; Paul wears a big gold ring through his ear; Ginger Paddy has a shock of ginger hair which sticks out at each side. More often the beats appear scruffy or dirty-looking, with frizzed-out or straggly long hair, and are dressed in insignificant looking old clothes and usually jeans and jumpers, handed on from one to another without washing. The beat group became accustomed to a state of grottiness which often would not be tolerated by the ordinary citizen. They may be seen as striving to remain outside of, and untouched by society.

Herewith is the curious contradiction. Although the beat group may go to great lengths to hide their personalities from being known (by using fictitious names, by acting completely passively in a given situation so that they give no clue as to their real feelings), the result is a state of alienation or loss of contact from society. They may have their freedom, but alienation also results in a sense of being lost and denied the good things which society offers, such as shelter, security, status, goals, and a sense of purpose. Many of these things are basic to survival, which, therefore, looms as one of the beats' biggest problems. Without National Assistance payments (for they may not be able to withstand the questioning, or else the local office has cut them off thinking that this would encourage them to seek jobs) or any other income, food has to be obtained by other means. Thus the so-called independence from society means that the beats are utterly dependent on chance acquaintances for a meal, or for a bed in cold weather. Thus these young people are laying themselves open to exploitation by others. This can result in a loss of self-respect, even though the original intention in going beat was a bid for freedom. Workers soon become aware of those beats who find the hardships and indignities of their way of life hard to bear, and frequently these are the ones who put a lot of pressure on the worker to make life easier for them.

Besides having time on one's hands, having no obligations to fulfill, and needing to rely on one's own resources, time with nothing to do can weigh heavily. It is hard for us to imagine what it would be like to be on holiday all the time, with no visible end to it and no doubt it can become a rut like everything else. Many of the beats may be seeking some kind of routine to which they can relate in order to recover some sense of belonging. Maybe the demands which are placed on them periodically by the courts are just what is required to prevent some individuals from slipping into oblivion. Equally well it may have the reverse effect if the young person becomes embittered by his experiences and chooses to run further away.

The denial of social benefits to an out-group may have several consequences. Firstly, help may be demanded as a right due from society. Secondly, it may provoke a need to hit back at society in some way, either by doing the very things which are socially unacceptable, or by using society in order to demonstrate one's contempt of it. A third alternative could be to set up an anti-society which provides the very things which society fails to provide. The beat group illustrate the first point by their demand for money, food, a place to go, and status, all of which they expect to be given gratis. The need to hit back is illustrated perhaps by their drug-taking, passive resistance to social demands, growing of long hair (which frequently makes them unemployable), and the state of being unwashed. The fact that society treats an addict and an occasional cannabis-smoker alike in law as dreadful junkies and demands that a person prove that he is "bad" (by having large quantities of a drug in his body at the time of examination) before he is given legal supplies of a drug, invites an abusage of the social services by an exaggertion of their symptoms.

The anti-society is happily demonstrated by the way in which the beats look after one another, share property, and provide company and comfort for anyone in their midst without needing to know the person first. They are extraordinarily sensitive of each other's needs, tolerant of much antisocial behavior within the group, and attempt to be loyal to the ideal of an egalitarian, libertarian society. Occasional status hierarchies have been introduced to distinguish the real beats (who are self-sufficient and asocial) from the pseudo beats (who are more dependent on social props); the real junkie (who is registered, or needing a lot of the hard stuff) from the rest (who don't really need it).

The lack of commitment to any social obligations makes for pseudo freedom. It is an effort for most of them to arrive anywhere on time, and the longer the situation is left the less practice they get in coping on any level. Beats have difficulties reconciling their present circumstances with their ideal self-image, e.g. facing the fact that nobody in Brighton knows or even cares who they are. Some beats will make efforts to break any familial and social ties in order to retain their freedom, and more usually will adopt an attitude of normlessness in which anything goes.

In a social out-group, it can be expected that their isolation from society creates enormous barriers to communication. Yet their very way of life can be seen as a communication to a society which sets up some "white" expectations of fulfilling family committments: working for a living, being clean, and remaining chaste if not married. It is not clear how much of beat behavior is provoked by the acting-out of the polar opposite of society's expectations. If a young person fails to conform to the "white" image, for whatever reason of his own, (whether guilt, need for independence, need of attention) then he has the "black" image ready-defined, he must leave house, bum around, live off the state without working, and be irresponsible, dirty and promiscuous. If he achieves some notice in this state which he has failed to achieve within society then the dye is cast. Even when he tries to get back into society, the odds are against an employer accepting someone with long hair and a history of prison and unemployment. Besides, one needs to be bad in order to get understanding help or to have any notice taken of you. As a confused person on the borderlines of beatdom is of no interest to anyone. There are all degrees of commitment to the beat philosophy which may serve as either rationalizations for past failures or else as seeking an individual expression, but the important thing is that society demands that the beats conform to their image of an out-group, so that they may be judged. Therefore, one way of getting back at society would be to conform to the "black" image which is both expected and condemned, and one way of acting out guilt feelings, would be to become "black" and, therefore, punishable.

How far the beats internalize this conventional view of themselves as worthless outcasts of society, or as the black sheep of the family, is another question. A rebellious adolescent who finds a group of others who are somehow like himself, finds that he is classed with a group and is expected to adopt their standards. The situation is taken out of his hands as he chooses his dress and way of life to fit in with the group's norms. Thus, he may be rewarded by having friends behind him, or gaining the security of group norms, he may submerge in anonymity or make his own contribution to the group. Somehow, the uniform of the beat group is to be different, sometimes bizarre in dress. Unlike other groups the beats will accept into their midst anyone who is lonely and of the right age. Frequently, there is puzzlement that people can stoop so low to help them. Although an essential part of the beat philosophy is that of non-violence, they did accept a violent beat into the group. Many people come to terms with their feelings about violence, yet the beats have great difficulty in accepting someone who described himself as a sexual maniac and preferred to shun him. He posed a problem which was less easy to understand and, like beats, they ran away.

The normal permissiveness of the beat group, however, allows most of them to find expression and feel noticed. The most frequent expression is often that of strident denial as if they don't care what happens to them, e.g. by taking a drug overdose, laughing their way through a court case, and not bothering much who they are with. Yet when one of the group attempted suicide by gassing himself, the rescue was rapid, indicating that maybe they do care. Others, of course, are so apathetic that they will not lift a finger for anyone, but it is hard to know whether this is a death wish. Whether they secretly hope that someone else will step in, or just that they habitually detach themselves from any feeling is hard to say. The idea of setting up a community where they can all look after themselves is peculiarly attractive to this group. They have high ideals of a caring society (certainly they press any worker to be concerned about them) so that society is bound to fail them each time it is put to the test. Certainly the beats tend to adopt an attitude of passive resistance to society and will even let someone tip rubbish over them. They passively seem content to do exactly as they are told without the interlocutor knowing anything about their circumstances. We have come to view beat as that behavior of people who do exactly as the wind happens to blow. They accept what happens to them as an act of fate. This behavior is, of course, not exclusive to beats. They have one area of violent resistance, that of resistance to authority, and a number joined the Grosvenor Square riots just so they could have a go at a policeman. Otherwise, they can be seen as a basically depressed group, questioning every social value, "Why work?", "Why cut hair?", "Why get married?", and acting as though they are nothing.

We saw work with the beats as consisting of a holding situation where the beats would be able to relate to the worker if they wished but were principally allowed to explore their own meaning and value, in their own time and place. Making sense out of life seems to be a full-time occupation for some of the beats and the quest for identity takes many strange forms.

Identity can be revealed or else hidden from others by the use of false names, such as Ireland, Canterbury John, Sparrow, Witless, Bernard Blue, Ancient, Spirit, Pot Mary, Tripsy, Ugly Pete, Romany, Big Joe.

Maybe it is the quest for identity which makes the beats often latch on to the nearest clear-cut role — that of being a junkie. A brief description of a habitual drug peddler emphasizes this point. Vince has been known to use since 1966, when he was 17. He did not take many drugs but rather liked the idea. However, he paid a visit to Scotland, where he was picked up for possession of heroine, and rather than face a court case and prison, he said he was a heroin addict and was put into hospital. He was discharged sooner than if he had served a prison sentence. He returned to Brighton where the probation service found him lodging with a landlady who was supposed to look out for any sign of drug-taking. Eve met him once trying to walk off the effects of cannabis and heroin before returning home, for although Vince always took his responsibilities very much to heart, he was torn by the conflict of wanting to rejoin the scene. At this time he was withdrawn, he sulked around and was paranoid about people watching him. In fact, nobody would have looked twice at this inconspicuous, blue-denimed, short-haired youth.

Eventually, Vince made the break with his landlady and moved into the Mermaid hotel, a beat center, becoming more and more involved with taking various drugs but never actually becoming hooked. Vince enjoyed his own drug experiences so much that he was always willing to share them, and so he set himself up as contact man for the others. The greatest compliment he could pay someone would be to "turn them on." He was over-sensitive to any of the workers' rejection of his offers to get them some "shit" as this was the only form of living to him. Later he was genuinely puzzled at the thought of someone taking an acid trip once and saying that once was enough. In fact, he took his drug-peddling so seriously that he was continually on the lookout for contacts, and in the summer, would take a walk around the beach just so that people could approach him. By this time he had long hair and wore brightly colored clothes, and walked with a swagger which made one wonder who he thought he was. This role of pusher gave him an identity, without which he seemed lost.

Life, however, did contain other things. He became anxious about his health and confined himself to natural things (a rejection of much of the artificiality of everyday life.) He did not, however, see this as applying to drug-taking, for which he used all the props of colored glasses, music, and even listening to classical records under the influence. He saw it as a legitimate technique to con a doctor into prescribing sleeping tablets for his nervousness, and then to sell them to his friends. It is probable that he saw himself as performing a great service and thought he was being completely honest about it. For he held up certain ideals such as being trustworthy, honest, generous, happy, which he always strived to be. He was hurt and shocked if the worker ever saw him as being anything else, for it offended the ideal image of the state of heaven for which he was aiming. Beatdom was halfway there, as one had to reject much of the modern world in order to know yourself. When he as put on probation (for allowing his flat to be used for the smoking of cannabis), he questioned the probation officer's words that he should be industrious and finally took them very seriously. He had been toying with the idea of making himself legally not responsible for his actions by becoming a psychiatric patient. At the court case, he told the court that he did not believe in working, which finally left him with the dilemma of how to be industrious while not actually working. He compromised by doing casual work, such as painting the archway (for which he was not paid) and making candles to sell.

After this court case (perhaps frightened by his legal position), Quince became a registered addict. Subsequently, he began to take more and more drugs, until even his best friends said that he was no longer the same person to talk to. At this stage, Quince took fright, and went in for a cure saying that junk had done something to his mind to make him selfish but he really wanted to do things for others, as preached by the Buddhist religion. He agreed with the worker that this would be difficult for a junkie; 10 weeks later he announced that he had not touched drugs for three weeks and that he was doing this to enable him to join the Scientologists.

Quince is perhaps an example of the real beat: sensitive, sincere, and trying hard to justify his way of life with a philosophy while at the same time being able to use society for his own needs. It is interesting to note that he was psychologically addicted to drugs at least two years before he became registered, and even then he did not become physically addicted until he had his regular supply. Once hooked he was frightened at the change in his personality, for his ideal had always been that of mind over matter, and decided to come off drugs.

It may also be important that he had to go through the process of being registered and cured, which is now the institutionalized way of being an addict. Is this Quince's way of asking society to accept him?

The history of employment/unemployment, living in/living out frequently follows a pattern of the beats being scared by the police for them to make any real effort. It is quite convenient to a dosser to be picked up as winter approaches and conning is scarce, for a prison provides shelter and food over a difficult time of the year. Flat-dwelling rather depends upon the generosity of the rest of the group, who know very well that if a landlady finds ten people on the floor of a single room, they will be chucked out. In spite of this, most of the beats find it very difficult to say no to any of their less fortunate friends. The complications involved in getting a flat, therefore, and in paying the rent operate against any real settling down. A few, like Black Mike and Matthew, prefer to keep their addresses secret from the others but again it does not last long if they want to keep their friends. A few people around town will provide a bed. For example, Bert Mason (who sleeps with the girls), Alan, Sara, and Mrs. A. who has organized her house so that she can accomodate a few young people. The Mermaid hotel served as a cheap grotty place for beats with flats until the landlady was frightened by the police. The houseboat at Shoreham served as a home for many and later another boat at Newhaven, which was useful for those beats who wanted to work for a few days on the docks. Those who managed to keep flats all the time probably come to less notice than those who are continually getting a flat and losing it. One individual, Phantom, has a reputation for charming his way back into houses when everyone else had been chucked out.

Very negative attitudes frequently herald an attempt to get out of the scene. Sometimes it is the declaration that it is a bad scene, that drugs ruin you, that the life they are now leading is stupid, that there is nothing that you can call your own, and that they are fed up, or sick of it, or choked. The curious thing is that we do not know very much about the ex-beats who have found their niche in society, we only see the unsuccessful ones coming back when they could not cope.

Ways of becoming a beat are even harder to establish, especially when it is mixed up with a fantasy-filled background. The most obvious example we have seen is that of Portslade Pete, who came into the arch from school as a Bank Holiday helper. He originally saw the beats as worthless people and could not understand any attempt to help them. A little later he was expelled from school for refusing to cut his hair, and got himself a laboring job. He still had to endure a certain amount of ostracism from his workmates for having long hair, but he found that as long as he had friends among the beats he could identify with them in dress. He keeps his job and keeps his money to himself, and pays the rent for a flat for two. But he began to experiment with drugs, saying, "Once I was scared of an injection but when you see people fixing all the time you're not scared anymore." He saw himself as having nothing to lose since society was sick and not worth his while contributing to; he experimented with shoplifting although he didn't need to, and became very involved with one of the beat girls, Jamie. In the archway he still worked as a helper "if you think I'm responsible enough" but was often out on drugs when he should have been working, and seemed to be trying to sort out his own values within the context of the arch and the beat group.

Sean, on the other hand, had finished with being a junkie when he was asked to leave university after his beat friend had died of an overdose. It scared Sean into taking a cure. When a love affair had broken up, he attempted to gas himself but said again, "The will to live is too strong" and he sought help. His parents, however, got fed up with having him around the house, being too depressed to work, so he teamed up with Pudding and both of them set off to go around the world. They only got as far as Brighton in summer '68, where they parted company. Sean went off hop-picking, came back to Brighton and settled into a hotel job, and enjoyed playing the role of beatnik for the hoteliers, and Pudding drifted around the London and Brighton scene before being scared away on the run. Sean is enjoying his state of being a beatnik. He will not go the full way of sacrificing his financial security, and he has a firm conception of the other life which he will eventually return to. He gets his kick out of having long hair, standing for free love and irresponsibility. He sees society as "dragging you down" to the stage of being beat but once there you have "nothing to lose" so can afford to look down on society. He keeps reminding himself that Christ was just as bad as the worst of the conners on the road, and therefore, there is something noble about the beat way of life. However, Sean needs to toe the line between conventional society and the beat group in a way which does not suit Pudding. Pudding seeks anonymity, and retired to a remote cottage in the Pennines for the summer.

Both Sean and Pudding come from middle class homes, but were more or less thrown out by their parents. Sean still visits home fairly frequently, to see his mother, but he does not talk to his father. Many of the beats seem to have come from very much poorer backgrounds, some from the Glasgow slums, and many are from disturbed or broken home backgrounds.

As a group, they accept into their midst all who are of the right age group. Although the group is made up of some very inadequate personalities, they have a high degree of tolerance and involvement with each other which enables them to relax in company with other beats. We noted the huge need of the beats to use the arch as a playroom, although it is not clear whether this is an expressed need or for action as opposed to words. The tendency of the group to stick together when they are on the road frightens people who fear the contagion of habits such as drug-taking. Mrs. A. prefers to work with small groups only (perhaps three or four) to whom she rents flats in her house, and finds that she can get much further in rehabilitative work if the individual is removed from the rest. On the other hand, individuals can become very lonely when they are surrounded by nothing but square people, and long to get back to the old scene. This feeling must operate against the cure of drug addicts in hopsital, who are abandoning not just a drug, but a whole way of life. Many of the beats find that feelings of shyness, feelings of difference, and boredom, interfere with their few contacts with ordinary, nonexploitative, people. For this reason, we hoped to encourage large numbers of helpers to the archway who would present some gentle social experience. We found that the average student helper did not relate too easily to this particular group.

On the other hand, it would seem that on humanitarian grounds, even the beats have a right to some kind of warmth and shelter in winter when everyone else is indoors. Other people are able to recover a damaged self-respect by having a wash when they feel like it, or an occasional change of clothes; the beats also needed these. For people like Mrs. A. to work, there must be a catchment area from which she can find the individual, who is most in need of help, whether this be the beach or a social center. The unattached worker can move more freely than the worker who is tied to premises, but when premises are made available, a whole group may make use of them as opposed to the one or two contacts of the unattached worker.

We would have liked to have provided emergency sleeping accomodation either on the floor of the archway, or else in flats. We were not able to build up a network of kindly motherly people that, for example, would nurse a girl with flu, take in somebody who was out on drugs, or give some security and friendship to individuals. It would have been useful to be able to fill a hostel with young people who were trying to lead a more settled life after coming out of prison or hospital. It would have been very useful to have had access to a houseful of cheap flats or bedsitters where the more settled beats could begin to set themselves up. Frequently, beats try to settle down with a girlfriend, who can act as a valuable stabilizing influence provided that they are allowed to live as man and wife. Within the present laws, no public or private house can afford to allow drugs on the premises. There would seem to be some value in trying to work with a drug-taking group by excluding the use of drugs and trying to focus more on personal interaction, but we are not sure whether this is being fair to drug addicts.

A number of ideas have crystallized out of the archway project. The Brighton Health Department are recognizing their responsibilities in accomodating the beat group in an archway-type setting which would have access to emergency sleeping accomodation and a small hostel attached. A church wished to set up a hostel for ex-addicts and ex-prisoners. There remain the problems of the unmarried mother who is a prostitute in order to get money for drugs and for her children; couples trying to settle down together without legal marriage; the addict who is afraid to be alone and cannot save any rent; the girl who wants to escape from home for the weekend but is not sure that she wants to sleep in a derelict house, and many, many other problem youngsters.

Formal Attempts To Consolidate, Maintain And Further The Aims Of The Project: The Consultative Group

Throughout 1966, Klein and Biven approached many different people in Brighton who might be suitable members of a support group for this new project. Many of these people did eventually become members of the first formed committee.

The people who Klein and Biven invited to be sponsors of the project were Lady Albemarle, Lord Cohen, Sir Elwyn Jones, Mr. W.G. Stone, Mr. Dennis Hobden, Rev. Geoff Whitfield, Mr. Barry Wood, Alderman Knowles, and Lord Hunt. They were asked if they were willing to be associated with a project which would, on a voluntary basis, cope with the Bank Holiday traffic of young people in Brighton. It was suggested that the organization could be called Brighton Weekenders Holiday Scheme. Also during 1966, considerable contact was made with the Brighton Police Force.

An initial approach was made to Mr. Cavey, Chief Constable of Brighton Police on 19th April, 1966 by Biven, one month before the first Bank Holiday weekend. The intention was to inform Mr. Cavey of the nature of the project, and to get some useful discussion started. However, the reply from the Chief Constable was:

> ". . . . I am not prepared to meet you on this subject and, therefore, I am not able to assist you."

On 5th July, Klein who had volunteered to be responsible for the August 1966 weekend, wrote again to Mr. Cavey:

> "It is hoped to provide a service for young people on the lines of the project run at Whitsun from Archway 190, for the August Bank Holiday weekend, and I have been asked to be responsible for the general supervision of the weekend . . ."

Following this letter, as there was no reply from the police to the letter, Klein telephoned Police H.Q. and spoke to the Assistant Chief Constable. On 14th July, Mr. Cavey wrote to Klein saying:

> *"Further to your telephone conversation with the Assistant Chief Constable, I have made arrangements for you to discuss this matter with Superintendent Probyn . . ."*

It was important, at this stage, that a relationship should be built between the police and the project because, during the Bank Holiday weekends, the feeling amongst those working on the project, was that the police who did make contact with the Archway were actively trying to upset the work. Visits by individual or groups of policemen often disrupted any peaceful atmosphere that may have been created in the Archway. The way in which some of the kids were treated in the sleeping centers made the helpers, as well as the kids, hostile to the police.

By the end of 1966, contact had been made with the Chief Constable, the Assistant Chief Constable and Superintendent Probyn, who was the officer in immediate charge of the seafront area. Much contact had also been made with many of the policemen on the beat at the Bank Holiday weekends.

In November, 1966, Klein and Biven applied to the Department of Education and Science for grant aid for the project Brighton Archways Ventures, and following this, wrote to Mr. Cavey on 3rd January 1967:

> *"Following our telephone conversation yesterday, I am enclosing a copy of the original application to the DES, submitted early in November and now under discussion.*
>
> *I have received a letter from the Department which is, on the whole, favorable to Stage I, but the Minister would wish to be assured that the scheme is acceptable to Brighton and, following enquiries by Mr. Leyden, the HMI concerned with 'Other Further Education,' i.e. concerned with young people who may no longer be at*

school, we have been asked to discuss the scheme with the Director of Education, Dr. Stone, Mr. Leyden and yourself. Dr. Stone has suggested January 17th (1967) . . . Mr. Biven will also be there. Mr. Biven is the originator of the scheme in the first place. He is an experienced youth worker, now reading for a degree at the University of Sussex.

So much for introductions. I have been thinking where the points might be which would cause most discussion among us. On the Archway-and-hostel scheme, I believe we have worked successfully together. This is not where the problems will lie: police control in previous years, a change in the type of youth coming here, and the effects of a good night's rest seem to have made for a more peaceful town. It is on provision for the beats and beachcombers that there may be issues between us and, as reference to them in the application is brief, it may clear some ground to be more explicit now.

*This is a growing problem and a national one. Brighton is a sort of reception area for them. Some are delinquent and this is where the police do their part, others are 'predelinquent' and this is where other agencies are needed **for preventative and rehabilitory work**. Neither the youth service nor social workers are as yet catering for this group, which needs a great deal of attention if the problems are not to become aggravated in the next ten years. It is vital to begin to tackle this now. In the first instance, an experienced social worker is needed to get to know these people and to use his opportunities to reconnect them to normal life, helping them to appreciate the implications and consequences of their actions so that they may live their lives in a way which brings them greater satisfaction and society a greater benefit, making contact with employment agencies for some, treatment centers for others, parents for others, and so on. It will need an outstanding person to do this, but it needs doing.*

This is the kind of thinking which lay behind the original application. You will appreciate that it stems from

*one kind of experience with young people and is to that
extent limited. If we pool our knowledge, modifications
of what we had in mind will naturally come about and
the scheme will gain by it. At the moment, there is not
a formal organization (since as yet there is no definite
grant) but I hope that you yourself, or one of your
representatives, will feel able to sit on the Responsible
Body which will be formed to administer the scheme, for
further help and consultation. Meanwhile, I look forward
to our meeting."*

Several people were invited to be members of a responsible
body, who would guide and support the workers, once the
grant of $30,000 had been agreed upon by the Department of
Education and Science.

The responsible body was formed with the knowledge that
a good supportive group of people, who were well-known in
the town, could be a tremendous boon to the workers. The
original conception did not expect this group to be responsible for the progress of the project, by making the important
decisions which would affect the work.

Those invited to join the group formed a wide cross-section
of the professional people in the town. Most of the people who
had originally been asked if they would be willing to be sponsors to the Brighton Weekenders Holiday scheme were not associated with the new group. Correspondence with one of these,
Alderman Knowles, illustrates the difficulty involved in forming a useful group. As early as July 1966, he was asking that
assurance could be given:

*". . . . That what you and those associated with you are
doing will not in your considered opinion result in many
more youngsters coming to Brighton to take advantage
of your half-crown 'flop-joint.'*

*"That measures will be taken to ensure that supervision
from the health point of view is much improved. That
blankets will be properly cleaned. That sleeping bags at
the Salvation Army will be provided additionally.*

That no charge of any kind will fall on the rate-payers
as a result of the activities or any extension of them."

Alderman Knowles remained unassured, because he did not attend the first group of meetings, and was not invited to attend the first meeting of Brighton Archways Ventures, and did not respond to overtures from the founders.

The first meeting of the responsible body was held on March 2, 1967 at the Brighton Social Services Centre.

"It was readily agreed that Dr. Klein would be Chairman and Mr. Biven Secretary. Mr. Worthington, Youth & Community Officer, was present as an observer. He referred to a letter by the Director of Education, Mr. Stone, which said:

'The question of official participation on this body was discussed at the last Youth & Community Sub-Committee and it was decided that it would not be the right course for the committee to appoint an official representative, although naturally individuals acting in their private capacity would make their own decisions. In the circumstances, I think there would be objections to senior officers of the Corporation becoming members since when later discussion or evaluation takes place it might be embarrassing for an officer advising a local authority Committee to be officially associated with the project itself.

'This is, of course, not to say that I should not be happy to learn what is happening. Indeed, I should value the opportunity of hearing from time to time how the scheme develops and any difficulties which may be encountered. It might even be possible, if this were agreeable to you, for me or a representative to attend occasionally at meetings.' "

Mr. Cavey, the Chief Constable, attended the first meeting of the responsible body. He was not willing to belong to the body himself, but a later letter shows that at the meeting he agreed that he would find a suitable officer to serve on the responsible body. [On 13th March 1967, Mr. Cavey wrote saying that the Superintendent Probyn was willing to serve on the committee.] The minutes report:

> *"Mr. Cavey was also present and expressed goodwill toward the scheme. He foresaw difficulties arising when the youth workers' reports dealt with matters of which the police were bound to take cognizance. The position is to be clarified and reported upon at the next meeting."*

The Easter Bank Holiday weekend was the next important event. A student volunteer had agreed to be responsible for the weekend. This was the first weekend run as Brighton Archways Ventures. Following the successful use of Archway 190 during the Bank Holiday Weekends of 1966, Biven and Klein decided that the two vacant Archways 141 and 167 would be ideal for premises for the new project. Negotiations with the corporation took place during February and the leases were signed on 15th of March 1967 by Klein, Biven, and Mr. G.L. Brown, who was then the acting treasurer.

Archway 167 was in a very bad state of repair before the project used it, and all facilities had to be built in. Electricity had to be connected, a floor had to be laid in the main room, the plumbing fixed, and the whole place redecorated. Storage heaters had to be left on permanently throughout the year as water was always oozing through the ceiling.

It is situated at the bottom of a slope. This is a favorite area for holidaymakers throughout the most of the day, because here are the traders selling ice cream, doughnuts, hot pies, and fish and chips. During the evenings, many people use the three pubs which are open during the summer months. On the lower promenade at beach level, thousands of holidaymakers walk enjoying being by the beach. This meant that a very high proportion of the young people who were visiting Brighton would walk past the entrance to the archway.

Archway 141 was very much smaller. It had two rooms, one above the other, each 15 feet square. It was used to store blankets until the August 1967 Bank Holiday weekend, when it was opened as an information center for the volunteers, and the center for the beats. The only alterations which were necessary were for a stouter door and side shutters to be fitted.

141 was in an ideal situation for the beats because it is only 20 yards from the spot that they usually occupied on the seafront.

Some people working at the weekend felt that since the police were now represented on the Responsible Body, it would be easier to work with the foot patrols during the weekend. However, there seemed to be no noticeable change in the attitude of the policemen who were on duty at the holiday weekend. One volunteer at a sleeping center reported:

> *"A radical change of behavior in the young people occurred during Sunday night such that its causation must be sought outside the sphere of general progression. Many of the young visitors had suddenly begun to help whereas, on the previous nights, they had been uncooperative. This cause was clearly the visit of the unsympathetic police inspector and his companions, whose aggression was largely directed against the helpers."*

Reports from other sleeping centers gave evidence of the police visits disrupting peaceful atmospheres. Volunteers involved with the project at this weekend felt that the police were testing out the helpers, rather than being simply antagonistic. Unfortunately, their way of testing out a hall full of sleeping youngsters was to wake them all up, get them excited and then see how helpers coped.

Before the next meeting of the responsible body (the meetings were scheduled to occur every two months) Klein sent this letter to each member of the Body on 31st March 1967:

"Note from the Chairman

Since our last meeting, various queries have arisen as to the function of the responsible body. We ought to discuss this at our next meeting. My own views extracts from a letter I wrote in answer to such queries — are set out below.

'The question of how decisions are made is a very tricky one. The money is, of course, largely earmarked. We are not free to use it except in the way laid down by the terms of the grant. What is left is, e.g. the appointment of the workers, the midweek uses of the Archways, the sorts of activities that take priority over others.

'It is difficult to know in advance what decisions will need to be made. My main concern is that the workers should never feel that they have to wrestle with an unsympathetic committee as well as with their own clientele. They should not be asked to pursue courses of action against their own judgment of the situation.

'In those circumstances, what is the function of the rest of us? Ideally, everyone should be in close touch with everyone else concerned. This is open equally to me, to you, to anyone who wishes to get involved in this work. In practice, it will not work out that way, because people have a lot of commitments. I, therefore, thought of a responsible body which would receive and consider reports, make their views known and mutually consider how best to do things. I hoped that with a set of people all feeling equally responsible, it should be possible to reach consensus. I now think this is no longer feasible, since the Brighton Council of Social Service's position is uncertain, and the LEA officials and the police have signified they are to be observers only. In those circumstances, since power without responsibility is not desirable, I propose at the next meeting to define the responsible body's function as consultative.

'In that case what about the sponsors? That is, Lady Albemarle, Lord Hunt, the NAYC, and the University of Sussex. I do not think they should be distinguished from

173

other full members of the responsible body/consultative committee. As I said above, it is hard for me to imagine an issue on which we cannot reach a common mind, but if such an issue did arise, then the Chairman would be required to put it to the vote (from which observers would be excluded) in the responsible body/consultative committee.

'Having said this, it seems important to impress again on everyone that the whole venture exists for young people, and that the three paid workers are paid to work with them and to know what is going on. The power of expertise lies with them, and with those who make it their business to be in close touch with them. To my mind, there is no legitimate power other than competence — that is what I mean as responsibility. The center of gravity lies, therefore with the workers.' "

Following the Easter Bank Holiday weekend, a businessman who lived close to Archway 167 wrote this published letter to the Evening Argus Newspaper.

"Dr. Klein says the aim is to cater for those who, at Bank Holidays and weekends, visit Brighton without knowing anything about the town and being prepared to sleep on the beaches.

She says considerable numbers were coming to the arch between three o'clock and five o'clock in the morning.

I know this to be true, as it was impossible to sleep during the early hours due to noise of those, sometimes in gangs of six or more, coming and going to the cener, shouting and singing.

. . . For a long time past Brighton Corporation has endeavored to clear the seafront of the beatnik type, and I would have thought by allowing this all-night center on the seafront we can look forward to the encouragement of more of this type.

. . . Over the Easter holiday we saw and heard the damage and complete disregard for other people's property when young people in gangs walk the streets . . .

If a center is needed does it have to be on the seafront?
. . .

Signed Mr. K.

This was the first major public attack that had been made on the project. Klein replied to Mr. K. personally rather than through the press.

At the same time, Biven and Klein were having difficulties with the application for a grant to the Department of Education and Science. The advisor to the minister had supported the scheme but the minister had rejected it. However, it was eventually possible to meet the minister in the House of Commons for five minutes before he was due to catch a train. Biven and Klein were given a few minutes to explain why they thought they should receive a grant instead of many other equally deserving projects. It was certainly no time for compassion and they did think that the project was truly experimental and innovatory. The grant was eventually offered on certain conditions which Biven and Klein thought were quite generous and more than acceptable. All monies would be clearly earmarked, the categories of expenditure were broad and flexible. It was also recommended that the project be sponsored by well established institutions in the youth work field. The National Association of Youth Clubs and the University of Sussex were happy to accept the invitations and did indeed remain sponsors throughout the duration of the project.

At the next meeting the responsible body on March 4th 1967, at which only nine people appeared (three more apologizing for their absence), Ashwell was introduced as the first of the three workers.

Klein explained the function of the committee as a "**Consultative Group.**" The minutes indicate that no discussion followed. Since Superintendent Probyn was unable to attend the

175

meeting, Inspector Hall and Sgt. Stemp attended in his place. They brought up three points relating to the Easter Bank Holiday weekend which Superintendent Probyn had raised in a letter to Klein prior to the meeting:

> "(a) The failure to segregate the sexes at several premises;
> (b) The need for rules to govern the conduct of the premises;
> (c) The provision of a simple form of register at each center. This is most important in the unfortunate event of a fire occuring and the need to check inmates."

Those at the meeting, who had been involved during the Easter Bank Holiday weekend, disagreed about points (b) and (c). The police felt that because no rules had been made, the sleeping centers could develop into a free-for-all. They felt that the existence of rules would stop this happening. The argument made against this was that the evidence showed that the visitors behaved themselves and that stated rules were, therefore, unnecessary.

When Klein asked the committee which rules they felt should be made, Sgt. Stemp suggested that a rule be made that anyone who broke up the furniture, for instance, should be made to pay for it. The argument against this was that to advertise such a rule would probably put the idea into people's minds, since evidence showed that it was furthest away from most visitors' thoughts. The other point made was that the person who was likely to break up chairs was hardly likely to stay and pay for the damage afterwards. No other suggestions were made.

The ideas of those who had worked at the weekend on the subject of making a register at each sleeping center were shared by more members of the committee than in the previous argument. Ashwell said that if a register were set up, the youngsters would probably put down inaccurate and false information, so there would be little point in the task. A further argument was that this would be another barrier through which youngsters would have to move, before they could be properly welcomed by the helpers. This would make our work even more difficult.

These discussions well illustrated the lack of understanding of the committee in the nature of the work, mainly because most members had not visited the archway or a sleeping center, and were mainly ignorant of the working atmosphere. This reluctance by the founders to concede to the recommendations of the police put the project in a new light for some of the members of the group, because the authority of the police was questioned.

Ashwell announced that he would be responsible for the Whitsun Bank Holiday weekend arrangements.

Eight people were present at the following meeting on the 22nd June, 1967, four more people sending their apologies for absence. Jago was introduced to the committee as the second paid worker.

Reports from the volunteers at the Whitsun and August 1967 Bank Holiday weekends indicated that the police were being much more cooperative with the project volunteers. There were no reports of the police being difficult although one policewoman was apparently sending many old people to one of the sleeping centers, saying that all the others were full up, and that the volunteers in the center had no option but to take them.

The paid staff worked together for the first time at the August Bank Holiday weekend, which started on 25th August, 1967. At this stage, the beat worker was a volunteer, but had been invited to apply for the post. The workers had a quick introduction to the nature of local feelings about the project when they were confronted by irate neighboring traders complaining about the weekend arrangements. The workers found that their defense of the project went unheeded because it appeared that the traders were complaining more about the types of young people using the project.

A local businessman encouraged the traders to make formal complaints to the council about the project and, as a result of these complaints, the archway team was asked to meet, with the traders, and with some representatives from Brighton Entertainments and Publicity committee to discuss the situation. These were the complaints:

". . . At this time of 1 a.m. I saw inside Arch 141 and I saw a crowd of undesirable people in all kinds of states. Some were drunken outside Arch 141 using foul language and shouting loudly. I saw girls and boys lying on the floor and completely covering the floor space of the arch. They were lying on what appeared to me to be blankets. They were creating a noise with music.

I was worried that a fight might develop with the drunks outside so I called the police. I was informed by the police that they would keep an eye on the place" . . . Mr. B.

"The type of person attracted to the arches being used as rest centers are a complete nuisance to all who are decent and have some respect for their fellow men. They tend to congregate in large numbers outside the arches allocated to them for hours on end, in fact they congregate all the time the centers are open, whether this be day or night. In most cases they are dirty and most undesirable . . ." Mr. M.

"Whenever Arch 167 is open I suffer badly business-wise. This Arch is usually open on our busy trading bank holiday weekends. They tend to hang around my shop premises and it is noticeable to see the ordinary family type of person walking wide of my shop premises. They openly smoke joss sticks outside my premises and the terrible smell penetrates into my archway where I trade . . ." Mr. R.

"On Friday 25th August Arch 141 opened under what I deem to be a pretext that it would be used as an information center to help get off the beach those who had no place to sleep. When this arch opened about 20 of the flower type of person and beatniks arrived. When they had got settled down all hell broke loose, they were

screaming, shouting, dancing, with music playing . . . All appeared to me to be in some state of embrace and in my opinion looked as though they had found their haven. Their haven was my hell, as although there were still people about who would have purchased from me they would not stop as the smell was overpowering. Many people passing by put their handkerchiefs to their faces to walk straight on. I had no alternative but to close down even though I could have remained open until 11 p.m. . . "
Mr. W.

"Whenever Arch number 141 is open it is noticeable that this reflects in our shop taking. The people using Arch 141 are dressed most peculiarly and invariably are dirty. People who would stop to look at our display always walk two or three feet away from our shop premises in order to avoid these characters." Miss S.

"During this year when I have been exercising my dog on the lower promenade I have seen some of the goings on of the people who frequent Arch 167 and of recent date Arch 141. Whilst walking with my wife after 12 midnight we have both seen the type of person using these centers. We have seen them leave Arch 167 and urinate against the adjoining properties. Toilets are open to the lower esplanade and when once I told this to a young beatnik a string of abuse was thrown at me. At every Bank Holiday weekend long trails of urine can be seen running down the slope where the rest center is situated. I have seen five youths leave the rest center, just in front of myself whilst walking down to the lower esplanade, and tip over eight full litter bins which are placed in the uppermost part of the beach opposite Middle Street. The flower people that are attracted to the lower prom because of these centers have actually picked geraniums from the garden surrounding the putting green then offered them to the passing public. Both my wife and myself were offered them. During the August bank holiday my wife saw 15 of the type of person using these arches come out of Arch 167 and immediately in front of the these premises they commenced painting each other's

179

*bodies stripped to the waist. When the whole operation
was completed over all their bodies the bearded leader
placed a sheet over his shoulders and proceeded with two
pages holding the sheet and the rest of the retinue along
the lower promenade and returned along the top
promenade. Many times when I have walked down to the
lower esplanade there have been crowds of these young
people outside Arch 167. Sometimes they sit like a lot
of birds on the railings. It is quite easy to see that some
are carrying knives and it would not be practical to tan-
gle with them" . . . Mr. K.*

*"The type of person frequenting Arch 167 are absolutely
disgusting in their behavior and habits. This is especially
so when I have seen them leave Arch 167, go over opposite my premises, where I am manageress, and actually
engaged in the act of making love. They have a couldn't
care less attitude and do not seem to mind who might
be watching . . . have heard little children asking their
parents what they are doing and have seen the parents
quickly take the children away from our trading area"
. . . Mns. B.*

A consultative committee meeting was held on September
7th 1967 and was much more eventful. Thirteen people were
present and four people sent their apologies.

During the August Bank Holiday weekend, a week previous to this meeting, the local traders complained about Arch
141 being used as a boat center on the Friday evening of the
weekend. This had resulted in the local paper announcing that
a group from the entertainments and publicity committeed were
wanting to meet the project staff to discuss the traders' complaints. A small group from project committee agreed to meet
the entertainments and publicity committee.

Two opposite pressures were occuring within the consultative committee at this stage. There was pressure being brought
to bear on each member to become more committed to the
project, while at the same time the project was being drawn
into conflict with the town fathers. It is hardly surprising then

180

that the discussion that followed the invitation to meet the entertainments and publicity committee was concerned with the function of the consultative committee.

It was suggested that the function of the committee needed to be clarified. Was it a steering committee that would throw out ideas, a policy making committee or an executive committee? Who thought out the policy as regards the overall venture? What should we do with the under-16s? Drug-traffic? And so forth. The committee were unable to settle the question of legal responsibility. It was clear that the committee could not be held legally responsible for the Archway premises but that the founders and lessees might be. The committee should be able to assess the situation and calculate the risks involved in alternative policy decisions. What was the nature of the work that needed to be done with those in trouble with the law? It was obvious from the content of the discussion that many of the members had not considered what any form of membership meant with regard to legal issues. Once the situation of having to defend the project occurred, many members demonstrated a lack of support. The situation must have been even more worrying to some because the workers had just previously rejected two recommendations from the police.

One member of the committee articulated his fears concerning the basis of the project in a long letter to Biven and Klein.

23 September, 1967

> . . . You know that for some time I have been expressing concern about the way in which the Archway Scheme has been developing. From time to time I have spoken to you about my doubts, and I am sorry that you have not been able to remove them. I do feel that the way in which you are working is so far out of sympathy with the aims and methods originally envisaged that I must withdraw from the Committee . . . I am particularly anxious about the following points:

. . . The voluntary workers. No attempt has been made to employ any standards of selection for voluntary workers in the scheme. Consequently, as you are well aware, many young people who are themselves in difficulties of some complexity have been involved in the scheme as "helpers . . ."

. . . The "professional" workers. Those whom you have so far appointed appear to have neither training nor experience in social work with adolescents. These salaried workers, who must bear the brunt of the work, are above all in need of an advisory committee which takes ultimate responsibility for their actions and determines broad lines of policy within which they should work . . .

. . . The general anti-authoritarian atmosphere which is at present pervading the whole project, and the disregard shown by "professional" and voluntary workers for "officials" in general seems to be alienating professional social workers . . .

Sincerely, ...

Shortly after this letter was received, Jago and Biven arranged a meeting with Mr. Williams, the Chief Constable of Sussex. It should be noted here that Mr. Williams was one of the original contacts in Sussex when Paddy McCarthy and Biven first planned an accomodation scheme and the Chief had been enthusiastic at that time.

When Jago and Biven met Mr. Williams, Biven was careful to make it known that he was one of the original group and reminded the Chief Constable of his interest. Mr. Williams sought to give us the assurances we needed and very quickly understood what we were trying to do. It was a refreshing change to find a senior officer striving for similar goals.

After a short talk with the drug squad where Jago made the plea for renewed pressure on the traffickers of drugs and more sympathy and fewer arrests of the drug-takers, we left the meeting feeling that a major step had been taken in police/project relationships.

This was exactly the kind of cooperation we had been working for for so long and which seemed so difficult for the committee to understand. Many of the members of the committee seemed to be obsessed with the letter of the law and were quite unwilling to see that we were incapable of helping a large number of boys and girls unless we were able to operate in an environment free from harrassment from the police and pressures from pushers.

What was clearly needed on the consultative committee was a mature group of people from a variety of walks of life and allied professions who were prepared to meet with the workers regularly and listen to what were doing.

This experience told us that politically motivated men and women who had vested interests in management and directorial skills would be unlikely to act in the passive role of supporter and clarifier. In any new experiment the experimenters need to know that there are a few people close to them who understand and support their efforts. This does not mean that the support group merely listens and does not contribute. What matters is the quality and style of the contribution. There needs to be sensitivity to what the workers are feeling and what they have been through. Unfortunately, in the Brighton committee, due to some pressure from the Department of Education and Science, Klein and Biven sought out people with status and authority. Although many of these people were highly trained they had been holding executive positions for many years and were insensitive to the new approaches in social work and youth work generally. One also sensed that they felt, initially at least, that a seat on the committee might be politically astute. Many of the committee had become set in their ways and found it difficult to accept the underlying philosophy of the work. Klein and Biven often felt in their more depressed moments that the committee represented only a more liberal version of those traders and councillors who wished that these young drifters would just go away.

In retrospect, it was probably the most expensive mistake the project made. It would have been wiser to try to persuade the Department of Education and Science to give us time to find more supportive people. It is obvious that it is easier to find such people once a project is a reality and staff have been appointed. The Department's circular made the formal committee of responsible local people a prerequisite for receiving grant aid. Although, this may ensure that the work is favourably received and increases the chances of the project being adopted by the local authority at the end of the experimental period, it does hamper genuine experiment. Such innovation must at times question the values and actions of those very people who make decisions for and on behalf of others, in whatever capacity.

We have no way of knowing to what extent the town council were influenced by the departure from the project committee of some of the more eminent people engaged in the social services in the town. But it is likely that this had some hidden effect on the status of the founders and their ability to conduct themselves properly according to the opinions of the town fathers.

However, the committee was never the hub of resistance to the archways scheme. That lay with some aldermen, Mr. K. and a few traders. The precise reasons for their dislike of the work and the clients was unclear but their opposition is documented elsewhere in this report.

It is doubtful whether any committee, however favourable and openly supportive of the project, could have coped unless they had managed to win the confidence and public support from more powerful men and women on the council. It is always possible to make out a strong case for ridding a town of dirty, unkempt itinerant young beggars. As one councillor remarked, "Brighton is a family resort." There was an active attempt to discourage young people from coming to Brighton whether they were well behaved or not. But a critique of the actions and attitudes of the council to the town's natural assets which have over the years been neglected and destroyed, would make another separate report.

Perhaps ironically, many of the holidaymakers found the beats an added attraction and enjoyed listening to them play guitars and sing. Often they could be seen sitting chatting with the beats engaged in some earnest discussion and the workers saw very few incidents of holidaymakers being repelled by their presence.

Some committee members were seduced by the arguments of the local opponents and since they were more comfortably aligned with the status and positon of the opponents it is understandable why they preferred to dissociate themselves from the project. But it remains unforgivable that some of the committee and the opponents did not even bother to accept invitations from the workers to see for themselves what was going on. If there is one thing that can be learned from this unhappy chapter, it is that experimental projects must be given the time and freedom to draw to them interested and useful people once the work has got underway. Far better to start with a loose association of individuals and allow them to grow into a formalized group as the situation demands.

Relations Between The Project
And The Brighton Town Council: Litigation

After considerable opposition from the town fathers all the staff met to redefine policies for the project. This was a lengthy meeting in which Ashwell and Ross appeared, to Klein, Biven and Jago to be uncommitted to the future of the project. Conversations toward the end of the meeting about trust and mistrust were partially resolved and everyone left the meeting feeling little depressed.

January 15th was the day of the court case. The formal notices terminating the tenancy of Archway 167 on Christmas Day 1968 (these had been received on 13th June 1968) also stated that:

> "The landlord would oppose an application to the court
> . . . for the grant of a new tenancy on the grounds that
> (i) you ought not to be granted a new tenancy in view
> of the substantial breaches by you of the obligations
> under the current tenancy and (ii) on the termination of
> the current tenancy the landlord intends to occupy the
> premises for the purpose of a business to be carried on
> by the landlord."

It was discovered that the corporation was intending to use Arch 167 to store and mend deck chairs and beach huts.

The workers felt that although considerable discussion had occurred at the time when the lease was being drawn up the corporation still felt tricked into allowing the premises to be used as they had been. It appears, from clause 10 in the lease of Archway 167 which concerns itself with the user of the premises, that the type of young person who would be using the premises had clearly been discussed. The clause says:

> "(10) Not without the prior written consent of the Corporation . . . to use or permit or suffer to be used the

demised premises or any part thereof otherwise than for
the purposes of a reception center for young people and
for the carrying out of general social service work . . ."

The archway team was convinced that the corporation was,
therefore, doing its utmost to close down the project. The archway team had no alternative but to take the matter to court.
In the brief for Queens Counsel, the object of the litigation
was summarized into four paragraphs:

1. In the opening speech of Counsel to present a plat-
form giving a precis of the objects of the Venture and
the antagonism which it has received at the hands of the
Local Authority who have been inclined to visit upon the
three leaseholders the sins of the beats and misfits who
they seek to look after and shelter.

Instructing Solicitors feel this as a sort of anti-Christ reac-
tion and it is quite clear from the newspaper cuttings that
the attitude of the Council . . . is that if the archways
closed the problem will be removed from Brighton or,
at least, swept under the carpet. The venture argue
. . . that but for their organization and interest the beats
and other disturbed persons would not be taking shelter
and congregating upon the arch but would be roaming
over the town and on the beach . . . It is no fault of the
Venture or indeed of the Corporation that these disturbed
people selected to visit Brighton at those (Bank Holidays)
and other holiday times and indeed the Venture was con-
ceived out of a desire to know what prompted or moti-
vated the mods and rockers of 1965-66 to alight on seaside
resorts. It is felt that if Counsel can indicate the stupidity
of the attitudes of the Councellors in Brighton to a legiti-
mate venture which undertakes social obligations which
an enlightened local Authority would otherwise under-
take of its own volition, the relief might be felt ultimate-
ly in the attitude of the other Local Authorities to other
organizations undertaking similar ventures . . .

2. The next object of the litigation is to repudiate the al-
legations of breach of covenant.

3. The third object . . . is to attack the intention of the Corporation to occupy the premises for their own purposes. Counsel will note that both Archways 166 and 168 are empty . . . and will note that the Beach Huts in question were adequately stored on the caravan site the previous year.

4. The final object of the litigation is to avoid an order for costs being made against the lessees . . .

As part of the preparations for the hearing, the members of the consultative committee had been invited to support the project by giving evidence, either in writing or in court, of the professional way in which the project had been handled. Only two members of the committee were willing to support in this way, and one of these withdrew at the last moment following a conversation he had had with a previous member of the committee.

Also in the way of preparation for the hearing, the archway team contacted various members of the press so that public notice could be drawn to the way in which Brighton Corporation had been treating the project. It was felt that there were other projects in the country were similarly treated and the publicity of this case might help draw attention to their cases as well. The team also felt that should they win the case, this might give other projects heart to make a similar stand.

The hearing lasted the morning only. The judge did not need to be convinced of the professionalism of the archway team, and the case rested on whether or not the corporation could prove that it held a genuine intention to use the archway for their own purpose. In spite of admitting that out of all other available premises the corporation had chosen the only one occupied by the Venture in which to store its beach huts, they were able to prove that their intention to occupy the premises for their own business was genuine. The corporation had moved correctly through all the legal steps and was, therefore, able to win the case on a technicality.

Although the case had been lost, the team was pleased when the court gave the project three months and three weeks in which to leave the premises. This meant that the archway could be used up until, but not including, the Whitsun Bank Holiday weekend.

That evening the local paper, the "Evening Argus" printed a story headed:

Wednesday, 15th January, 1969

"TOWN WINS A COURT FIGHT FOR ARCH 167

At Brighton County Court this afternoon Judge Sydney Noakes refused to extend the lease of Archway No. 167 to the Archways Venture for beatniks. The organizers who had been operating under a $30,000 grant from the Department of Education, were given until May 26 to get out.

The judge said: "It is perhaps with some regret that I have no option but to dismiss this application. But I am satisfied that there is a genuine intention by the corporation to use the Archway premises for business — namely for the storage of chalets."

The judge said he had heard no evidence of the alleged breaches of covenant and of the allegation that a business was being conducted on the premises.

The original lease came to an end on Christmas Day last year. The council refused to renew it.

During the hearing, Mr. John Bartlett, principal assistant in the management section of the council's estates department, admitted that the council had deliberately selected Archway No. 167 in which to store chalets so they could oust the beatniks.

"The majority of the council are against this Venture," he said. "The council were concerned about the alleged activities that went on in the archway. They were being used for sleeping throughout the night, cooking in

189

unhygienic conditions, and there was only one toilet being used by a considerable number of people of both sexes."

Mr. Bartlett conceded that there were many other premises in which the beach chalets could be stored. There were even seven vacant archways which could be used to store them.

But, he said, the council would not use them for this purpose because they were in a prominent commercial position.

"We need No. 167 — the premises of the Venture. At the moment the chalets are out in the open at Black Rock and being damaged by the weather. The locks rust and the doors warp. Last year it cost the council $160 to repair them," he said.

Mr. John Alliott, counsel for the Venture, asked Mr. Bartlett: Do you accept there is a deliberate selection of 167 for the storage of chalets in order to have the basis for turning the Venture out, irrespective of breaches of covenant? — "Yes, I accept this is the case."

Mr. Alliott said his clients were accused of breaking their obligations and occupying the premises for the purpose of carrying on a business there.

Unhappily, the Venture had aroused "implacable hostility" from members of the council. But it had such eminent supporters as Lord Hunt and the Attorney-General.

Mr. Alliott said the three main people running the scheme were Dr. Josephine Klein, Barrie Biven, and Leo Jago. What they were doing was a genuine and worthwhile venture. They were helping beatniks and shiftless young people, and researching into their problems.

Dr. Klein, who said she was a doctor of philosophy and of Dutch origin, told the judge that the original concept of the Venture was to help these wandering people. Many of them found that with the Venture they had a home from home.

If the lease was not renewed "it would have a very distressing effect on our clients, who would feel this was another official rejection."

After the hearing, Dr. Klein was dubious about the future of the project.

Dr. Klein added that the Department of Education and Science grant of $30,000 would be "coming to an end." Costs for the case would not be coming out of that. "We are raising that money ourselves. If we had lost the case today we would have been faced with getting more than 1,000 blankets out of the center and now, at least, we have until May to think about the future," she said.

Nicholas Swingler, of "New Society" spent some time on the day of the court case with the workers, learning about the project. He wrote a long sympathetic article which was printed in the following week's edition of "New Society."

Later in the month, on 27th January, 1969, Sebastien Brown of the "Evening Argus" had this to say:

"I Like Brighton But I'm Amazed At This Treatment

Seven years ago I found and fell in love with Brighton. It had, I persuaded myself and my friends, all the appeal of a metropolis and all the warmth of a village. But I sometimes wonder if that very special flavor which makes Brighton a unique and stimulating place to live in, has anything to do with the men who run the town.

Their Brighton is a dreary, humdrum never-never land. They have to be coerced into joy, cajoled into charity and

191

heckled into humanity before the boundaries of their dull borough blur with the promised land many of us hope to inhabit.

The Archways Venture did not invent the beatnik problem for Brighton as the council and their officials delude themselves into believing. It seeks only to solve it. And solve it in the only way possible: by thoroughly investigating its roots, its causes and its effects.

I can only speak for my own experience of their work in its early stages when, during the summer nights, the archway in dispute formed a center and a community shelter for many young people who had lost touch with any form of community life.

The reciprocal benefits from their meetings on a basis of absolute equality with the Venture workers and their helpers was obvious to anyone who took the trouble to go down to the archways to see for themselves what the scheme was all about.

Links and contacts were formed, however tenuous, with the society from which they had came adrift, while the reasons for that drift could gradually be studied and analyzed over the months and years . . .

. . . The alternative to the Archways Venture is to sweep the problem under the carpet and pretend it doesn't exist. The council's carpet is getting too small and too threadbare for all the dust it is expected to cover."

One of the regular users of the archway also wrote to the "Evening Argus," and several other articles appeared in the local press during the week following the court case, and a brief comment appeared in the national daily "Guardian."

Since the grant from the Department could not be used to finance the court case, an appeal was launched to cover the $200 needed and $100 was quickly received by the project. This was an indication of the degree of support there was for the project from people in Brighton.

Since there was no immediate change in the circumstances of the project, the work continued as before.

At the consultative committee meeting on 23rd January, several matters were brought up. The press coverage of the court case was discussed and there was some concern about the "Evening Argus" headline to the article read "Town wins a court fight for Arch 167." People in the committee thought that this was misleading; it was not the town but Brighton Corporation!

The Reverend Geoff Whitfield had been invited to the meeting to discuss his ideas and plans for the future of the beats, but no one seemed interested.

The problem of premises after the end of May was discussed and it was suggested that Ashwell should contact the estates department to see if the arch could be used until it was needed for storage purposes.

The workers said that without Arch 167 it would be difficult to organize the usual Bank Holiday facilities at Whitsun, and impossible at August. They thought it would be necessary for another group to be ready to take over the Bank Holiday scheme by Whitsun.

The future of the project was discussed. Jago's statement that he saw 31st March as the deadline for forming a group responsible for any work which would follow this project produced some consternation amongst the committee.

Taking up the previous invitation, Ashwell paid a second visit to Mr. Stone, the Director of Education, on 29th January. Mr. Stone had read the reports in the local press, and appeared concerned about the future of the project. He began to think about a possible site for a beat center, and spoke of the impossibility of putting it anywhere where it could be seen. He seemed less interested in the coffee bar consultation service, yet fascinated that the training scheme might still be a possibility.

Also on 29th January, Ashwell visited Mr. Rostron, Chief Superintendent of Brighton Police. Following up the suggestions made in the previous committee meeting, Nick had written to the entertainments and publicity committee members individually about the possibility of remaining in the archway until after the summer, or at least until after the Whitsun Bank Holiday weekend, and he had also contacted Mr. Rostron asking him to support the project in their request.

Mr. Rostron asked to see Ashwell because he wanted to explain carefully how he, representing the police, had not wanted to take sides in this matter which was, as far as he was concerned, between the project and the corporation. He had not wanted to give evidence in the court case against the project (the police were subpoenaed) and he would, therefore, being fair, not become involved with the project's request for an extension of time in the archway.

On 4th February, Ross met Geoff Whitfield to discuss his future plans for the beat project, and 10th February, Jago met a Mrs. R. who had offered to provide some financial backing for the coffee bar consultation service. On 11th February, Ashwell saw Mr. Antcliffe, the deputy director of education responsible for further education in the town, about the possibility of Brighton Education Committee providing finance for the Bank Holiday project once Brighton Archways Ventures had stopped running it.

The consultative committee met for the last time on 27th February 1969. At this meeting the workers spoke of the proposed run-down of the project and asked for assistance in closing down the project in an orderly manner. The feeling was that the committee should disband itself, and be available individually to the workers. The workers felt that the committee could have been more supportive than this, and that as a group they could have offered advice, time and encouragement to some of the developments for the future.

During this period, Ashwell was making the necessary arrangements for the Easter 1969 Bank Holiday weekend. Roger Else, the coordinator of Voluntary Service by Youth, had decided that he would be responsible for the Bank Holiday projects, and he met Ashwell on several occasions. As part of these preparations, he went with Ashwell to meet Mr. Rostron of Brighton Police, in order to talk over the arrangements for the coming weekend. Ashwell was also able to introduce him as the person who would be continuing the Bank Holiday work.

On 17th March, the workers decided that the archway should be closed immediately after the Easter Bank Holiday had finished. The application to the entertainments and publicity committee to remain in the archway after 25th May had been refused, and the workers felt that it would be less confusing to close at the Bank Holiday weekend rather than two weeks later.

Lord Hunt visited the archway team on 19th March. The workers got a tremendous boost from his visit, since he was very much in touch with what the project had been doing, even though he had not been in Brighton.

On 29th March, the archway was redecorated for the Easter weekend, which took place on 4th to 8th April. The workers felt that this was one of the best weekends that had been organized. Although there was not the same pioneering spirit as at the earlier weekends, there were fewer hitches. The volunteers worked hard and some very useful discussions took place about the future.

A trainee sociologist who was working on a research project into out-groups and then presenting this material to groups of school children to see their reaction, contacted Ashwell on 11th May. He was wanting material about the living habits and behavior of the beats. He took away with him information about the project, the workers, the users of the archway, the set-up withthe corporation and some poetry and art composed by users of the archway.

On 21st May, the last item was removed from the archway. The accumulated rubbish was dumped, clothing left behind was distributed among the beats, the refrigerator sold, and a few effects left behind in the archway for future use by a B.B.C. team.

The Bishop of Horsham convened a meeting on 23rd May in which the beat problem was discussed. This meeting only helped to confuse the issue, since new people, with different approaches and ideas inevitably caused divisions in the group.

On 25th April, the workers realized that yet again the Department of Education had not paid the first quarter's grant. Ashwell contacted them to find that they had been waiting for him to tell them of any additional money the project might be wanting connected with a move to alternative accomodation. This was clarified quickly, since no alternative premises had been found and it was possible at a meeting with Miss Quick and Mr. Baines, of the department, on 23rd June, to discuss the amount of money needed for the remaining six months of the project. The audited accounts for the year 1968/69 were also accepted with little comment at that meeting.

A further meeting of the new beat project occurred on 29th July but little new ground was covered.

During August the office was cleared out and for the time being moved into a small room. This was finally vacated during October. On 23rd September, the project treasurer, Biven and Ashwell met to clear up any remaining financial commitments.

During the last month of the project, all accounts were closed with local businesses, and the final bills paid. Having completed this, it was then possible to close the office.

Volunteers

Volunteers At Work In The Archway

The main Archway was open for 24 hours a day each Bank Holiday weekend, during which time a large number of young people made use of the facilities. They came into the Archway for a host of reasons. Some were seeking information about accomodation for the night, asking about the entertainment in Brighton, hoping for a cup of coffee, wondering if their friends were in the Archway, wanting to use the left-luggage facilities, wanting to wash, or simply wanting to rest from having to move around the town continuously. Many helpers were needed to meet the demands of these visitors. A desk was set up close to the front door of the Archway to provide information and also to help the visitors walk into this strange, unfamiliar place. Some of the work for the helpers, involved in these demands, was reasonably straightforward. There was no confusion for the helper when making a cup of coffee. And similarly, looking after the left luggage was one of the easiest jobs at the weekend.

The idea of what help was became uncertain when it was obvious that the visitors were using the Archway for reasons other than those very practical purposes already mentioned. A very large number of young people used the Archway for meeting other young people. Some indicated that this is what they were there for when they played their guitars and sang, or added to the decorations on the walls in the back room. Many visitors sat in the Archway day and night, in case they missed anything. It appeared that most of the young people simply enjoyed being in the Archway; no other reason seemed necessary.

Prior to the first Bank Holiday weekend at Whitsun 1966, Biven, Jones and Haywood made contact with many people whom they thought would like to be involved in the weekend. Biven spoke to many students in the Education and Social Studies Common Rooms at Sussex University and wrote to many of his friends already involved in youth work. He also wrote to several of the colleges which ran youth leadership courses, suggesting that they inform their students of the weekend arrangements. Jones and Haywood made contact in this manner with people they knew. As a result of this chatting up, more than 100 people arrived at Archway 190 volunteering to be involved during the weekend.

The concept of a helper grew out of this weekend. Biven, and others more involved with the organization of the weekend, could see that several of the volunteers had been able to offer more to the atmosphere of the weekend than had others. This set a pattern in which the people who were invited to volunteer were called helpers.

Five or six weeks before each of the subsequent Bank Holiday weekends, circulars were sent to all of the old volunteers asking them to help again, and also to send names and addresses of people they knew who might also be interested. Attempts were made to communicate this to new helpers before they arrived at a weekend. This extract from a circular sent to prospective volunteers prior to the Easter 1967 weekend, refers to the two Bank Holiday weekends of 1966:

> *". . . People helped with the Archway, coped with left-luggage, distributed information, took people to the centers in cars, worked there with other helpers, and generally enjoyed themselves talking to everyone from university lecturers to the most hardened down-and-out. Success largely depends on the volunteers. The main qualifications are an absence of the need to take charge, a quiet voice, and a basic liking for young people. Can you come? You might be needed just to be around, ready to talk, make coffee, and receive people at the sleeping centers all night; perhaps you would prefer to work from the Archway or do odd jobs . . . ."*

Helpers were encouraged to add to the atmosphere, which the visitors were enjoying, in an unobtrusive way. This meant that the left luggage, coffee making, was going smoothly, but it also meant ensuring that the atmosphere remained friendly, warm and accepting. The uncertainty involved in not knowing each time how to greet a new group of young people complicated the concept of the helper, particularly since each group of young people had different reactions to the Archway.

Much of the tone of the work in the sleeping centers was set by the senior people who were on the desk in the Archway late into the night. Between about 10 p.m. and 2 a.m. each night, many young people (up to 200 on the busy nights) approached the helpers at the desk in the Archway asking for accomodation. The helpers would make a rapid assessment and send them on to a sleeping center.

In the sleeping centers, there were up to eight helpers ready to receive the visitors who had been sent from the Archway. It was much easier to define the work of the sleeping centers to helpers, because the sole purpose of the centers was simply to provide somewhere to sleep. Of course, there were many groups of young people who insisted on staying awake all night, but the service being given could still be considered as rest. Helpers sometimes had to stretch their patience and imaginations when they were involved with a really lively group. One group of 30 boys played football in a church hall at 4 one morning.

New helpers were asked to work in the sleeping centers because work in these centers provided an easy introduction to the way in which contact was made with the visitors. In the sleeping centers, people arrived in manageable numbers, and the more experienced helpers could encourage them to go to sleep. Most found that they preferred to run a quiet center, though there were notable exceptions which will be mentioned later.

Many helpers saw themselves as providing a very definite service for the young visitors to Brighton. This approach, though not entirely accurate in practice, meant that the new helpers were in little doubt about their role in the sleeping centers. They were there to take on practical tasks such as: meet each group as it arrived at the door of the hall; take the money from each person; give each person two blankets; make the group coffee if they wanted it; show people where they could sleep, where the lavatories were situated, and talk to those who wanted to stay awake.

This was a particularly straightforward service which was being given for 30 cents. The more experienced helpers, usually one or two in each center, had additional jobs such as collecting the money, making friends with the caretakers, bringing up the supplies to the center, welding the group of helpers into a working group, and answering questions.

Although the basic administrative structure was set before the young people arrived at the centers, their mood determined the way in which the center was run on any particular night.

Leafleting

Many leaflets had been printed, setting out the basic services which the project was offering. On several Bank Holiday weekends a team of people were used to distribute these to all young people whom they met in Brighton. This distribution was usually confined to the hours between 9:30 p.m. and around 1 or 2 a.m., which was when the streets were most heavily populated with young people at a loose end.

This was a vital part of the scheme, because it caught many of the young people before they hid themselves under draughty boats, and in derelict houses.

There were often several helpers who were younger than the rest, often from such organizations as the Weekenders, who had tremendous enthusiasm for working on projects such as the Archway. Their liveliness and enthusiasm were qualities which did not fit very well in a sleeping center where the emphasis was on quiet, calm and emotional neutrality on the part of the helpers. Also other helpers felt wary of such lively groups being around in the archway, since they tended to be more interested in their own fun rather than in their effect on the people in the Archway. These people were ideal for leafleting. In a lively group, there were few inhibitions about giving another lively group some leaflets, and the atmosphere they created about them as they bounced along the street encouraged other young people to search out the Archway.

The leafleters simply covered all the streets which formed the boundaries of old Brighton. The most important street was West Street, because this was the entertainments center of Brighton. As the two cinemas began to empty, the leafleters would walk up and down West Street until it was empty. This was at about 12:30 or 1 a.m., when the last fish and chip shop closed down for the night. The leafleters then wandered around the town again, looking in the passages between the buildings, under the boats on the beach, in bus shelters, under park benches for any young person who was trying to get some sleep. At this later hour, about 2 a.m. the leafleters and the police were usually doing the same job.

This job had the least amount of role uncertainty about it. The leafleter's had a straightforward task of giving out information to young people who might want to make use of the Archway. The only worry arose when some leafleters had to decide whether or not to wake people asleep in cars to tell them about the Archway project.

Sleeping Centers For The Volunteers

Volunteers were given a special center during Easter 1968, but it was not until the following year that this was run at its best. Individuals were asked to be responsible for the few major jobs that needed to be maintained in this center. It was the intention that there should always be one person awake in the center who could give any information about the project to a helper. At the Easter 1969 weekend, three people worked a shift system so that the others could get some sleep.

A cook was usually appointed at the beginning of the weekend, to provide the breakfasts. One weekend, a professional cook appeared on the scene; on another, a helper offered to cook who had obviously not cooked for a large number before and the result was inedible.

At breakfast time, volunteers were encouraged to write reports on the previous night's work. A few experienced helpers joined in this recording of information to help jog memories, and generally to liven up the process. This was a difficult task because many of the helpers tended to be somewhat diffident about what they had done on the previous night.

Methodology And The Volunteer

No overall method of working was imposed on any volunteer. The belief was that the person himself has the best idea of his capabilities, and that he will make what he can from a situation without being told in every detail how to do it.

The only major imposition that has been made, and this has also been passed on to the visitors, was to state that a warm, quiet, accepting atmosphere was necessary for the archway. In addition, the feeling among the instigators of the project has been that the archway was there for the use of all young people in Brighton, and the atmosphere which was created within those premises was to be created by the young people for themselves within the above limitations. This has meant that each visitor was more than a client; he was a contributor as well as being a participant. When this happened, which was at all the weekends to a greater or lesser extent, the role of the visitor became uncertain. This was illustrated beautifully one weekend when Dublin, one of the beats, appointed himself as compere to an impromptu show of singing and poetry recitation.

This uncertainty in the role of the visitor, who had shown either in the archway or a sleeping center, that he was not a simple client, meant that the helper necessarily became uncertain of his role as well. This had two general effects on the helpers: the first was the defensive reaction. Many helpers were conspicuous in that they were always helping with left luggage, or making the coffee, or some such similarly well-defined job. The uncertainty was too much for them, or they tended to behave in a manner reminiscent of that of a client, and often had to be approached as if they were clients. The second effect was that the helpers were able to experiment in their interactions with others, and in doing so, many began to learn a lot about their own behavior, which they were then able to feed back into the job. These people found the work very exciting. The overall administration set few limits on the ways in which people could behave in the Archway. This meant that the more enterprising helpers felt no restrictions on how to work. It could be argued that those who felt that they were being restricted in their movements were building the restrictions themselves.

The collective philosophy, among those who have been very closely associated with the project for a long time was that the Bank Holiday weekend provided a fundamental service by making accomodation available for young visitors to Brighton, at the same time as preparing an atmosphere where interesting exchanges could occur between many different kinds of young people.

In order that helpers should have some idea of the nature of the weekend work, group meetings were arranged at each Bank Holiday weekend, so that the many questions which were appearing in people's minds could be answered, or begun to be answered. Many of the final answers to such questions as "What do I do when . . .?" were only discovered when a helper found himself in that situation. Much of this desire to know how to cope with different situations was linked to a helper's wish to experience what he could at a weekend, and also to make what he could out of as many situations as possible.

Use Of Volunteers In The Archway

So many different types of young people used the Archway, that it was impossible to predict how best to approach each new group. There were so many factors at stake; the mood of the young people, the mood of the helper, the expectations that the young people had of the weekend, and preconceived ideas of the helpers about the young people viewing them from their dress. New groups were met in two different ways in the Archway. At the desk the helper sitting behind it would have to gauge the right amount of warmth to put into his tone, as he asked "Can I help you?" Helpers found the necessity of trying out different sentences to start the contact, or of letting the young people start first. In the main part of the Archway, the helper might see a group sitting on its own. The ways in which that helper managed to get himself into the center of the group needed constant experimentation.

Often helpers found that they were engaged in conversations with young people at the door of the Archway. This gave rise to many events which the helper used. For instance, as a young person came to the door to peer in, the helper could introduce one of the young people already in the archway. Some helpers managed to build up a conversation in this manner with a policeman as the third party.

Late in the evenings, as the young people were seeking information about cheap accomodation, two people were usually assigned to the desk to send the young visitors to the sleeping centers. This could be tackled in many ways. Most helpers simply made judgments about the young people, such as mod, rocker, beatnik, lively or tired or very young, and sent them to the center which they thought was best for them. It was sometimes a precarious way of handling the different groupings of young people. In a more fancy piece of work at the first Bank Holiday weekend, one of the helpers on the desk sent a large homogenous group of young people to a center which already had such a group. The interaction between these two groups gave both something to think about. This type of flexibility had some startling results. One time a group of boys from Ealing realized that they had been in conversation with another group from Acton at one of the sleeping centers. Usually being rivalrous neighbors, they had been less willing to talk with each other, and now some of them were delighted at the interchange.

One of the more experienced helpers in the archway noticed one evening that the coffee area was terribly untidy, and needed cleaning up. With young people helping themselves, a considerable amount of coffee, sugar, milk and water became mixed with each other. One obvious way of tackling this job was to simply clean up as quickly as possible, and then move away again. However, this helper noticed that there were several other helpers sitting close to the mess, who were obviously finding the work hard to cope with. Very soon after beginning to clear up the mess, the more experienced helper had managed to start a conversation between the other helpers and the visitors who were within listening distance.

There is no way of telling whether that conversation was useful to anybody involved, but the helper had increased the potential of the situation by creating contact between the different people.

Also if she had felt that her role as a helper was to clear up the mess, or to talk with the visitors, then she would have missed the opportunity of encouraging the others to talk to the visitors.

A good contrast to this situation concerned a helper who had assigned himself the task of sending the visitors to the sleeping centers from the desk. Ashwell, who was responsible for that weekend, was not too happy about this arrangement but let it continue because no one else was available to do this job and the helper seemed able to make the right type of decisions about which groups to mix with others. Maps of the route through Brighton to each sleeping center were piled on the desk from which the helper was operating. He had found the work quite straightforward. Groups of young people had been asking him where they could sleep, and he had been able to describe the layout of a sleeping center, telling the visitors it would cost them 30 cents each, and that the sexes were segregated. At about 11 p.m., however, soon after the pubs had closed, a noisy drunken group barged into the Archway and demanded sleeping accomodation for the night. There were many alternatives available for the helper. He could have sent them to a sleeping center, thereby acknowledging their request; he could have made a joke of their drunkenness; he could have told them where the coffee was. Disappointedly, his remark to the group, in a rather surprised and hurt manner, was "Mind the papers!"

At another weekend, one of the helpers who was working on the desk in the Archway in the early part of the evening, found that a young deaf mute was making an effort to find out about the services provided by the project. She was able to interest this young man in explaining the philosophy of the work via written notes. They discussed the values of a beat way of life for about an hour.

After the pubs closed along the seafront, many older men tried to get into the Archway, because it was often the only place still open at that time of the night. One of the helpers found that he was quite proficient in keeping these people out of the Archway. When confronted with a rather belligerent man, this helper was usually able to convince the man that, although he was too old to be in the Archway, it was not the sort of place in which he would want to be anyway. The helper did this by carefully describing the way in which all the young people contributed to the place, and that any result would not be what a man of his older years would be wanting. Sometimes a man would march straight into the Archway and then the helper had to stand in his path and keep talking to him. This was not always effective because there were some men who insisted that it was their right to be in the Archway. Short of calling the police to remove them, it was often wiser to allow these few to sit in the Archway. Once they were in, they could sometimes sit quietly. There were one or two who felt that they should be part of the atmosphere, but this so often finished in a fight that helpers had to be firm and had to keep them out of the archway. On occasions, the police were called.

One man, Irish Jim, caused a considerable nuisance. Ross had called the police on a few occasions and he still persisted in coming into the Archway. However, at the Bank Holiday weekend, when both Ashwell and Ross were sitting at the desk welcoming people to the Arch, Jim lurched into the Archway and began to read the notice board. The helper, who was good at keeping people such as Jim out of the Archway, began to approach him, but Ashwell and Ross caught his eye and suggested that Jim be left on his own. This approach, or lack of approach, worked and Jim found that no one spoke to him so he walked out.

Many helpers found that they had to cope with police visits. Sometimes the police were hostile to the helpers, who they often felt were encouraging the young people to visit Brighton. Often the police attacked the helpers' ideas in such a way that made helpers become hostile to the police. Some helpers were able to cope with this in a way that was better than being provoked. Sometimes long conversations took place between the helper and a policeman, each arguing the pros and cons of a Bank Holiday project.

One weekend, a large group of 30 boys had visited the Top Rank Suite. They had managed to start a fight and several of them were either taken to the police station or to the hospital. The group had stayed in one of the church halls on the previous night, when they had played up the helpers. This was the time when the group had played football at 4 a.m.

Following the fight in the Top Rank Suite, the boys had returned in ones and twos to the sleeping center and, in the coffee area, they talked through the night with each other and with the helpers about the fight.

As well as offering an uncondemning ear to the boys, the helpers by slipping in the right comment helped the boys to see how they had started the fight themselves. In the course of the night, the boys came to clarify for each other the effects their behavior had had on the others.

Sometimes, helpers were totally unable to make anything out of some situations. A good example of this concerned a first year university student, who was sitting in the kitchen of one of the church halls, listening to a conversation between one or two visitors and two other helpers. The conversation became more complex — relativity was discussed — and instead of the helper seeing that this may not have been to the liking of all the visitors present, he saw this as for him to read his book. It was interesting to know that this helper was totally bored by the weekend, because he saw nothing that was interesting.

There were many situations of greater benefit to the helper than to anybody else. An argument had developed between two helpers over a matter of whether or not a group of boys and girls could sleep beside each other in the kitchen. One helper said it was not permitted to have boys and girls sleeping together, however innocent it might be, and the other helper said that it made no difference to the visitors anyway, and therefore it could continue. Both the helpers became very angry about the other and, at one stage, one of the helpers started to pull off the blankets which were covering the young people in the kitchen. The situation was resolved but the helper who thought that the situation could stand said afterwards, at breakfast in the volunteers' center, that the situation had taught him how he could say no to some people. This was something that he previously found difficult.

The leafleters found that most of their time was spent in searching out the people who might have needed the project's facilities. But there were occasions when a street worker, with no other purpose than to hand out leaflets needed to assume a more therapeutic role.

One pair of helpers found that they were following a small group of young men along one of the streets in Brighton, while they (the helpers) were distributing leaflets. The helpers saw that one of the group, who was exceedingly drunk, tried to hit everyone his own age and, at one stage, he grabbed a shoe that someone was holding and threw it into the road. The two helpers realized that an ugly situation could have developed if the various people, who had suffered from the drunk man, were not pacified. So the helpers walked close behind the small group talking to each person who was hit by the drunk.

At the Easter 1969 weekend, a few young men found that their suits had been stolen from the cloakroom of the Top Rank Suite, while they were changing into more informal clothes. They had made a fuss but the management had called the police. One helper, who was simply street walking, came across the situation just as one of the policemen was shouting at the young men "Go away or you will be arrested." He was unable to offer an assurance that the loss of their suits would be looked into, and he appeared to have no faith in the CID by the way he suggested to the young men that they should go to the CID. The situation was agonizing for the young men, there was simply nothing they could do, and, at this moment, another policeman started to move into the group and push them away. At this crucial point, the helper managed to push into the group alongside the second policeman, and hold a conversation with him, while the crowd dispersed. The helper was certain that had the second policeman joined in, the young people would have started to be abusive, which could have resulted in a few unnecessary arrests.

Role Expectations Of A Helper

There was no clear cut way of defining a helper, and this made it difficult to communicate to a new person what he should do to become a helper. This was not to say that there were no covert expectations. These were numerous. The problem was that what each person could make of a weekend was of his own choice, and depended considerably on his personality. The realization, as a weekend progressed, of what a person was like gave an indication of the type of work to which he would best be suited. Usually, by that time, the person had already found what suited him. The circulars sent to volunteers before the weekends, gave a brief idea of what a helper was expected to do.

Until the volunteers had experienced the atmosphere of a weekend, it was difficult to explain to them the nature of their role as a helper. Group meetings were arranged at various times before, during and after weekends, so that the nature of the work could be discussed, and the circulars served as an introduction to the type of work in which the volunteers would be involved if they wanted to help.

Plainly, many of the volunteers were not helpers, and others tried too hard to be useful (some of these being people who had arrived originally as visitors) and it was necessary to attempt, on several occasions during the weekends, to encourage the person to stop doing something so that he could merge into the atmosphere more naturally. Many helpers found that they were being given advice like "You don't need to do anything — just hang around." Some of those who were given this advice felt that they were being told to keep out of the way, which was not always true. An emphasis on the helper being able to recognize what constituted a good atmosphere in the Archway was encouraged.

The difference between a person who was helping and a person who was not helping was often obvious, but the border between a helper and a nonhelper was always kept purposely broad and vague so that anybody could contribute in any way he felt he could. This meant that, on several occasions, a visitor to the Archway would be found making the coffee, or looking after the left luggage. People were also able to contribute to the friendly atmosphere by sitting quietly or, conversely, by wrestling with each other on the floor instead of simply sitting quietly. There were several jobs that had to be done, like manning the left luggage, ensuring that the supplies did not run out, which had to be done unobtrusively. It was important that people who made themselves responsible for these jobs did not make too much fuss about being in charge of the luggage for example, in such a way as to create a gulf between them and the visitors who were using the left luggage facilities. This gulf could easily be misinterpreted by the visitors as a show of authority, which would have disturbed the spontaneous atmosphere. The reference to one of the main qualifications being an absence of the need to take charge, in the circular sent to people before the Easter 1967 weekend, was the first check against helpers unwittingly creating a gulf while helping. It was a point which students and qualified youth leaders particularly, found hard to learn.

As a very simple guide, helpers were seen as people who could be expected to be able to contribute to the atmosphere of the weekends and, at the same time, be able to share the experience of the weekend with all the other young people also

210

in the Archway. This called not only for sympathetic, though not condescending understanding of the behavior of many of the visitors, but also for a basic liking for the young people on the part of the helper. Many helpers, in fact, found that they were unable to enjoy the company of one group, for instance the beats or the hard mods, and so were unable to work with this group of young people successfully.

Most of the people who volunteered to help at the weekends were able to meet these expectations, but there were, in addition, several other people who were expected to be able to do much more than those tasks already described. As an illustration, there were several conversations that were between helpers and visitors which were carried beyond a simple talk-and-listen relationship. Some helpers could be expected to add to the conversation in such a way that the conversation took on an added relevance to both people. Much of this was that of the skill of the helper slipping in a relevant question or two at the right time. Any more could have been construed as moralizing. A rather boisterous conversation held between a group of helpers and a group of boys in one of the sleeping centers, serves as a good illustration of this point. The group, which had one black member who fitted in with the group very successfully, were talking about the "spades" (the black people) being the cause of all the troubles in the neighborhood. This conversation continued for some time, and eventually, one of the helpers pointed out to them that one of their members was colored. Their immediate answer was "He's different," but the remark may have set some of them thinking about the situation. Another illustration mentioned already, is of the large group who had trouble in the Top Rank Suite but were able to see that the trouble had been started by themselves.

There were also people who could be relied on to cope with the awkward situations which occurred from time to time. Before each weekend got underway, these people were singled out, given the jobs of greater responsibility, and were expected to be responsible. These were jobs such as looking after a sleeping center and the volunteers in that center, keeping out the

the older men and the drunks at the door of the Archway, coping with the fights that broke out, and helping out less experienced helpers who had difficulties with aggressive policemen.

Eventually, it was expected of some of the helpers that they would be able to discuss openly their feelings about the weekend. Many needed considerable prompting to do this, often because they felt that any action they may have taken with some young people would be considered as wrong. Few of the helpers were able to be this frank with the full-time workers or with each other and so many of the problems of working in this setting remained hidden. It was obvious that as people became more involved with this type of work, they found that they were questioning their own values. An example of this is the helper who was horrified by the beats way of life when he first made contact with them and did not know them. As time progressed, he was able to appreciate some of their values for himself. The transition took more than a year, and he is now more contented with a permanent job, and yet looking very much like one of the beats on the beach.

Once people could discuss their feelings about the work, it was possible to begin discussions about the role of the helper in this setting. Some then began to feel that they had been presumptuous in imagining that they were able to help visitors in the Archway. One person became so concerned about this that he began to worry when he found that he had been useful in the Archway. The full-time workers were pleased when helpers could see their limitations in the unstructured setting of the archway project although this made their job harder, because they then had to supervise the helpers who felt embarrassed about being a helper.

More Enterprising And Less Enterprising Helpers

Successful is too strong a word to use in this context. It is not even possible to say definitely that an encounter in the

Archway was successful, because a conversation in the Archway occupies such a small part of a person's life. There are not ways of following up a person to see how he has fared. It has only been possible to say that there was a chance that an encounter, which might have been relevant at the time, might be relevant to that person sometime in the future. Little more can truthfully be hoped for.

New helpers were most contented to begin working in well-structured settings, such as on the well-known left luggage, and the coffee making. Some of the more successful new helpers were seen as those who were able to build more out of this job than simply coping with the straightforward task. This was the ability to be able to use the task in hand to contribute to the atmosphere around them. For example, a helper has been described as turning the task of clearing up the coffee table into a much more adventurous encounter with other people. Another helper found that this was also possible when driving visitors from the Archway to the sleeping centers; some of the conversations which were held in the van proved fascinating. One incidental difficulty was that some of those who could see more to this work than that offered by the left luggage, tended to leave their post and hope that someone else would do the work for them. On the other hand, it remained necessary to recognize that people can only be enterprising to the extent their inhibition permits. Ross noticed one helper who had been stuck on the left luggage for about four hours. She knew what a bore that could be and so offered to take his place for a while. She was very much surprised by his vehement reluctance to leave the post. Eve felt that the helper was using the left luggage as a safety measure and could not as yet move to more expansive work in the remainder of the Archway.

The following descriptions of four different people serve as good illustrations of the variety of the helper.

Mr. and Mrs. P., age around 35, were able to understand the behavior of many of the more ordinary young people who used the Archway scheme. They were aware of what the young people needed in the sleeping centers, and their sensitivity enabled them to cope with the playing up that occurred in the sleeping center in a mature and noncritical manner, which the young people were able to respect.

On the other hand, John was keen on being involved in the project. He saw working very much in terms of doing jobs, such as taking people to sleeping centers, giving out blankets, finding out where people came from, and was close to being insensitive to other people's needs. He had a habit of going out from the Archway, doing a useful job such as taking people to a center, or distributing some leaflets, then telling everybody in the Archway how he had done that job, often to the annoyance of other people in the Archway. His lack of perception is best illustrated by an event at one of the sleeping centers. John visited the center with three of his friends at about 2 a.m. The hall was deadly quiet as all the visitors were asleep. John burst into the hall, and nearly shouted "How are things going?" Ashwell, who was responsible for the hall, very rudely ushered the offending group into the kitchen, from which their voices would not be so loud. John did not see why Ashwell had pushed him out of the hall and reminded him that he was a helper and not a visitor!

Jack was an unattached worker from London. He was able to understand the behavior of the visitors, the more so since he was working with some of them in their home surroundings. Jack was certainly a successful helper in the sleeping center where he worked. He was able to respond to the atmosphere created by himself and the visitors in such a way that his approach to the young people was fitting. This called for flexibility of approach and attitude which Mr. and Mrs. P. did not have. His perceptive skills enabled him to be able to respond to the collective needs of the young people, which was different from responding to individual needs of one person to the exclusion of others, as in the case of Mr. and Mrs. P.

In contrast, Ralph was fully conscious of the atmosphere within the sleeping center for which he was responsible. He felt that it was all important that the atmosphere should be right for the visitors. He was flexible in that he could respond to the changes in mood which were required of him, for instance in playing his guitar, but he was insufficiently flexible to allow himself to make any suggestions to the visitors about where they could sleep, or even to collect the money from them. Unfortunately, he could see no point in the basic administrative tasks such as getting a coffee or showing people where they could sleep and, in fact, became so caught up in the atmosphere created with these people who like guitar playing and singing that he lost sight of his own purposes for being there. Once, after Ralph had been singing for some time, he decided to have a walk and left the hall with no one person responsible for its well-being. He visited other centers for about two hours. At one center, he upset another helper by telling her that she was not running her center properly. He was one of the people who was unable to reconcile having to do the basic jobs without, at the same time, making those jobs appear all important.

Success has been described in terms of people rising to the challenge of the weekend, and several incidents illustrate a few successful occasions.

A group of art students came into the Archway and started to have a go at the beats for the way they lived and behaved. One helper began by refereeing the exchange, and eventually managed to get the interaction operating more a discussion, by which time the helper left the groups on their own.

The boy who said, as he walked out of the Archway, "That's the first argument that I've been in without hitting the other person at the end of it."

An experienced youth worker said "I've learned to say no this weekend, at the same time maintaining a liberal attitude."

A girl, who was attending a psychiatric center daily, said "This weekend as a helper has meant so much to me."

This has helped build up the concept of people "coming through" the Archway. One ex-drug addict was able to use the project to build up sufficient confidence within himself to eventually be accepted at a Leicester College for youth leadership training. Other people have volunteered to work in a sleeping center, and have been responsible for a sleeping center at the following weekend, and finally been responsible for the total weekend at the following Bank Holiday.

Communication

The smooth running of each Bank Holiday weekend depended on good communication links between helpers and those responsible for the weekend and, hence, between each sleeping center and the archway. Some weekends went better than others and this did depend a lot on the degree to which people knew what they were meant to be doing. A considerable amount of avoidance of repsonsibility on the part of some helpers was linked with uncertain communications from the people responsible for the overall administration. Often this uncertainty was related to a lack of information about the helpers.

Many ways have been tried to improve the communications at a weekend. One person made himself responsible for knowing as much as possible about what was happening during a weekend; he acted as a sponge for information. This person was able to make decisions more confidently with the information and was able to cope with helpers and other people with more ease.

At the first three weekends, Whitsun and August 1966, and Easter 1967, the three people who were responsible, Biven, Klein and Ross, respectively, realized that there should be this one person who was sufficiently in evidence to be able to accumulate the information. They also realized that for this to happen in a fully successful way, one person would have to be awake for the whole weekend.

At the Whitsun weekend 1968, Ashwell, by then a full-time worker, had been responsible for the weekend with a helper, Anna. It is difficult to assess how useful that arrangment was

216

because of other circumstances: very few helpers had volunteered that weekend and alarming gaps kept appearing in work rotas. However, few of the helpers seemed able, or willing, to accept much responsibility which, in itself, could have been an indication that the arrangements had not been very successful.

Jago made himself responsible for the August 1968 weekend. He decided that to ensure that he knew all that was happening, he would stay awake for the whole weekend. He was encouraged to get some sleep after 70 hours. By that time he was so tired that he was less willing to be bothered with the helpers, who were constantly needing his attention and assistance. No one else attempted to stay awake for a whole weekend.

At Easter 1969, the three full-time workers divided the work of being responsible for the weekend between them. Ross looked after the archway during the day. Jago concerned himself with the volunteers and ran the volunteers' center. Ashwell looked after the sleeping centers and the evening work of the archway. This division of labor helped the weekend run very smoothly.

As a means of keeping in touch with what was happening in a sleeping center, and also to know how the group of volunteers in a center was coping, the person responsible at each weekend made a habit of visiting each sleeping center once during each night. Another very simple means of improving the links between the archway and the sleeping centers was to encourage the sleeping centers to telephone occasionally to the archway through the night. After the first year, this did not occur with any regularity, even when helpers were given the money with which to make the phone call. It appears that many saw little point in phoning to say that all was calm, and others felt that to telephone for assistance was admitting that the helpers could not cope. However, several centers did phone through to the archway on occasions when they were in need of supplies.

It was important that the helpers who arrived to start a new shift in the Archway should overlap for a short period with those about to leave, so that one set of helpers could tell the others what had happened on their shift.

So that some written communications could reach the helpers and person responsible for the weekend, log books were provided in each of the sleeping centers and in the archway. These were introduced into the archway at Whitsun 1967, but not into the sleeping centers until Easter 1968. Helpers arriving for a new shift at the archway very quickly got into the habit of reading the log book before they did anything else. Most of the helpers found that they had no difficulty in recording an event in the log book as soon after it had happened as was possible.

The uncertainty of many helpers as to what they were expected to do during a weekend was alleviated by briefing meetings arranged on the Friday which started the Bank Holiday weekend. These meetings took place in the early evenings. Arrangements were usually made for follow-up meetings to occur either on the Saturday or Sunday evenings, but often these did not take place. In the first year, meetings were held after the Bank Holiday to establish how well the weekend had gone. This was too late for one purpose, namely to have an atmosphere in which helpers could communicate with each other and give each other support or information in the course of just talking things over. The answer was found in the provision of breakfasts in the volunteers' center. The helpers were then tired, since most had come away from working in a sleeping center all night, but they were also excited and had lots to talk about. In the often boisterous and very noisy atmosphere helpers felt that they wanted to talk to each other. A few more experienced helpers were there to facilitate and to record as far as possible. In the course of this the helpers realized that they had a lot of information to offer and many wrote some of it down or used the information sheets which were available.

A further improvement in encouraging the helpers to communicate with each other was made at Easter 1969, when it was decided that the archway should be freed from being the source of the information which the helpers needed. Supplies, information and discussions were all centered on the volunteers' center. On previous weekends, the supplies had been kept in the archway, and some of the information in the volunteers' center. With the volunteers' center being firmly established as the place where you could find things out, and a person with the necessary administrative information was always available, helpers began to drop in to see who else was around.

Helpers were encouraged to take on responsibilities within the project, and were, therefore, considered as status people within the set up. Status, responsibility and expertise can be closely linked but all three tend to foster envy. This happens easily in unstructured situations and when it happens, status is seen as divorced from expertise or responsibility. Communications then become inhibited and distorted.

The biggest responsibility was, of course, that of running the whole weekend. This has usually been the task of one person, though Nick and Anna tried together at Whitsun 1968, and the three workers managed a joint effort successfully at Easter 1969. The person responsible for the weekend selected, from all those who had volunteered, a few key people to be responsible in the sleeping centers.

Another level of responsible work was that of directing the young people to the sleeping centers from the archway desk during the night. This required a perceptiveness and an accurate memory that few of the helpers appeared to possess.

Less structured work, in fact, of tremendous importance included the jobs in which a person was asked to be in the archway and to do what was needed. Some of the helpers who were asked to do this felt they were being pushed out of the way, and saw themselves as low-status people because they were given nothing definite to do. This job was one of the more important ones because it required the helper to be able to perceive situations and to be able to predict how they could develop. An example of this would be that of coping with a restless person, who was angling to make himself a nuisance to other visitors. In this case, the responsibility was of a much more personal nature; the helper was expected to keep his eyes

219

open while in the archway and to make his own decisions about what he should or should not do. There was no obvious result of a helper's effectiveness in this role, apart from the fact that nothing untoward may have happened. There was, of course, no way of knowing how effective or ineffective he might have been.

Many helpers would appear at a weekend to help and then show they were willing to take on responsibilities. Those helpers, who volunteered for several weekends running, were given jobs which demanded more responsibility. For instance, any helper who had survived working in a sleeping center for a weekend or so was usually considered competent to run a sleeping center. There were naturally a few who did appear regularly at the weekends but who were unsuitable for taking on jobs of more responsibility.

As helpers took on more responsibility their status rose in the organization. The helpers, who took on the more responsible jobs, found that other helpers saw them as status people, and so gave them information about the project. Having this information, they were, therefore, seen as status people by others. The interesting point was that a person could only become high status if he was able to work effectively with the responsibility that he had been given.

It was not until the arrangements for Easter 1968 were being made that the workers fully realized that they were not concerned enough with the status of the helper in the project. It had been recommended in the August 1967 Bank Holiday report that this point be considered before the next weekend.

Miriam Wiltshire, a youth leader, became involved with the project at its beginning. She was concerned about the way in which the helpers were treated at weekends, and she pressed that separate provision should be made for them. This was when the importance of a volunteers' center was realized. It was also seen that the helpers should be treated well, because the smooth running of the weekend depended on them. The outcome was that the helpers felt that they were being treated as people that mattered and, therefore, they felt that they could contribute to the weekend by talking to people about what they had experienced. The helpers had been treated very well that weekend and a large number of the helpers wanted to join in the discussion group, whereas at previous weekends the helpers had seemed reluctant to join in.

Out of this some helpers saw the importance of being able to talk to others about their problems of working with the project. This helped the person, who was prepared to talk in this way, to understand better his own role in the weekend. This supervision of helpers took place at an informal level; certain individual people were known as those whom "you could talk to."

Chapter 5

Summary Of The Study

Bank Holiday Weekends

Although the Bank Holiday weekend scheme came into being on the wave of the mod and rocker riots up and down the country, it was never intended that it should combat the violence, such as it was, or be regarded as an instrument of juvenile control.

The scheme was originally set up because of the obvious need to provide cheap accomodation and an information service. In thinking about this idea of service, it was realized that there would be many other functions for the workers. Since there had been no similar projects it was not possible to accurately predict in what way the workers would be used. It was also seen that the teams would have to work with the young people's expectations of the town, of their holiday and of those who might be in the town at the same time. We had some ideas on this theme but we could not be sure what to expect.

However, as stated, the major purpose was to provide a service and in this respect the aims of the project were fulfilled. On numerous occasions we exceeded the fundamental provision and were able to set up ancillary services. Some of these were the ideas of the young people themselves. For example, the left luggage scheme was thought out and organized by some of the young visitors assisted by a number of students.

But it would be wrong to create the impression that we were just providing services, or that it was our sole intention. In many ways we were wanting to contribute to bringing about social change with those who were most conscious of the need. The fact that little can be achieved in a weekend led us to formulating plans for a full-time project.

But if we are to consider the weekends from the standpoint of the workers they were a resounding success. Many hundreds of students, teachers, youth workers and lecturers over a period of years have felt that they were a part of something new and valuable. They have given up their holidays to work on the scheme and in so doing have learned a great deal themselves. All those who headed the teams for each Bank Holiday have remarked on their personal growth over the weekend and have been surprised that such insights were possible in so short a time.

The weekends were a happening or to some a trip without drugs or artificial stimuli. The similarities with wartime days in the underground or the C.N.D. marches of the '50s were numerous. In both of these illustrations survival was the reason for people being found together in large groups. Regardless of the possible consequences they found a sense of unity, acceptance, camaraderie and personal intimacy which was often lacking in their normal lives. The young who visit Brighton at Bank Holidays are often overwhelmed with a sense of personal obsolescence. They know that there is no work for them. If there is, they know that it is unproductive and has little meaning. They are often concerned, as volunteers are, with the seemingly purposeless complexity of modern life. They have no power and no voice.

In this respect the weekends provided an accepting platform for their thoughts and feelings. Since the organization and structure of all the archway work was intentionally flexible, there were many opportunities for the young visitors to experiment with latent skills. Some wanted to run accomodation centers, some wanted to help with the transport services some wanted to collect the money for the bed and direct people to a place, while others were happy to make coffee, to run errands, deliver leaflets and so on. It was necessary for a worker to initially keep an eye on the young visitor for a few hours. If he was satisfied that the young person could cope, then they were given a free hand. If it was judged that they could not cope they were given unobtrusive support and encouragement. Each encounter a learning process in itself.

There were some discouraging elements in the weekends. There were problems with the traders but given time they could have been overcome, as they were eventually with the police. It is inevitable that innovatory schemes cause some anxiety but it is the responsibility of the town council to support such schemes and help the organizers to interpret their work to the general public.

There was also the problem of the press presenting a distorted view of the young visitors and, more dangerously, the degree of violence. On checking records with the police it was discovered that there was no more violence in the town than exists on a normal weekend. But there were incidents which were unusual and could be attributed to such a large influx of young and energetic men and women looking for a good time. It has to be faced that there is little in Brighton for young people. Brighton has deliberately discouraged the young in an attempt to maintain a family holiday resort. But the young will continue to come to Brighton. It is vital that they feel that they are not surrounded by hostile adults.

In order to meet young people and wanting to help in some way, it is essential that the worker holds a strong belief in the young. He must feel that they have something to say. It is the experience of the workers and volunteers that if you meet young people because you recognize their worth and, hopefully because you like them, they will respond positively. If this much is accepted then it follows that the organizational structure of the meeting places with the young must tie in with this very basic philosophy. Great attention has to be paid to the layout and the furniture. But most important of all, the young need to feel immediately welcome. Most volunteers needed some help in acquiring skills to work in unstructured and informal settings.

To meet this need the archways team set up training and feedback sessions for all volunteers. Because of the rota system it was not possible to meet all volunteers together but a regular meeting each day helped to overcome some of the problems that arise from time to time.

The person responsible for each sleeping center was usually the one in most need of assurance and some clarification. They felt the weight of responsibility keenly and in the main worked extremely well considering the unfamiliarity of approach. Sometimes one or two volunteers were a little anxious about the sexual activities of the young or the presence of drugs or the fear of being hit by a young aggressive visitor. Many of the problems were overcome by using a team of troubleshooters. They were usually experienced youth workers who could tackle such situations and were at the end of a telephone, should one of the centers feel they could no longer cope. The fact that as many as two or three groups of some 30 or 40 young aggressive East-enders out for a bit of fun were contained in a church hall all night, indicates the level of skill required to run a center. In addition there were numerous medical requests from poorly prepared youngsters.

The archways scheme attracted a number of able people who have wanted to continue the work even though the Department of Education grant has come to an end and we no longer have the archway. They now operate from one of the church halls in the town center. It would be true to say that the scheme has lost some of its attractiveness since it has been denied the ideal point of contact, a seafront archway. However, the newcomers to the scheme are not aware of this and still find great enjoyment and satisfaction in working on the weekends. The demand for space to sleep has not lessened.

It would be encouraging to add that we were able to extend the scheme to those towns who have expressed a need for a similar scheme. But we were without the resources. However, no scheme of this nature will survive unless it has a small local group who are able to supervise and hold the whole thing together. What is not essential is that the scheme be supported by the council, but it is certainly highly desirable and efforts should be made to achieve this. And it is inevitable that if one chooses to work with the undereducated and the underpriviledged, there will be problems of some kind.

There are many people in all communities who do not feel that such people ought to exist at all. Any worker who attaches himself to one of these groups immediately becomes a focus for this latent aggression and fear. It is important that all backers of such schemes should understand the dynamics of this process so that they are prepared when the resistance begins. Such work suggests to many a lessening of standards and values and as such the young people are seen as threats to the stability of that community. The Brighton Bank Holiday Weekend scheme was seen in that light and as a result attracted the attention of those with the greatest fears and anxieties.

But to conclude on a brighter note.

If nothing else happens we are sure that for many young people they will remember a weekend in Brighton with pleasure.

Full-Time Project

We feel that those young people who had made the most use of the Archway on a regular 24 hour basis had been the ones who had been stuck in some sort of experiential rut. They seemed unwilling or unable to create new experiences and situations for themselves from which to learn. Life for them had become boring and dull and often so depressing that suicide or drugs were the only way out of a desperate situation. The archway provided something new. It was somewhere where they could experiment with new indentities and be taken for what they wanted to be. They could practice with new relationships, particularly those who were unsure of their sexuality. They were stirred out of inaction into being more positive and for those that were judged more fragile they could find comfort and company. The workers made contact with some three hundred young people in the two Archways, apart from the thousands who came down at Bank Holidays. We doubt very much that we were able to help the more severe cases. There were those young people who just did not seem to possess

226

any inner resources that could be tapped. All the team could do was to comfort and befriend. Our successes are clearly remembered and we can see that very soon after establishing some sort of relationship, we were aware that there was potential. The fact that the young person was on hard drugs, very promiscuous, showing symptoms of severe skin disorders, physically handicapped, and showing signs of psychological disturbance, were in no way a deterrent in themselves. The worker had to satisfy himself that there existed a desire by the young person to change his way of life. Many of the Archway users were delinquent. Most offenses were for drug misuse and petty theft but a number had been convicted of assault. There was also a number who had been convicted of sexual offenses and quite a high percentage who had been victims of a sexual offense. A few of the girls were subjects of Fit Person Orders while others were known to be in care with a local authority some distance from Brighton. Many of the users had one or both parents dead, divorced or had never been known. They came from all socio-economic levels and represented fairly accurately the percentages of the general population who had received state and private schooling. Again, it was judged that they would be representative of the range of intelligence and ability to be found in the world outside the Archway. What distinguished them from other young people was their degree of isolation, their alienation from generally accepted behavior and their inability to think and plan for the future. It seemed as though a number of genetic and environmental factors had come together to create a situation which prevented them from coping with most mundane and normal demands of life.

Workers

All the workers were largely self-selected, were committed to developing the project, and all had gained experience in the Archway as volunteers. They had all received formal training in related fields but were attracted to the greater flexibility of the unstructured setting. The one worker who resigned early in the project lacked previous training and had had little experience as a volunteer. They saw themselves as professionals but without the status and defined role of the office worker and inevitably found themselves personally exposed. They believed that a wealth of varied experience tends to nurture creative growth. They were primarily themselves as individuals in the work rather than fulfilling a role and kept each other informed. They trusted each other enough not to be played off against each other by some of the more disturbed archway users. They shared case loads, and confidences were maintained within the team. They recognized the need to be flexible yet consistent. Each worker had a separate area of work. They met regularly for team meetings every week. They were paid the same salary and drew the same expenses. They were all supervised by a trained supervisor once every week. They all found work on the project "exhilarating and stretching, a happy and painful period of personal growth." They all confirm that they have not found such conditions in their subsequent employment. They could not agree on many issues, e.g. that the Archway existed to influence social change and bring about changes in attitudes of the users. They did not often agree on work methods but accepted the necessity of making decisions and deciding as a team on a course of action.

They did not always get on too well, but they remain friends. They all believe that the Archways Ventures was an important and valuable piece of work.

Method Of Working With Youth

We began with a philosophy which was vague but which suggested to each person involved in the scheme that this was a piece of work which somehow externalized our feelings and thoughts about the good life. We were realistic enough to know that we could never bring this about but the work suggested some direction. All discussions of method and techniques

228

tended to emanate from this point. But since we were all very different people we interpreted this in our own way. That is to say each worker had his or her own style but we freely borrowed techniques, notions, insights and diagnoses from each other. This being said, it is not difficult to understand why the project could not readily be incorporated into the Local Authority Services. Local authorities have statutory obligations and these define the work which in turn defines the goals and methods. The local authority workers at ground level tend to be interchangeable because the work relationship is defined by the goal and obligation. It is obvious that the Archways could not operate in this way since the whole team were oriented to each individual user as an individual, and as a member of a particular group. There was no precedent for this way of working in an unstructured setting. We had no obligations or standards of professional contract to observe, only those we chose to adopt ourselves. We had no allegiance to any political or religious group. Since many of the users were suspicious of many of the statutory services, we considered that our methods were the right ones in first establishing meaningful contact with the young people. We felt we understood the unresolved rage that many of the young people felt, which is often internalized, since these particular young people tend to feel impotent and helpless. This rage sometimes breaks out into violent verbal attacks on society and sometimes wanton destruction of public property. We feel that it is important to be neutral and detached from the public services in order to help this sort of young person. And finally, our method was how we behaved all day and every day. We tended to talk a great deal about views and feelings since this is what the young people wanted. Because of this, it became important to them and to us to be seen to live up what we professed to be our stated goals.

The Support And Supervision Of The Project

A great deal of trouble was taken to establish a solid support network. A paid supervisor and a psychiatrist were made available to the workers. The workers were also encouraged to form friendships with people of varying skills and interests who could offer a wide variety of advice and assistance. The founders also saw it as part of their contribution to support the team both informally and formally. One worker writes, "Unless a worker can remain clear headed and accurately perceive the work, he is useless. The importance of supervision cannot be overstressed." Not only did the team feel that this was important for them but they recognized the need to supervise and train the helpers. Training groups were set up on a one-a-week basis and were run by the workers themselves. The whole concept of supervision in the youth service needs to be examined and clarified in depth. Like many words in youth work language, supervision seems to be inappropriate. It is recommended that all progressive and experimental youth work find the necessary funds to employ adequate support. It is important that the workers themselves select their supervisor and consultant. It is often too late to effectively employ the services of a supervisor once the workers hit a serious crisis in their work. In their doubt and confusion they will find it very difficult to make best use of what he can offer in a short space of time.

The Finances

There were a considerable number of differences of opinion and procedure between the department and the ventures. Although some of these disagreements concerned simple matters of calculation, the majority centered on expenditure on items which were not readily agreed by the department as allowable under the terms of the grant. A major problem developed due to the interpretation of the original conditions under which the grant was given. It was recognized by the two founders that there needed to be a certain degree of flexibility in the way money was to be spent since we could not predict with any accuracy just what kind of work we might face.

It appeared to us that if monies were to be provided to finance experimental work, then the donors and the administrators of the work must be prepared for certain experimental expenditure.

Unfortunately, it took some weeks to sort out the differences between the ventures and the department and the workers had to live with some considerable anxiety not knowing whether payment of the quarterly grant would be made. The workers had to draw their salaries from this check and on two occasions it was delayed by some difficulty, while the department and the treasurer tried to find a basis for agreement. Some of the conflict obviously arose due to the fact that we were unable to predict just how much we might have to spend on such things as refreshments and consultancy fees. We had earmarked a sum of $600 for medical expenses for the workers and consequently had under-estimated the amount of money required to provide adequate support and supervision. However, in spite of our difficulty in estimating correctly, we feel that the situation was exacerbated by the Department's reluctance to forward the project's quarterly grant and thus making the workers' task that more precarious and worrying.

These negotiations were made all the more difficult due to three complete changes of staff at the department and a change of government. It seemed to the archways' team that the new D.E.S. staff were unable to catch onto the notion of an experiment and all that that entailed. All the money had been earmarked under general headings and was spent accordingly. The difficulties arose in interpretation and the fact that these headings allowed some degree of flexibility and detailed accounts were unnecessary. Where we felt that the D.E.S. might be justified in querying an item of expenditure (e.g. the payment of the fine), and was probably not covered under any of the headings, we were happy to finance this from our other source of income, namely the Bank Holiday Weekend Scheme.

It is certainly tragic that the relationships with the D.E.S. should have deteriorated after a very sympathetic launching. It is more the so, since the areas of disagreement were always

231

questions of finance and rather minor, inconsequential ones at that. However, if we can forget our differences for a moment, we can look at the D.E.S. with some sympathy and gratitude. We are, of course, very pleased to have received a grant from the department and we remember the interest shown by Dennis Howell, M.P., when we first floated the idea. We hope that it might be possible for future experimental projects and the D.E.S. to resolve some of the problems we experienced before the work begins.

The Town

One of the greatest problems we had to face was being totally identified with the attitudes and actions of those we worked with. Many colleagues in related professions saw us in this way as did many of the traders, councillors and members of the public who chose to voice their opinions in the local paper.

It is certainly difficult to maintain radical criticism, at the same time trying to work out ways in which problems can be overcome. Although it was not readily known to our critics outside the Archway, we were under some considerable attack by our clients for adopting a neutral stance. Many were in such a state of depression that they could only advocate total destruction of the existing social order. This often gave them an edge over their more liberal friends and the Archway workers. It certainly made us feel at times that if we had a good word for programs of social change under way or expressed any possibility of hope, we were told we were naive or that we had sold out. Since those who advocated some sort of negative action were in the majority, it became extremely difficult for the workers to nurture the creative and life-giving elements that existed in the arch. Often we did not know whether our efforts should be directed to the individual or to the group. A further difficulty was that this radical negativeness, not to say nihilism by our clients was often seen by many of them as a verbalizing of all the latent aggression and hatred of a society which had dealt them all such a cruel blow.

What we feared was that there would never be sufficiently strong collective will to act humanely to one another nor the impulse to externalize these feelings into some form of magnanimous action. There were certainly times when this happened and the workers worked hard to support those who tried to break out with the result that the one or two individuals changed the direction of their lives while the remainder of the group slipped back into their familiar way of life.

None of this sort of work was known to those outside although we all made strenuous efforts to inform them. But, the fact that we made attempts in this direction meant that we identified ourselves and, therefore, became what one worked called "the focus of disapprobation." We were seen as the representatives of a way of life which existed mainly in the imagination and morbid fantasies of uninformed observers.

When our critics could not anger us with criticisms about the people we chose to work with, they began to criticize us. We were accused of being "airy fairy intellectuals" or reported as being students in a context which sought to show that we were untrained and unsuited for such work. It certainly seemed to us that many people in the town were prejudiced against us from the beginning and long before we began any serious work. In our view, they had a mistaken idea that the sort of people we worked with made the seafront less attractive and thereby damaged the tourist trade. The fact that the tourist industry in all South Coast resorts had taken a serious knock with the advent of cheap packaged tours to the continent and the Mediterranean was never mentioned. Nor was the condition of the Archways all the length of the seafront. It was never reported that the council had been deliberating about what to do with the seafront archways for some 20 years. As a result, the seafront traders have been reluctant to spend large sums of money on renovation. Consequently, the arches present a tatty, dilapidated appearance. Conditions in the kitchens of the cafes are far from ideal and the whole area reeks of sausages, onions and candyfloss. The beach during the summer is always littered with beer cans and ice cream papers. No one seems to have thought that these factors might have something to do with the decline in visitors. Accomodation in the town generally is poor.

By comparison, the presence of a few dozen dishevelled and hairy young people seems of no consequence. In fact, our experience was that the holidaymakers were delighted to find a unique diversion from the slot machines and hard pebbly beaches. They were amused and fascinated to listen to the young people play guitars and sing and lark about.

In a way we saw a parallel between the town fathers and the young visitors. Those who sought to protect the town seemed to have no sense of history. They bled the town of its heritage without contributing anything and what they did do seemed to work against all that people wanted to find in a place like Brighton. The young people on the other hand, had an anti-historical bias. They seemed only concerned with the present. As an indirect result they certainly confronted old problems in new forms and gave a freshness to those who were able to reflect on their actions. But one sensed a genuine intellectual and personal deprivation. And in the meetings with the traders, the councillors and the opposers of the project, one sensed the same intellectual and personal deprivation. They sought to protect a way of life and a style of living that was no longer relevant. In many ways, Brighton is typical of British seaside resorts in that it has lost touch with the needs of the holidaymaker, young or old, and can no longer see how to compete. No amount of poster publicity of well-developed, sun-tanned young women is going to convince people that Brighton is the place where it all happens. All of the Archways' team fell in love with the beauty of the old parts of Brighton and were saddened to see so much being spoiled.

It can be seen that we often found ourselves at odds with decisions made by the town council for the apparent benefit of the holidaymaker. It was as though the council genuinely wanted to improve the town but had not the slightest idea how to do this. Suggestions made by us and other interested residents were swept aside. For example, one of the team felt that the Archways would look much better if they were painted in bright colors. We devised a scheme whereby each Archway tenant would contribute to the cost of the paint and we could find the volunteers. This suggestion was dismissed by the council who maintained that the uniform corporation colors of cream and mid-green were best. In this case the worker decided to make a personal protest and took part in a "paint-in" on two unused archways.

The archways staff were not alone in these feelings and many people wrote to the local newspapers or contacted us voicing similar misgivings about the future of the town.

Since we identified ourselves with these thoughts, we probably did our work a disservice in that it was likely that the opponents of the scheme would not be able to separate our personal actions from our professional concern in the Archway. This was certainly difficult for us too, since many of the clientele held similar views as ourselves.

But we felt that any attempt to improve or reform requires minimal organization and thought about the possible consequences. We discovered that many of the clientele felt that there is something intrinsically evil about any form of action which has organization in it. They became very involved in the idea of action and were particularly attracted to action which might lead to direct confrontation. Consequently, we were not too keen to express our thoughts and ideas so openly in the arch since the whole thing tended to get out of hand. Even when a quite minor course of action had been decided upon, it was very difficult for any of them to decide upon areas of responsibility.

But much of this sort of Archway work was on the periphery of the real work, which has been explained in some detail in the main report. Frequently, we made attempts to link the people in the Archway with those adults in the town who held responsible positions of one kind or another.

What was interesting was that many of the young people had a passion for democracy and self-government but when finally given the opportunity to get something done, became autocratic or, at the other extreme, quite woolly and inefficient. We learned that we could not easily allow them to be exposed to too many painful experiences for it became a self-fulfilling function. After yet another rejection, they were able to demonstrate how hard-nosed and unfeeling were those in authority and maintain that Brighton had had it and leave.

From time to time we gave interviews or submitted articles to the local newspaper in the hope that we could clarify our work to the local people. None of this resulted in any positive response. In more private conversations with people we explained the personal tragedies and anguish that lay behind the lives of the Archway users. We talked of the unfulfilled cravings for love and for a sense of belonging and sought to show how our approach might go some way toward meeting these needs or at least help the individual to find ways of meeting them himself. But to no avail. Many of those we talked to felt that we were too soft and that what the young people needed was more positive direction and discipline.

After many months of this sort of activity, we became depressed when we realized that we were not going to win over the council to our way of working. It was a hard thing to accept that it was very unlikely that the work would continue beyond the time covered by the D.E.S. grant. However, we were not pessimistic about the survival of our sort of approach to young people, for it will continue without us, and with or without funds. We chose to work with the derelicts and the rejected but in spite of the severity of their problems, they demonstrate in exaggerated form the weaknesses and the strengths of all young people. They see with astounding clarity, which no ideology could match, that a society that is unjust to its poor and its minorities and is organized for the benefit of a privileged few, is too often ugly and artificial. They see also the phoniness and hypocrisy of much adult life and realize that, as individuals, they can only meaningfully contribute to society as long as they refuse to support the existing social structure. They see that they cannot influence the quality of life by being themselves. If we enabled them to withstand some of the enormous personal demands inherent in their way of life, then we have performed a useful function.

Expansion

For the young drifters — many of whom made repeated visits to Brighton — it would be a good idea to have a national network of small projects. The recent troubles in the various towns could no doubt be substantially reduced by an archway project. These projects would offer similar, though not necessarily identical, facilities to the Archways. These centers would be hospitable drop-in places which the young people could use when they wanted to make new contacts and renew old friendships. The workers at these centers would benefit not simply from knowing that similar centers existed, but also from contact with each other and exchange of information and ideas.

For the local young people, we feel that any town should offer as wide a variation of facilities and support as possible. A variety of experience is a good nurturing ground for creative development. There is a need for imaginative, commercial provision which should include pubs, restaurants, discotheques, cinemas, bowling, and should be designed to attract young people. Further facilities, up until now seen as alternatives would be theatre groups, arts labs with provision for activities, including drama, poetry, film-making, arts and crafts. Perhaps, with a little imagination, these could be related to the town's adult education program. Some of these facilities could be staffed by attached support workers or be work-venues for itinerant workers. Formal advice and consultation facilities should have complementary informal facilities.

Since a common difficulty of both drifting young people and local young people was finding congenial accomodation,

237

we feel there is a need for suitable accomodation. For single-night stops, a pool of welcoming stable families would be advantageous though we know this is very difficult to arrange. For stays of one or two weeks, there is a need for a nonmembership youth hostel. It would be desirable if such a hostel also had bedsitting room accomodation and flatlets with adequate supervision by suitably trained support workers.

However, it is our experience that to provide such a range of facilities is difficult. The difficulties increase in proportion to attempts to provide for young people who are perceived as deviating, however slight or imagined the deviations may be, from the accepted stereotypes of young people.

The nature of experimental work now appears to be defined more by the lack of money than by it being new. Many experimental projects are working in ways, pioneered more than two decades ago, with people whose problems are not new to the youth or statutory agencies. That work is still labelled experimental and is a reflection of local authorities' refusal to face reality and provide the necessary money and to stand by their action when ratepayers criticize. The local authorities have some sympathy due in that their attitudes are reflections of their voters' pathological attitudes to the non-successful members of present society.

Working with young people in these circumstances will be difficult and we suggest that any group initiating experimental work take steps to become informed of the success and failure of similar work in this country and the United States.

If the challenge of working with young people in informal settings is accepted then, in our experience, a support group for the workers is necessary. However, a management committee with executive power to make decisions is not our vision. Decisions can only be made by the workers since their actions will, in themselves, have policy implications. The workers will need a support group which enables them to clarify their thoughts and feelings. A group then, which listens and aids exploration of alternative actions and thus helps the workers to become more effective.

Brighton Corporation

The Estates Department, after consulting the entertainments and publicity committee agreed to lease Archway 141 to the project as "an office for social workers" to meet their clients, and Archway 167 as a "social center for young people." Considerable time was needed to explain the less obvious use of Archway 141 as an office, in which the social workers (the full-time workers) were meeting the beats.

During 1964-65, when the young people were having their most disturbing time in Brighton, the Brighton Education Committee did nothing. At that time, it was the general policy in Brighton not to provide a service for any young people from outside Brighton. When the Department of Education and Science became interested in the scheme, they stipulated that the local youth and community services should be involved, so that the services provided by the project should not cease when the proposed grant came to an end.

The first committee to be directly involved with the Bank Holiday work was, therefore, the education committee, and the principal youth and community officer was invited to attend the consultative committee meetings, which he did as an observer.

The second committee with which the project became directly involved, was the Entertainments and Publicity committee. The workers met a sub-committee of this committee following complaints made by traders in other archways on the seafront. The complaints were initiated by a local businessman, who lived in a flat on the promenade almost directly above the Archway. He had complained about the noise of cars drawing up outside his premises. He had rallied the support of traders on the lower promenade to make statements about the Archway to show how trade had suffered.

The education committee had asked that the workers should report to the youth and community sub-committee about the work and, as a result, the education committee had shown its approval and sent a letter of appreciation to the project. This was in direct contrast to the opinion held by the entertainment and publicity committee.

Only two councillors even ventured into the Archway to see for themselves what was happening. One of these was a member of the education committee, and she popped her head in the door for a very brief spell. She was recorded as saying, "There appears no harm in them." The other councillor was accused by a town alderman of "showing an interest in a large number of matters to which the council as a whole takes the greatest exception." He usually visited the Archway at each Bank Holiday weekend, and made several suggestions as to how the services could be improved.

The Church

The church has been one of the major supports of the project at the Bank Holiday weekends. A total of 13 different churches have allowed their halls to be used as sleeping centers, and none have ever charged rent. There have even been cases of the church feeling that it could even pay for small amounts of damage that had occurred during a weekend. One or two halls did suggest that the project might make some payment to cover the cost of gas or electricity for the nights that the halls were used, but most felt that by offering their halls free of charge, they became part of the project, and made a contribution to a worthwhile cause.

The workers have found that the clergy and the caretakers have been, on the whole, much more straightforward to deal with than many other people they have met. There have been several instances of the clergy being unsure about allowing the hall to be used again, and most of them have been able to give their reasons in a straightforward manner. There was one clergyman, who informed the project that they could not use the hall because a new floor was being laid. After waiting for the floor to be laid, the workers applied again, but were refused on the grounds that he was not sure that the project was not creating a problem.

The other halls, which were very close to residential areas, politely refused to let the project use the halls again as sleeping centers, on the grounds that they had to keep the peace with the residents. The people involved had wanted to participate in the scheme, and had been unable to because of the noise element. Both appeared pleased that they had found a way of joining in again.

One vicar had to withdraw from the scheme because of the noise that the motor scooters had made during the night. However, by Easter 1969, he managed to persuade his church council to allow the hall to be used again.

All denominations in Brighton have offered their assistance at the weekends.

Two other churches allowed the project to store the blankets in their halls.

The Press

The workers felt that they needed to have some control over what the press printed about the Bank Holiday work. It was obvious that the press had made more out of the disturbances than may have actually occurred, and several people were of the opinion that the press managed to invite the young people to certain towns, by freely advertising which town was providing the excitement.

Klein and Biven visited the editors of the local newspapers. The *Argus* agreed to print nothing until after each weekend, and the editor of the *Herald* wrote ". . . I fully appreciate the importance of avoiding advance publicity for the Weekenders Holiday scheme and we will therefore, be making no reference to it in the Herald . . ."

At the first Bank Holiday weekend, members of the press were asked to leave the sleeping centers. It was impressed on them that no mention of the scheme would be best for the project and the town at such an early stage. Several newspapers printed items on the Whitsun 1966 weekend.

During 1967, relations were built up with the reporters, who were then encouraged to concentrate on the full-time work rather than on the Bank Holidays. A full account of the role of the press during the Brighton disturbances is described in *Folk Devils and Moral Panics* by A.S. Cohen.

Counseling, Support And Supervision For The Staff

When the scheme was still in the early planning stages, Biven and Klein had a meeting with David Lloyd-Jones of the Department of Education and Science, to clarify a number of items of expenditure in the proposed grant. From his experience in other projects, Biven felt there was a very strong case for a sum of money to be designated "Workers Expenses." Other workers in experimental projects have also discovered that they have great difficulty predicting the hundreds of minor expenses which are rarely covered in the budget. These items include such things as small gifts of a few cents to homeless young people to buy a meal, a dollar or two to a runaway girl for accomodations, the cost of hundreds of cups of coffee, tea, occasional beer and cigarettes, the price of a taxi or rail fare to enable destitute youngsters to get home. (There were occasions in B.A.V. when donations were received from grateful parents.) A number of small loans are inevitable.

The Department of Education Advisor, David Lloyd-Jones saw how these expenses would play a vital part in the ability of the worker to be flexible in the job, and this item was agreed and budgeted for, under the heading "Estimated Workers Expenses."

It was also felt that there would be occasions when the workers had something that they could not discuss with other members of the team. For this reason, the idea of the support network with a variety of informal and formal supervisors was put forward as the best way of ensuring the survival of the project. This, too, was accepted in principle although the department were unable to give us the kind of financial support we had in mind.

However, the above two examples give an indication of the way Klein and Biven tried to predict some of the needs of the workers and their clients and build into the project a flexible system whereby these needs could be met swiftly and without time-wasting complication. One can see elsewhere in the report that our basic assumption throughout was that we were a team of people who would need to be sensitive and receptive to mutual needs — a do-it-yourself support system. But it was also thought that such unity may not be there at the outset, or that it would necessarily evolve. There had to be ways of ensuring that the work continued at a superior level during those inevitable periods when the group might be seeing things differently. A system was needed that would allow the team to temporarily dislike each other but for there to be no serious or traumatic disruption as a result. It was, therefore, arranged as a beginning that each of the full-time workers would see a psychiatric social worker once a week, to talk over whatever they wished.

It was also arranged that they could go and see a local psychiatrist at need. He was known to the workers and to the organizers because he had helped interview the staff before their appointment. No bill was ever received and, as far as we know, he was never consulted.

For a period the three full-time staff members also met with Biven at a stated time each week to talk over the underlying philosophy, the aims and objects of the project. This group was intended to provide opportunities for developing the peace of mind which is needed to work steadily in that unpredictable situations. The planning of this was sound and included theories, methods and techniques from the social sciences. Collection of data to meet the requirements of the research assignment, and the methods by which this would be achieved was central to these meetings. In retrospect, it looks as though the timing was wrong. The group started as soon as the third worker was appointed, and after some weeks the need to discuss pressing practical problems and to shake down as a team began to interfere with the learning process. This might not have happened if this particular approach had been tried three months later. The group continued to meet to talk over the events of the week and to be guided to connect these events with more basic philosophical, social, and psychological ideas. The original intention, which was the more valuable investment, could not be fully carried out.

In addition, the very severe personal problems facing the first beat worker were becoming more apparent in every session. Many of the intellectual challenges thrown out by the group were interpreted as an individual criticism. She refused to discuss her worries with the PSW or the psychiatrist. In this atmosphere, try as they might, the group were unable to discuss anything remotely connected with the task in hand. Often the group found themselves confronting the beat worker. She would present the group with a crisis situation in her work but which, in reality, only existed in her imagination. She often felt that the kids did not like her and thought her "silly." She could only use the group to cry a little and attack Biven as the man most responible for putting her in this situation.

After 12 sessions, during which time the group tried to find ways of communicating usefully with the beat worker, it was decided that the sessions were probably more damaging than helpful to the whole group. It was unanimously agreed that the sessions would end and that Klein and Biven would meet with the beat worker to discusss her future in the project.

Some weeks later the beat worker eventually agreed that she was unsuited for the work and resigned. The project again offered the free services of the psychiatrist and the supervisors on her resignation but they were never used. A clean break with the work took the beat worker out of contact with the other members of the team for many months.

From time to time the workers also met with Klein on a more formal basis. These sessions were similar in nature to those quite often found in traditional youth work. It was necessary for the workers to be able to consult someone who could apply a vast amount of experience to a teaching situation. Often the workers found difficulty in writing up their records and it was more helpful for them to be able to consult someone in this formal setting. With hindsight it was probably not wise for the founders and directors of the project to act as informal and formal supervisors. This fact certainly created some difficulties and probably hindered the progress of particular pieces of work from time to time.

This being said, it is hard to visualize how the team might have worked using other techniques of direction and support. Klein and Biven were unpaid supervisors and unpaid directors. This came about because the Department of Education and Science was unable to give the project the finances needed to employ senior personnel. It meant that Biven and Klein felt very strongly the need to support and supervise and to give of their time than if they had seen themselves as only responsible for direction and policy making, or if they had been able to employ people who could provide the supervision on a part-time basis.

Given all these obstacles, it is surprising that the three full-time staff members and the two founders have remained friends. But this is no recommendation that this sort of situation should be allowed to develop in other similar projects.

The PSW, the paid supervisor, seeing very clearly that the work could be quite damaging to one's self-esteem, appears to have provided a good antidote. In a relaxed setting, he gave unlimited quantites of warmth, respect, support, fun and zest, and, on occasions, psychodynamic interpretations of workers and client actions. He made it possible for the workers to carry on, rending the thoughts of depression far shallower than they would otherwise have been.

On the other hand, it may be that this approach did not help the workers to work through their problems, to use a boring and over-solemn phrase. If they were failing in some aspect of their work, this could not be brought into the open, nor could the workers come to terms with each other's very different personalities just by means of being cheered up.

These then were the more formal supervisory aspects of the project. One and a half hours a week for each worker with the paid supervisor, two hours a week for each worker with the paid supervisor, two hours a week with Biven to discuss social and psychological concepts related to the work, and an hour or two a week for each worker with Klein on recording difficulties and discussion of more general committee strategies.

As the work progressed, the network of people grew and a number of professional people at the university and in the local services were used in a consultative capacity from time to time.

But all this contact with each other was in addition to the regular business meetings and in addition to the normal friendly interaction between people who saw each other every day. It was not always possibe to say when supervision began and ended. There were often problems and ideas and strategies which needed more concentrated thought and frank expression of feeling than one usually finds appropriate in a conversation that is mostly light-hearted chat and gossip.

Nor were three informal supervisory meetings limited to talk and the exchange of views. Sometimes Biven and Klein wanted to be involved at a different level and sometimes they were asked by the workers to accompany them to meet high-status people, sometimes to help in the drafting of a statement regarding the project policy on drugs, to help with an interview with the press, to help move blankets, to drive a van, to meet a senior police officer, and so on. Sometimes in the course of these events, e.g. moving blankets, a conversation would begin which would result in a reversal of roles. Biven presented the worker with a problem that had been bothering him and the worker was able to help him clarify his thoughts and reach a solution. It was this sense of shared responsibility and concern that served to blur the roles of supervisor and worker. However, all those involved in the work knew that ultimately Klein and Biven were responsible to the Department of Education for the finances and general administration of the project. With a local bank manager, they were also responsible for the leases of the two archways. These facts in themselves obviously limited the workers and their ability to make radical changes in the policies of the project without the consent of the founders.

The quality of support is always difficult to assess. It would be safe to say, however, that our situation was more complex than is usual, because our work was experimental and depended to an unusual extent on the perception, inventiveness and endurance of the workers, which in turn depended on their individual strengths and weaknesses. For this reason, it was rare for the whole group to say clearly and definitely, "this action must be taken in such and such a way by this date," for only the person directly involved knew whether such a procedure was feasible. Therefore, the kind of support which is given by clear directives and sound advice was lacking, compared with what happens in other places of work. With hindsight, all of us regret particular occasions when this or that could and should have been done, and would have proved beneficial to the work.

It may be that we solved all these different demands — for flexibility and imagination, for warmth, zest and courage, for work that had to be done, for being a perfect team — in an optimum way. The solution was imperfect, but it appeared that there was only a range of imperfect solutions to choose from. On the credit side, a lot of work was done and only one of the six left the team during the three funded years. On the debit side are many ideas for the development of the work which were never pursued. Occasionally quite painful strain in the team occurred. Until we understand more on the nature of informal support, it is impossible to evaluate the degree of success attributable to our system. However, it does seem to us that the notion of a wide and varied network of support people interspersed with those whose task it is to remind the workers of the project's original brief and ensure that this is followed, is on the whole a good one.

We have not had contact with or ever heard of any other projects where so much time and consideration has been given to this area of the work. (It has been estimated that Klein and Biven each spent 15 hours a week on project work which could be defined as supportive or supervisory.)

For those looking to this chapter for a model for support systems, they will be disappointed. In the main much of what we feel and know about support and supervision is contained in the total report. And there has yet been no theoretical analysis of informal support systems which would make it easier for us to describe what we did in a few paragraphs. Much will obviously depend on the personality of the worker and his own perception of his needs. He must be able to seek out the appropriate support. We fear that many workers in this field do not readily accept the idea of being supported as though this detracts from their skill and control of the work and implies that the supervisor is more knowledgeable. In the insular world of much experimental youth this is not a belief that could be easily tolerated.

We would like to have spent more time on the whole business of support and supervision, since in many ways we feel we were led into considering that we might have created something like a nonresidential community in the original, proper sense of the term. No doubt, we would do well to look again at the literature relating to the theory of groups but we doubt that there are many parallels.

The Police

When the project first started at Whitsun 1966, the police were categorically uncooperative. A letter from the Chief Constable of Brighton in answer to a previous letter from Biven suggesting that they could talk together about the project says:

> "... I am not prepared to meet you on this subject, and therefore, I am unable to assist you."

However, after the Whitsun weekend had taken place, and there had been no apparent trouble in the Archway, it was possible for Klein to meet and talk with one of the superintendents about the work and the way the police viewed the project.

The police were skeptical and communication was difficult with the men and women on the beat. Young people had crowded into Brighton during the first weekend, and the police had learned to be wary of any large gathering of youngsters. Numbers of young people did gather in the Archway and the sleeping centers. As late as Easter 1967, there were reports of policemen visiting sleeping centers in a rush, and searching many of the young people who had been asleep. A helper at Whitsun 1966 reported this incident:

> "A policeman came in at 3 a.m. for a second round. J.K. stood in her way but she barged past without a word followed by an entourage of four officers this time. She asked why we didn't find out how old people were who asked us for accomodation; why we didn't send her any girls under 16. We talked to the other less obstreperous officers, who became quite sympathic. They left quickly."

In a report from the NAYC this comment was made about the police at Whitsun 1966:

> "The attitide of the police was interesting. Though the Chief Constable had been informed, the constables on the beat seemed to have no knowledge of our proceedings in the earlier stages of the experiment; several were extremely hostile and sarcastic. As the weekend developed, the general relationship with the police improved considerably and their attitude changed to one of encouragement . . ."

At the Easter 1967 weekend, this report was made about a visit by the police during the night:

> "Entered flashing torches in sleepers' faces. Very hostile to the scheme on grounds of encouraging immorality, not knowing who the people were; sarcastically 'nice' to cater for layabouts, not running an entertainments center, etc.

249

> *Long and involved argument on what we were doing, apparently based on personal opinion (in conflict with that of the chief constable), how we controlled the situations, and so on. Inspector parted on friendly 'agree to differ' terms, sergeants unconvinced.''*

It was easy for helpers to become anti-police, since the police were creating considerable tension in the Archway and the centers. From their behavior, it appeared that the police were very critical of the project, and conceded nothing to it during the first few Bank Holiday weekends. They needed to be certain that the project was not creating more trouble in Brighton.

The police were often such a hindrance to helpers trying to keep the situation equable that many felt that they had coped in spite of the police.

The police had been invited to attend the meetings of the consultative committee. At a meeting after the Whitsun 1967 weekend, which an inspector and a policewoman sergeant attended, an intense discussion about the weekend work took place. The police were anxious that some rules should be made for the sleeping centers, and that the names and ages of the young people should also be taken at the door. They felt that a rule needed to be made about making people pay for any chairs they might break up, that drugs should not be used, that girls and boys were to sleep apart. The workers, on the other hand, felt that if these things were not highlighted by making the rule in the first place, then people were less likely to do them. It seemed that the police were reluctant to let people use the centers in the expectation that their common sense would prevail.

Reports about police visits at the following August 1967 and Easter 1968 show that the police had begun to trust the scheme.

At August 1967, this report appears in the Archway log-book:

> *"A Sergeant and P.C. visited. The latter walked through the Archway and no one was disturbed. Sergeant said that he was 'all for it' and had been to two of the sleeping centers where everything was fine. They chatted about fights that had occurred in the town during the night; most friendly."*

And at Easter 1968, a helper had this report:

> *"Police visit, very friendly, no special problems, just out for a cup of coffee."*

During this period from about Easter 1967 until the end of the project, many efforts were made by the workers to talk to as many of the policemen on the beat as possible. This involved having fruitless arguments with some policemen. The police wondered whether it is right to attract the young people to Brighton. Why should helpers provide these people a welcome? Why should people feel responsible for the young people so that they stood less chance of getting into trouble? Some of the conversations were rewarding, and a few of the policemen became friendly with the helpers in the course of a weekend. There was one policeman who spent about 30 minutes in each of the centers on his beat each night, talking to the helpers and to the young people who were still awake. From the reports, this policeman used to put people immediately at ease by sitting down and taking off his helmet.

This effort, on the part of helpers, to get to know the man-on-the-beat saved the policemen from worrying about a large unsupervised group of young people. The conversations that they were able to have with the helpers often dispelled fears of trouble.

An interesting phenomenon which did not change throughout the three years was, that in spite of the police station receiving the information about which halls were to be used, the man-on-the-beat claimed that they were ignorant of the scheme. They said that they had received no instructions that the scheme was in operation.

A reorganization of the Brighton Police Force took place during 1967 and afterwards helpers found it easier to talk with the uniformed Police. Several meetings took place between the workers and the new Chief Superintendent of Brighton division, when the philosophy of the project was discussed in some detail. It appeared that the new Chief Constable of Sussex was particularly interested in the project. However, the CID seemed to be unaffected by the relationship that had developed between the uniformed police and the workers of the project. Very little contact was made with the CID at the Bank Holiday weekends.

The relationship improved sufficiently well for the chief superintendent to ask about the future plans of the project. It was obvious that they were concerned that the scheme might not be in operation at the Whitsun weekend.

The workers were sure that the police had seen the value of the Archway technique by the way they behaved during the incidents of the Easter weekend. Ross phoned the police station to see how many arrests had been made. She was told that there were less than usual and that the police had been adopting an attitude of letting the young people run themselves out, rather than running them in.

Conclusions

The Brighton Archways Ventures was set up to provide an array of emergency services to itinerant and somewhat delinquent youngsters and to provide Her Majesty's Government (Youth Service Development Council) with information as to the special problems and needs of these young people.

Both tasks were completed in the given time frame. The project staff were in constant contact with H.M. Government advisors, Inspectors and other officials. Many local government officials were, as has been made absolutely clear, opposed to the project. But in other towns, council officers and representatives of voluntary and statutory bodies were keen to learn from the experiences of the B.A.V. staff. As a consequence many of the recommendations that the B.A.V. staff were able to make, were acted upon, to a greater or lesser degree. As this study is a retrospective essay the author merely wishes to note that many similar schemes are now in existence in seaside resorts and inner city areas throughout the United Kingdom. Not all of these have utilized the B.A.V. approach. Fortunately, some have a most fruitful relationship with the Town Council; something that eluded the B.A.V. staff. The importance of the B.A.V. project rests upon the need for carefully selected staff who are then entrusted with a most lonely, demanding set of responsibilities. The specific tasks as outlined in, for example, a job description were not in our view the essence of the work. In a service designed to meet the needs of young people presenting multiple problems it is neither necessary nor desirable to lay down hard and fast dividing lines, goals, intervention strategies or professional allegiances. The character of the worker is of paramount importance. Some idea of the kind of person we sought will be gleaned from a report by Leo Jago in the appendices.

We have discussed many practical problems and solutions throughout this book, let us, for a moment, consider some theoretical frames of reference.

In his book *Delinquency and Drift* Matza (1964) underlines the fact that while one naturally focuses attention upon the rebellious, aggressive, and impulsive nature of a delinquent's behavior, his behavior in general is not dominated by such anti-social acts. Within the appropriate contexts such as gang meetings, or effective therapeutic milieus, the delinquent will be civil, obedient, and conforming. A simple observation of a youngster in such a state of relative calm, reveals that he is also relatively happy. Studies which indicate the delinquent's low self-esteem, indicate that despite his deviant behavior, he yearns for a secure wholesome life, and condemns the anti-social behavior in which he is embroiled.

Accepting this view that delinquents are capable of a large measure of conformity and that they repudiate the values of the delinquent lifestyle, and believe in traditional values to which they cannot consistently live by, we would like to examine four concepts cited below.

Asch's (1951) experiments on conformity conclude that the greater the majority disagreeing with an individual's perception, the more he will tend to alter the judgment of his perceptions in the direction of the majority opinion. This is most likely to happen due to personal anxiety and discomfort. Soon thereafter he will doubt his powers of perception such as eye sight or hearing, because of the discrepancy between his judgment and that of the majority.

All four young people discussed in this book were uncomfortable with their delinquent tendencies which they saw as negative ones. With John and Jamie, the more delinquent of the four, this was particularly evident. John wrote "who led me to this life of sin" and Jamie wondered "whatever happend to that sweet kid Jamie."

John, embroiled in a life of violent crime and drug addiction, found relative calm in becoming a social dropout. In this sense his beat lifestyle at the Archway, dissolute and indolent as it was, was an improvement from his active delinquency of the past. During this quiescent period he made an attempt to conform with the mainstream of society in his anti-drug campaign. Unfortunately his personal problems which led him to delinquency in the first place, undermined these efforts.

In Jamie's case, too, her disturbance and her involvement with drugs was too profound, and eventually outweighed any efforts to lead a more wholesome life. Indeed efforts in this direction were minimal for Jamie. Her attempt at conformity was limited to her reluctance to register as an addict. She felt that this would be "an irreversible step" as indeed it was. After registration she underwent "a personality change" regressing to her original argumentative stance, and moving further away from the worker.

In John's and especially Jamie's case, one is left with the impression that the worker and the Archway offered a haven of solace in an otherwise embittered tragic life.

It is worth focusing upon the role of the Archway and the worker as symbols of majority opinion. The workers stood for wholesome conventional moral values, particularly in their opposition to the use of drugs, but differed from the mainstream of society in that they offered the young people the means of adopting these values for themselves. The means was the Archway process and the character of workers. As we have seen these efforts failed with Jamie and John, but met with greater success with Amy and Cathy.

Amy tried to make a virtue of the incestuous relationship that set her apart from the mainstream of society. She was convinced that she was special. Her attitude to her sisters was an attempt to rationalize and glorify the relationship to her father which was in fact the source of her sense of worthlessness and her estrangement from mother. Though Amy's search for a mother substitute dominated all her relationships, the relationship with the worker enabled her to see beyond this blind dependency to a more realistic and mutual friendship.

Similarly, Cathy worked through her devious testing of others to the level of trust and trustworthiness. Her self-esteem improved and she was able to resist the compulsion to buy drugs. Like Amy, her relationships with men blossomed and she did not need to substitute sex for love.

In all four cases, the young people clearly yearned for a conventional life, and used the worker as a gateway to normal society. The success or failure of these efforts depended upon the relative mental health of the individual.

Closely linked to Asch's experiments on conformity is the work that explores the degree to which people believe that what happens to them results from their own behavior, versus the degree to which people believe that what happens to them is the result of luck, chance, fate or forces beyond their control.

Other authors have pointed out, in our view correctly, that by defining the external forces as arbitrary and unstable, there is a tendency to slant "experiments" toward a natural preference for an internal, stable focus of control. Be that as it may, the delinquent's view of society (and the family) as an

255

unfriendly, threatening and unreliable force, drives them away from others and undermines their ability to trust.

At first glance this inability to trust the environment may seem at variance with the youngster's inclination to conformity described above. However, this inconsistency is superficial. What it means is that the young person's individual environment has not been stable or supportive and that they yearn to be a member of one that is.

Here again, the worker and the Archway provided a supportive environment that functioned as a large happy family. In this way the workers exhibited the leadership characteristics that some researchers have described in experiments dealing with political motivation. They state that in order to motivate the public, political leaders should exhibit qualities of personal integrity and should espouse values consistent with those whom they wish to motivate. This is exactly what the workers aimed to do, and in terms of making a meaningful emotional contact with the young people they were frequently successful.

Insofar as they were ultimately successful, as they were with Amy and Cathy, the workers helped them to replace an unstable internal locus of control, with a more stable one. This happened when Amy and Cathy were able to work through some of their insecurities and internalize the qualities of trust and worthiness.

Nevertheless, it is worth noting that regardless of its origin, there is in human nature, a tendency to see the majority of unpleasant events as a consequence of external sources. Thus Jamie blamed a "hated man who injected her with drugs" for her downfall. Similarly John's poetic question of who "led" him into sin absolves him of any guilt. Amy passively looked for a mother substitute to put things right, and Cathy regarded sexual encounters as something that happened to her.

Such rationalizations are bolstered by the syndrome of "learned helplessness" that Seligman (1975) describes. Basically, learned helplessness is caused by the repeated experience that "response is independent of reinforcement." Thus one inevitably believes that all action is futile. The resulting help-lessness is similar to a depression where hopelessness and despair predominate. It is easy to see how an unstable, (in-imicable) environment can teach a youngster that his responses are futile. It is equally easy to see how a person might long for a wholesome caring, conventional milieu.

Seligman's prescription for a person who has learned to be helpless, is to provide directive therapy which forces him to make responses which produce reinforcement. This is ex-actly what the workers did in first encouraging and then guid-ing John in his anti-drug concert. The worker, Eve, provided similar guidance in insisting that Amy view her as a real per-son, not a fantasy mother upon whom Amy would make ex-cessive futile demands. Cathy's workers also helped in encouraging her to say "no" to the drug dealers and "yes" to herself. In allowing Jamie such latitude in her abusive test-ing, the worker, in a less direct way, won her trust by remain-ing a benevolent figure despite provocation. This less direct response was necessary because Jamie was incapable of a posi-tive action at first. Later the worker responded to her guard-ed efforts to communicate in conversations.

The concepts of conformity, locus of control and learned helplessness are interrelated and hinge upon the young per-son's attempt to interact with a wholesome environment and gain a sense of inner worth. Militating against these efforts are the delinquent, hostile, impulsive tendencies that held sway in Jamie's case and probably in John's as well, while the balance favored health and emotional growth for Amy and Cathy.

In his work on obedience, Milgram (1969) describes phenomena that helps us to understand these negative forces and the ways in which they operate. Milgram states, "the most fundamental lesson of our study (is that) ordinary people, sim-ply doing their jobs, and without any particular hostility on their part, can become agents in a terrible destructive process. Moreover, even when the destructive effects of their work be-comes patently clear, and they are asked to carry out actions incompatible with fundamental standards of morality, relatively few people have the resources needed to resist authority."

Whether or not one ascribes to Milgram's notion of the "banality of evil" as something divorced from hostility is a moot point for the purposes of our discussion, since it is undeniable that underlying if not overt hostility is an essential element in all delinquency. Indeed it is this hostility, nurtured by an unsympathetic, unresponsive environment, that motivates delinquent behavior.

The delinquent peer group, where such hostile tendencies are socialized, exerts considerable pressure upon the delinquent, (or potential delinquent) to behave in an anti-social manner. The delinquent's low self-esteem is testimony to the conflict between his actions and his conventional moral standards, but this conflict is not sufficient to make him mend his ways.

Milgram mentions reasons why, in an experimental setting, the subject is unable to follow his conscience. There is a disinclination to be impolite, and a tendency to concentrate upon the narrow technical aspects of the experiment, avoiding the moral dilemma, which he leaves to the experimenter. In the real life situation of delinquents, one might add to the list his fear of rejection and his fear of physical retribution.

In this way one can see how delinquent peer pressure might allow, or force a youngster into anti-social behavior. In order to avoid his painful moral dilemma he might become immersed in the details of his life, particularly in the use of drugs. In the cases of the four young people cited here, this avoidance was largely unsuccessful. If Jamie and John did not manage to rehabilitate themselves, neither did they happily come to terms with their delinquency.

It would please us to state with some conviction that one cannot successfully avoid one's conscience, but we cannot be so sanguine. What one can say is that with disturbed young people, still searching for the means to become functional, independent adults, the means may simply be the offer of understanding and trust which might allow them to side with their better instincts.

Homelessness and running away are, rather obviously, serious symptomatic responses to a destructive home environment. These geographic escapes are futile but they are, in some respects, positive attempts to avoid "murder of the soul" (Shengold, 1989).

When they arrived on our doorstep we entered into an unspoken agreement with them. By our everyday conduct we disavowed the exploitative and did our best to protect them from further mental injury. We were not able to aspire to a standard of therapeutic neutrality due, largely, to the social and political climate which we have explained at length. The project then was a rather odd mix of research, social service, and counseling, bound together with a simple recognition of humanitarian need.

It is gratifying to see, with hindsight, that the core of our recommendations, the philosophical heart of our findings is now commonplace in youth work in the United Kingdom. We do feel that the Brighton Archways Ventures played a part in bringing about a more humane and relevant approach to youngsters not welcomed by, or attracted to established and traditional youth service agencies.

Appendixes

Appendix A

THE FINANCES

Financial Schedules: —
1 Revenue Expenditure for the period of the project
2 Capital Expenditure for the period of the project
3 Summary of Grant received and disbursement thereof
4 Schedules of Fixed Assets
5 Notes on Financial Schedules

INTRODUCTION

The following shcedules set out, in what I feel to be a reasonably self-explanatory way, the finances of the Archways for the whole period of the project.

The accompnaying comments and explanations with regard to certain items shown in the schedules may be of further assistance in understanding fully the financial picture of the Archways.

John Chapman (Treasurer)

REVENUE EXPENDITURE FOR THE PERIOD OF THE PROJECT

	Period 14.3 1967 to 31.3 1968	Year to 31.3 1969	Half Year to 30.9 1969		
Worker's Expenses					
Young People's Provisions	411	293	81	785	
Recreation and Art Therapy	89	64	6	159	
Travelling and Subsistence	61	66	68	195	
Loan Advance written off	77	--	--	77	1,216
Management Expenses					
Salaries and National Insurance	1,852	3,109	1,747	6,708	
Selective Employment Tax	102	203	139	444	
Consultancy Fees	353	480	136	969	
Treasurer's Remuneration	75	175	88	338	
Training Course Fees	9	--	--	9	
Audit Fees	5	7	7	19	
Legal Charges	28	--	--	28	
Secretarial Fees	--	4	--	4	8,519
Overhead & Recurring Expenses					
Rent Payable	296	206	89	591	
General and water rates	217	135	22	374	
Lighting and Heating	162	64	60	286	
Telephone	207	171	41	419	
Bank Charges	4	5	1	10	
Repairs to Premises	89	21	--	110	
Repairs and Renewals: Fixtures, Fittings and Equipment	52	31	7	90	
Advertising	42	59	--	101	
Printing, Postage and Stationery	98	169	20	287	
Reference and Research Literature	--	16	18	34	
Cleaning	8	40	5	53	
Medical Supplies	1	11	2	14	
Gratuities	--	2	--	2	
Sundry Expenses	14	17	18	49	2,420
Part Costs of Report			217		217
	4,252	5,348	2,772		12,372
Less: -Loan Advance Disallowed	77				77
	4,175	5,348	2,772		12,295

CAPITAL EXPENDITURE FOR THE PERIOD OF THE PROJECT

	Period 14.3 1967 to 31.3 1968	Year to 31.3 1969	Half Year to 30.9 1969	Total
To Fixtures and Fittings	858	36	--	894
Equipment	771	158	--	929
Office Furniture and Machinery	94	17	--	111
Initial Installations and Repairs	440	--	--	440
	2,163	211	--	2,374
Less Items Disallowed for Grant	18	--	--	18
	2,145	211	--	2,356

TERMS OF GRANT MADE BY DEPARTMENT OF EDUCTION AND SCIENCE

PERIOD GRANT   2 1/2 years from March 1967

AMOUNT OF GRANT

Revenue Expenditure	12,300
Capital Expenditure	2,700
	15,000

SUMMARIES

	Revenue	Capital	Total
Grant Received	12,447	2,204	14,651
Expenditure	12,295	2,356	14,651
	152	- 152	----
Grant Awarded	12,300	2,700	15,000
Expenditure	12,295	2,356	14,651
	5	344	349
Grant Awarded	12,300	2,700	15,000
Grant Received	12,447	2,204	14,651
Minus	147	496	349

SCHEDULES OF FIXED ASSESTS

1. FIXTURES AND FITTINGS

7	Electric Storage heaters	395
2	Water heaters	40
1	Refrigerator	19
1	Electric Cooker	10
	Carpeting	56
1	Storage Cabinet	193
2	Table top work benches	51
	Seating benches	66
	Divans	10
1	Table	2
1	Desk	6
1	W.C. Pan	20
1	Fan Heater	3
1	Electric Fire	3
1	Wood screen	3
1	Small Cabinet	5
	Electric fittings	12
		894

2. OFFICE FURNITURE AND MACHINERY

1	Desk	3
1	Chair	5
1	3-piece suite	10
	Carpeting	8
1	Typewriter	15
2	Filing cabinets	33
1	Duplicator	20
1	Electric Kettle	8
1	Fan Heater	4
	Sundry Small Fittings	5
		111

3. EQUIPMENT

1,250 Blankets and 750 Coil Mattresses	835
5 Electric kettles	37
2 Record players	15
Crockery, etc.	8
Tea towels and dish cloths	4
Dustbins	3
Mops, buckets, dustpans, brushes, etc.	5
Sundry tools	2
Padlocks and keys	1
Ladder	5
First aid equipment	9
Curtaining	5
Less items disallowed	18
	911

4. INITIAL INSTALLATIONS AND REPAIRS

Archway 167

Reflooring	297	
Rewiring	20	
Redecoration	55	372

Archway 141

Rewiring	58	
New door	10	68
		440

265

NOTES ON FINANCIAL SCHEDULES

Initial application was made to the Department of Education and Science, late in 1966, for a Grant, the total sum applied for being some 18,000 and for a period of three years.

The 18,000 was to be apportioned, over the three years, as follows:

Workers' Salaries	11,250	
Workers' Expenses	2,250	13,500
Capital Expenditure on Fixed Assets, Initial Repairs, etc.		2,550
Overhead and Recurring Expenditure		900
Capital Expenditure and overheads for a further Archway:		
Capital		150
Overheads	525	675
Provision for Medical Help, if required		300
		17,925

After due consideration by the Department and Minister, consequent upon negotiations between the department and the Archways Committee, a grant was finally made in February 1967 of 15,000 and for a reduced period of 2 1/2 years to be apportioned as to 12,300 fo current or revenue expenditure and 2,700 for capital expenditure.

The above original apportionments were proportionately reduced by one sixth to become as follows:

Workers' Salarics		9,375	
Workers' Expenses		1,875	11,250
Capital Expenditure			2,125
Overhead and Recurring Expenditure			750
Second Archway:			
Capital	125		
Overheads	438		563
Medical Help			250
			14,938

The revenue grant was to be paid in quarterly installments of 1,230 in advance and the capital grant was to be paid on periodic production to the department of all relevant invoices and, subsequently, a statement certifying that payment had, in fact, been made was to be sent to the department.

266

Appendix B

NEWSPAPER ARTICLES

Brighton and Hove Herald, November 10th, 1967

SEA FRONT EXPERIMENT

Brighton's Entertainments Committee have let two Arches on the Seafront to the Brighton Archway Venture, and now, through no fault of their own, are in a cleft stick until the lease expires next year. The B.A.V. is a unique experiment by a group of sociologists studying the young people who appear to drift into becoming beatniks or flower people and generally opt out of the responsibilities of life. The object of the B.A.V. is praiseworthy, and they are supported by a direct grant of $30,000 or more from the Department of Education and Science, which gives some indication of the importance the department places on their work. The dilemma the Entertainments Committee now finds itself in is that this experiment is being carried out slap in the middle of Brighton's shop windows, the seafront between the two piers. Traders have complained, and they claim an arch is being used as a "doss house" — which the B.A.V. deny. One thing certain is that very few visitors would class a group of beatniks as an attraction for a holiday town and Brighton must attract visitors. It is being argued that most of the flower people or beatniks behave as they do from choice; they are healthy physically, many are intelligent, but they do not wish to work or conform in any way. Most will have to be kept by the State, and as a problem they should be studied, but should they be encouraged? That is one of the strongest arguments put forward against this interesting experiment. Are they not in danger of encouraging even more people to opt out of life by their very interest in them? Perhaps the report of their experiment will supply an answer.

Evening Argus, November 16th, 1967

BEATS OF ARCH 141 UPSET TRADERS

. . . A report by the town's entertainments and publicity committee says the traders complained that the very presence of these young people on the lower esplanade, often in large groups, had the effect of discouraging less extreme members of the public from using the trading arches in the vicinity, and as a result the traders' taking suffered. They complained that the arches (mainly No. 141) were being used for sleeping purposes in contravention of the terms of the leases, and that on one occasion there was a performance by singers using amplifiers. A report from the chief constable said the two arches were used as reception centers from which young people were directed to one of the halls where they might sleep. But, it continued: 'It is increasingly obvious that the reception centers are not doing just this work of directing youngsters to a sleeping place. Youngsters are congregating at these arches and remaining there, in some instances all night.'' If there is indecent, threatening, abusive behavior and the like, these are clearly matters within the jurisdiction of the police, and should be dealt with within the framework of the existing criminal law where adequate powers exist.

Evening Argus, November 22nd, 1967

BEATS BECOME BETTER BEATS

. . . They assist them discreetly and in the most patient way possible to be themselves, to give expression to their personalities, to discover their potential as human beings. That is the simplest way of summing up in a nutshell the aims of an organization that had a complicated birth. It dates back to those disturbing Bank Holidays when Brighton was the venue for multitudes of warring mods and rockers. They brought with them in their wake social workers concerned over such mass violence . . . Plainly, youth workers and traders are likely to stay gulfs apart in their outlook. The interests of one are based on commercialism; of the other in making, to use the words of the beat worker, "beats into better beats." This illuminates the basic free-thinking philosophy of the Archways Venture. It is one of acceptance of young people, whether they are beatniks or not, as individuals. They are in no way ordered about. There is no preaching down, no attempt at facelifting their characters to something more socially acceptable. They are respected as being young people who in their own way are making a comment on society by rejecting much of it. But there is certainly no question of easing the paths of their rebellion . . . The Venture story is in the best traditions of welfare service, good leading to good. And it's as well there are such stories. It is those who turn their back on the world who often need most guidance from it, those who reject who sometimes need most acceptance and help . . .

Evening Argus, November 24th, 1967

BRIGHTON CAN'T FIND A WAY
TO BANISH THE BEATNIKS

Opening two of Brighton's seafront archways to beatniks had created "cesspools of iniquity" in the town, Ald. Leonard Knowles told the town council last night. And the chairman of the Entertainments and Publicity Committee, Ald. George Lucraft, agreed in the course of acrimonious debate: "We should never have let these archways to these people but now there is next to nothing we can do about it . . ." The debate on the beatniks was launched by Ald. Knowles, who said he had received innumerable complaints from seafront traders about the activities of people using the archways and had passed them on to the committee. The original proposal, to keep word of the archways quiet so that not too many individuals would be attracted, had obviously been lost, he continued. "The word has got around that Brighton is the place to come to. These people are moving in from far and wide in ever increasing numbers." The massive list of examples of misconduct prepared by the traders was too lengthy to read, said the Alderman, but he would quote one. A woman manageress of a store stated: "The type of person frequenting Archway 167 is completely disgusting in behavior and habits. This is especially so when I have seen them leave Archway 167, go over opposite my premises, and actually engage in the act of making love." They did not even mind being seen, she said. "In fact I have heard little children asking of their parents: "What are they doing?" Commented Ald. Knowles: "In this age they must have been very young infants indeed." In a recent article in the *Evening Argus*, the organizers of the scheme had stated that if their next two years were as successful as the first, they were hoping that Brighton council would take over financial sponsorship for the work . . . Said Ald. Knowles: "All I can comment is — what a hope!" Ald. Arthur Nicholls said the arches were not supposed to be used for sleeping in but merely as reception centers. Yet "only last week 14 mattresses were taken out of Archway 141 and dumped on our beaches by these do-gooders." Cr. Michael Cohen said, "It would be pointless trying to close the town to beatniks because they were obviously going to arrive. These people are coming to Brighton because they want to. The trouble is that we have closed all the coffee bars around the town so they can't go to them and they are attracted to the beaches. We can eliminate the problem at the beach quite easily by adopting a more enlightened attitude toward entertainment in this town." Cr. Ray Blackwood commented that it was a pity that more councillors had not gone to the arches to observe them for themselves. "People have told us in this council chamber tonight what is wrong. But I think a lot of it is hearsay. They should go down and look for themselves." It was a pity, he said, that Ald. Knowles, having initiated the discussion, should have left the chamber. He wondered where the Alderman had gone. Delighted shouts came of: "On the beach. He's gone to the beach. He's with the Hippies." It was a pity, Cr. Blackwood continued, that the council were apparently not prepared to help the unfortunate people unable to fit into society who had to use the archways because they had nowhere else to go. Councillors should do all possible to assist these people, "even if they do dress in a strange way," Ald. Knowles returned to the council chamber and observed: "Cr. Blackwood, if I may say so with the greatest respect, seems to have a great interest in a large number of matters to which this council as a whole takes the greatest exception."

Evening Argus, January 10th, 1968

NO ROW LIKELY ON ARCHES

There is unlikely to be any discussion on the controversial future of the arches on Brighton's lower esplanade at next Thursday's town council meeting. Unless any member deliberately raises the matter, there will be not debate about Arches 141 and 167. Instead of expected lengthy report on their decision to obtain forfeiture of the two leases, the entertainments committee has contented itself with a six-line report. Even this is listed as business undertaken as an item dealt with under delegated powers and "reported for information." The committee's report says that the town clerk has been instructed to serve notices on the tenants and failure to comply with the order would result in action to obtain forfeiture of the leases.

BAPTIST MINISTER BACKS ARCHWAYS

The chairman of Brighton's Entertainments and Publicity Committee (Ald. George Lucraft) today revealed that two members of his committee had visited the seafront arches which are to be closed at the end of the year by the corporation. The corporation is to take legal steps to end the lease on the arches following a police report that beatniks had slept there overnight. Sweeping in with a wave of fresh support, the Rev. Geoffrey Whitfield, of Moulscoomb Way Baptist Church, known to his parishioners as "forward-thinking," asked: "Has Ald. Lucraft and his committee ever actually engaged in the scheme to see for themselves what goes on and do they rely on second or third-hand reports?" Ald. Lucraft was quick to answer back. "Certain members of my committee have been there," he said, "but they had trouble getting in. As soon as these people saw anybody respectable coming they just locked the doors and didn't let anybody in." He added that two members, however, had succeeded in inspecting the arches and the manner in which they were run. They later made reports to the committee. But he refused to disclose the contents of the reports. "Legal proceedings are pending and, in the circumstances, no comment can be made." He contended that reports from these members could hardly be considered as second-hand information. As well, the committee had confidential reports from the police, beach inspectors and sanitary inspectors. They couldn't be considered unreliable. Mr. Whitfield, expressing strong support called for "a change in the recurring theme of the attacks on the archway venture." Was it not vaguely possible that some good was being done? "Surely we are concerned that Brighton should be a resort of excellence. This means that we will therefore endeavor to cater for all our visitors, even the unorthodox. If we can show care and understanding, a lack of bigotry and exploitation, it could be that a useful job would be done," he added. "Let Brighton's greatness be seen not

273

just in status symbols but in care, concern and constructive approach to a complex social phenomena. Let the petty-minded be educated to see that problems are faced and not hidden or ignored. It seems that blindness, jumping to conclusions and exaggeration is clouding the whole of the Archway project. Let people be careful in their appraisal, slow in their condemnation and fair in their judgment lest they be swayed by less responsible elements and thus too easily despise and reject what may be a fine and worthy venture."

Sunday Telegraph, February 4th, 1968

HAVEN FOR THE YOUNG OUTSIDERS

By Celia Haddon

". . . On a board inside is a notice asking people not to get "high" on the premises. But for all the cautiousness of the two ex-teachers in their 20s who run the center from day to day, a girl kept insisting to me last week: "I'm high. I'm a dosser. I'm stoned" . . . The corporation's offers of accomodation away from the beach have been rejected. Barrie Biven explained: Our clientele are on the beach, so that's where we must be. There's no particular reason why this center should be in Brighton, but that's where we are, and that's where some of the beats are."

The Guardian, June 1st, 1968

BENEATH BRIGHTON ARCHES

by Johnathan Steele

It was half past three in the morning and they were dozing uncomfortably in a glass-sided shelter on the seafront, when the policeman woke them. They had hitchhiked down from Langley, near Slough that afternoon, Easter Sunday, got to Havant and then struck out eastwards and reached Brighton at dusk. Both were 15. It was a cold night. So they stumbled up to the church hall which the policeman pointed out.

Inside the hall, their story could be repeated dozens of times. Kids who'd slept last night on a golf course in Oxted, or who'd come by bike from Chislehurst, a gang which had crammed into two vans and two scooters from Leatherhead — they drank the free coffee, chatted desultorily, and then paid their half-crowns for a space on the floor and two army surplus blankets. The Brighton Archways Ventures which started with an arch under the promenade two years ago, and now uses half a dozen church halls each Bank Holiday, is still the only seaside project of its kind.

This Easter more than 500 teenagers slept in the different centers. They expect it will be the same at Whitsun, even though numbers are down on the last August Bank Holiday's record of 700 and there are signs that the wave may be receding. The volunteers who man the centers are young teachers, child care officers, students, youth leaders, sittings up most of the night chatting to the kids who want to chat, and keeping them quiet enough for the others who want to sleep. By day they stagger off to a local Friends' Center where their own mattresses are laid out on the floor . . .

. . . Many of the kids mean to sleep rough on the beach, but regret it half way through the night. The Archways started naturally enough to give them a roof. It has since branched out and has won the support of several local churches, who are lending church halls. The Arch itself is now no longer meant

276

for sleeping but serves as an information center and an informal club room from which the youngsters are directed to the various halls.

The police keep an eye on the centers, and a constable usually looks in two or three times a night. After being suspicious at first, the police, at least at the highest level, are sympathetic to the scheme. Keeping kids out of the cells is a benefit which they recognize. At Easter this year a senior superintendent stepped in and reprimanded a constable who strode into a church hall and started asking a lad questions before approaching the youth worker in charge.

Rules are strict about keeping boys and girls separate and against drugs. The difficulty is to make these basic rules understood without spoiling the permissive atmosphere of the centers. The youth workers after all take pride in creating an environment where a stranger would hardly be able to tell which are the workers and which the kids. Or as they sometimes appear in the project reports — "the clients."

For the project is no longer just an emergency service for visiting youngsters; it has become a long term attempt to provide a permanent youth center. The weekenders who come down at Bank Holidays may be the largest group numerically but they are now the Archway's easiest challenge. Since September, it has opened its two Archways for three nights a week as a meeting place for local teenagers and for a group of beats who came down to Brighton and were living rough, or in a rented room for long stretches at a time. They are all kids, known in the jargon as unattached, groups which find established youth clubs dull, churchy or paternalistic; street corner gangs, frequenters of coffee bars, drifting in and out of delinquency . . .

. . . Like most other projects dealing with the unattached, the Archways Venture is experimental. Its aim is to provide a place where young people can talk to young adults and get help on an informal basis. Inside the arch the atmosphere is surprisingly passive, a few kids twanging a guitar, a game of cards here, a group talking there. None of the normal youth club pingpong tables or dartboards.

Kids who announce they are hitchhiking to Istanbul tomorrow, or that they want to set up a boutique selling leather pouches, are asked quietly how they are going to do it. Kids who throw their weight about are ignored, or reasoned with, but not forced out.

The beats, particularly, tend to build fantasies, project workers have found. They may go into long accounts of their life story, most of which is made up. They need help in doing basic things: finding flats or filling in forms. There was friction between them and the regular group of more extroverted teenagers, who used to use a separate arch, but were thrown together when one Arch was closed because of staff shortages. The project had also come to difficulty when boys absconding from approved schools have tried to shelter there. Youth workers make it clear that they cannot protect them, but try to find out why they are running away.

In its starkest form, this is the dilemma the project always faces: how to bridge the gap between the youngsters and authority. It is an unfinished task, for which the project has found no easy answers. But it is attracting growing interest from other youth workers in the field. This Whitsun, along with hundreds of weekenders, a number of youth leaders on training courses in other parts of the country will be down in Brighton too.

Appendix C

Correspondence Between Brighton

Archways Ventures and Brighton Corporation

To: Dr. J. Klein   29th September, 1967
From: W.O. Dodd
Dear Madam,

141 and 167 King's Road Arches

Further to my letter of the 19th September and in connection with your forthcoming meeting at the Town Hall with Alderman Lucraft, Alderman Nicholls, Councillor Theobald and representatives of the seafront traders to discuss conditions at King's Road Arches, with particular reference to Arches 141 and 167, I am enclosing, herewith, for your information, copies of the statements that have been supplied to me by a number of traders, in which details of their complaints are fully set out. You will no doubt wish to give consideration to the matters raised therein to enable you to be in a position to deal with them when the meeting is held.

It is only right also for me to tell you that I have received a report from the Chief Constable concerning activities at Arches 141 and 167 during the latter part of August and the early part of this month. He tells me that Arch 141 seems now to be used almost exclusively for beatniks and that on the nights of 26/27th and 27/28th August some 60 and 72 individuals respectively remained in the Arch overnight. Whether or not they sleep there, it clearly seems from what the Chief Constable tells me that the arch was certainly used for providing these people with accomodation on the nights in question and this is definitely not in accord with the terms of the Lease of this Arch, the relevant ones of which are set out below. He also tells me that on the early morning of Sunday, 10th September, his officers found a number of young persons congregating around the entrance to Arch 167 from the interior of which could be heard the voice of a man singing to the accompaniment of a guitar. It was found that he was singing into a microphone connected to a large amplifier and the singing music could be heard on the promenade immediately above. I gather that when you were seen you informed the police that the man with the amplifier had merely wandered into the Arch and started his singing and playing and that you were going to close this Arch in any event at 1 a.m. At 1:15 when the police returned it was discovered that the young man had moved to Arch 141, where he was again playing his guitar while, gathered outside, were some 20 or so persons. The interior of the Arch on the ground floor was, I understand, filled to capacity with persons described as being either beatniks or of the flower fraternity, while on the upper floor of the Arch it was discovered that there were a number of mattresses with some 15 or so people reclining upon them and that they had with them their bedrolls. I gather that when you were asked about this you, and also Mr. Biven, said that they would not be staying but would be going on to the Mermaid Hotel.

As you know, under the terms of your leases, Arch No. 141 is not without the corporation's written consent to be used or permitted to be used otherwise than as an office for three full-time social workers and Arch 167 otherwise than for the purpose of a reception center for young people and for the carrying out of general social service work. In particular, there is prohibited in the case of both Arches the carrying out of any business, manufacture or art, the use of the Arches or any part of them for the preparation, reheating or cooking of any food or for the service of cooked meals; the use of either of the arches for the purpose of sleeping; the installation of any machine which might be used for the purpose of amusement or entertaining or the playing, broadcasting, or amplifying of music which may be audible outside the Arches; the sale, distribution or supply of articles, goods or things to any person who requires the same for re-sale to the public, the holding or permitting to be held or any sale or auction, etc., the sale or service of any intoxicating liquor. In an attempt to keep this letter as short as possible, I have paraphrased the various conditions as to use but these are contained in paragraphs 13 (in the case of Arch 141) and 10 (in the case of Arch 167) of the respective leases and, although some of the prohibitions on use that I have mentioned do not seem to have relevance to the matters at present in issue between the traders, yourself and the local authority, I thought it as well, briefly, to refer to them above.

The particular complaint relates to last night (28th/29th September) when, it is alleged between 10 and 20 young people of both sexes slept the night through in Arch No. 141. Quite apart from the fact that you and your colleagues' tenancies of these Arches expressly prohibits persons sleeping therein; the tenancy of Arch 141 restricts its use as an office for three part-time social workers. Unless the use of both these Arches is properly controlled by you and your colleagues, and the terms of the respective tenancies strictly adhered to, there will be continuing complaints, and, whatever the motives of those complaints might be, if there are breaches of covenant I shall have no option but to recommend the council to terminate the tenancies forthwith. May I therefore, please ask you to look into this latest complaint, and let me have your observations. While writing, I would mention that it has been noticed that the door of Arch 167 has been painted in a similar manner to the unauthorized painting that took place on premises to the east. The design on this door is not considered acceptable, and I shall be glad to receive your proposals for repainting the door in a proper manner, in accordance with Clause 2(4) of the Tenancy Agreement.

Yours Faithfully,

(Signed)   C.D. DUTTON

Borough Valuer and Estates Manager.

To: C.D. Dutton   4th October, 1967
From: Dr. J. Klein
Dear Mr. Dutton,

Thank you for your letter of September 29th.

I wish again to assure you that it is not the case that people sleep the night through, either on September 28/29th or earlier. We now have a church hall to which people who need somewhere to sleep, go in the small hours.

Maybe your observers, who clearly were not there for long, were misled by a couple of dozing drunks. These are a problem to us and we would prefer not to have them in, but the alternative of sending them back on the highway seems less desirable to us. They are not encouraged in, either by us or by our regulars.

Our use of Arch 141 does not break the clauses of the lease though as an office it does present a very unorthodox appearance. 141 is proving extremely useful in allowing us to contact and get to know some of the beats which is one of our functions and one we could not fulfill on more orthodox lines . . .

. . . The surrounds and brickwork of 141 are being painted this week in corporation colors. The painting on the woodwork is giving pleasure to passersby, some of whom stop and look at it and talk about it appreciatively among themselves, as may be verified any Saturday or Sunday afternoon. The general appearance is considerably less unsightly than the old neglected-looking doorways or those disfigured by flapping posters advertising ice cream or sausages. A walk along the seafront, comparing our Archways with others, should convince anyone that we are adding to and not detracting from the amenities and cheerful appearance of the lower promenade. May we not leave this matter for six months, by which time I truly believe the people of Brighton will have become pleased with and proud of our unique doorways.

Yours sincerely,

(Signed)   Josephine Klein

To: Dr. J. Klein   10th November, 1967
From: W.O. Dodd
Dear Madam,

141 and 167 King's Road Arches

I am writing to you in your capacity as the council's lessee of Archs 141 and 167 and also on behalf of your fellow lessee's, Messrs. B. Biven and G.L.S. Brown, to whose attention I should be obliged if you would draw the contents of this letter.

You might well be aware of by now that the Entertainments and Publicity Committee of the council at their meeting on the 8th November considered the report submitted to them by the three representatives who met yourself, your associates and representatives of the seafront traders at the town hall on 24th October. After a very full discussion of all the issues involved, I was instructed to write to you and draw the attention of yourself and your fellow lessees to the serious concern with which the committee viewed the present state of affairs. I was also instructed to require you to ensure that for the future all the terms and conditions of your two leases are complied with without fail and would instance in particular the following matters where the committee consider there is evidence to support the allegations that breaches of convenant have taken place in the past:

(a) the supply of refreshment

(b) the playing of amplified music audible outside the Arches.

(c) unauthorized painting, and

(d) the use of the Arches, particularly No. 141, for the purpose of providing sleeping accomodation.

The committee requires you forthwith to set right those breaches which have occurred and still persist, and so far as the matter of the unauthorized painting is concerned you should get in touch with the borough valuer and estates manager to ascertain his precise requirements.

The committee also required me to inform you that the manner in which the activities at the two Arches have been conducted in the past and the manner in which they will be conducted in the future are matters to which they must inevitably give very serious consideration when the question of the possible renewal of your two leases comes up toward the end of 1968. I think it only fair to say, and at this you will no doubt not be surprised, that as at present minded it would seem most unlikely that the committee would countenance any extension of the present terms that you hold. Clearly, therefore, it must be in your own interests to ensure that, so far as is possible, the future conduct of the two Arches is such as not to give rise to the volume and type of complaints that have arisen in the past and at which the committee are most seriously concerned.

The committee's report on the position will be before the council when it meets on the 23rd of this month and, clearly, it would be of assistance if, by then, I could have your written assurance that henceforth every endeavor will be made by you and your associates to ensure that the terms of your leases are not broken and that any further cause of complaint is obviated.

Yours Faithfully,

(Signed)   W.O. Dodd

Town Clerk

From W.O. Dodd, Town Clerk   24th November, 1967
To: Dr. J Klein
Dear Madam,

141 and 167 King's Road Arches, Brighton

... As indicated to you earlier, the council would not wish you to be under any misapprehension as to the gravity with which they viewed the position and I felt it was only right again to draw your attention to their avowed intention to ensure that the convenants in your two leases are complied with. Moreover, unless there is some radical improvement and further cause for justifiable complaint is not given to the seafront traders you would be unwise to assume that your present leases will be renewed . . .

Yours faithfully,

(Signed)   W.O. Dodd

Town Clerk

From Dr. J. Klein   28th November, 1967
To: W.O. Dodd, Town Clerk
Dear Sir,

Mr. N. Ashwell, now the secretary of Brighton Archways Ventures, is away on a course for some days, and in his absence I have pleasure in answering your letter of the 24th.

We have indicated before that there is no cause for complaint, and I refer you to previous correspondence on this subject.

The position now seems to be that the Venture is nourishing the morbid fantasy life of some people in this town. No investigation of the complaints is made, because people prefer to believe curious things, as the council meeting last Thursday (reported in the Argus on the 24th) proves. For instance, although Alderman Nicholls tried in our presence to smoke a joss stick and found it could not be done, he nevertheless believes that others have a strange power which enables them to do this. A lady mentioned at the council meeting seems to believe that she saw two people engaged in sexual intercourse on the promenade outside her archway, and it appears that the councillor who reported this, and you, believe her.

In our work we try to help people confront reality with clearer vision. We try to do this in one kind of way in the archways, where we also sometimes have to deal with psychologically disturbed people, and we can do this in other ways with citizens less obviously adrift. We shall take legal advice on future communications if they appear libellous to us. We shall probably not do so in the case of the muddled and confused traders, but if you indicated our intention to Messrs. Kn. and K. for instance, it might well lighten your own administrative burden somewhat.

Another aspect of this same mode of working is to point out to you that leases are normally renewed unless there is a reason not to, and that the hearsay fantasies of others cannot be considered sufficient cause.

Yours faithfully,

(Signed)   Josephine Klein

From: W.O. Dodd, Town Clerk   30th November, 1967
To: J. Klein
Dear Madam,

141 and 167 King's Road Arches

I duly received your letter of the 28th November which, although referring to mine of the 24th November, makes no reference to my earlier letter of the 10th November in which I requested from you and your co-lessees certain assurances as to the remedying of existing breaches of covenant and as to the future conduct of these two Arches. These are still awaited and I shall be obliged if you will let me have them as soon as possible. It would be pertinent to mention here that I understand from the borough valuer that you have not yet been in touch with him with regard to the repainting of the exterior of the Arches and I should be obliged if you would contact him without delay.

I do not propose to deal in any detail with your letter now under reply except to say firstly that it is untrue to assert that the complaints that have been received have not been investigated (you cannot have forgotten the lengthy meeting at the town hall, attended by yourself and the traders specifically for the purpose of going into the allegations) and, secondly, that I do not propose to enter into debate with you by correspondence as to the value of the work that inspires it. Members of the council have (in some cases forcibly) made their opinions known but my concern in this correspondence with you is merely to underline the terms upon which you hold your two Arches as the corporation's tenant and to point out the consequences of failure to comply with those terms. You say that the renewal of leases is normally a matter of coure but I cannot indicate too strongly that this is not so and you would be misleading yourself if you nourished that expectation in this particular case.

Yours faithfully,

(Signed)   W.O. Dodd, Town Clerk

From: Nick Ashwell   5th December, 1967
To: W.O. Dodd, Town Clerk
Dear Sir,

141 and 167 King's Road Arches

With reference to your letter of the 30th November, I wish to assure you that we will be in touch with the borough valuer as regards the painting of the outside. Our only recent contact with him has been to complain of the rubbish deposited by council workmen outside Archway 141, which made it impossible to get in. Most, but not all, of this has now been removed; this section of the promenade is still closed to traffic.

To take up what appears to us the main point of your letter, we do not consider that the complaints were investigated at the lengthy meeting referred to. No evidence was adduced that the complaints were, in any way, justified. We denied the allegations that the traders reiterated. This cannot be called investigation. The upshot was that a lot of totally incorrect and irresponsible statements were, and continue to be, made to the press. Even this cannot make an untruth into a truth.

(Signed)   Nick Ashwell, Secretary

From: W.O. Dodd, Town Clerk   7th December, 1967
To: Nick Ashwell
Dear Sir,

141 and 167 King's Road Arches

It was good of you to reply on the 5th December to my letter of the 30th November addressed to Dr. Klein in her capacity as one of the co-lessees of these two Arches, especially since, despite your connection with the Brighton Archways Ventures, you are not one of the corporation's tenants. That you are getting in touch with the borough valuer with regard to the painting of the outside of the Arches I have duly noted but so far as other breaches of covenant of the two leases are concerned I still wait to receive from Dr. Klein and Messrs. Biven and Brown their assurances that these will be remedied and not repeated.

That you do not see eye to eye with me on the question of the investigation that the entertainments and publicity committee made into the seafront traders' complaints is regretted but for my part, I remain satisfied that, short of a full judicial enquiry, the committee looked into the matter completely impartially and without pre-judging the issues. You were made fully aware well in advance of the meeting of the substance of the complaints that had been made and the committee listened to everything that was put forward by you and your colleagues in answer to the various allegations. The committee have made it clear to the council that what they are concerned with is to ensure that the two leases are fully complied with and that the allegedly reprehensible behavior of those people attracted to your Arches either on the beach generally or in the immediate vicinity of the Arches is a matter which they, as Landlords, cannot control. This, however, does not prevent the members of the council from holding strong views about the value of the work you are doing and the general character of the persons for whom you cater. That you choose to deal with an extreme section of society will naturally produce equally extreme reactions from those more conservative persons whose ideas will inevitably be so very different from your own. Their statements are likely, therefore, to attract an amount of publicity which is probably completely out of keeping with what the problem deserves. However, I am not responsible either for what members of the council might say or for what the local newspapers print and I certainly would not subscribe to the view that merely because the press chooses to publish a statement it is thereby endorsed as true. It would, in conclusion, be pertinent to mention that I seem to recollect that the local press gave a good deal of prominence to what was virtually a full page article on your Venture and the work that you are doing. So both sides of the coin have been shown to the public.

(Signed)   W.O. Dodd, Town Clerk

To: Barrie Biven   11th January, 1968
From: W.O. Dodd, Town Clerk
Dear Sir,

141 and 167 King's Road Arches

At their meeting yesterday the Entertainments and Publicity Committee considered further reports on some of the activities which are allegedly being carried on at these seafront arches. Despite the correspondence which I have had with Dr. Josephine Klein, I have not received an assurance that existing breaches of covenants under the leases will be remedied. In the circumstances the committee have instructed me to serve upon you and your co-lessees formal notices under Section 146 of the Law of Property Act 1925. These notices are being prepared in my office and will be served upon you shortly.

Yours faithfully,

(Signed)   W.O. Dodd, Town Clerk

To: Barrie Biven   18th January, 1968
From: W.O. Dodd
Dear Sir,

141 and 167 King's Road Arches

Thank you for your letter of the 11th January and I would agree with you that it is a matter of regret that you should have first heard of the decision of the Entertainments and Publicity Committee through an approach to you by the local press. As you have pointed out, the committee members themselves were completely agreed that it would be improper for details of their decision to be released to the press before Dr. Klein, yourself, and Mr. Brown had been first informed.

The notices which the committee directed should be served upon you and your co-lessees are at present being drafted and will be served upon you as soon as possible.

Yours faithfully,

(Signed)   W.O. Dodd, Town Clerk

To: W.O. Dodd   January 29th, 1968
From: B.M. Biven
Dear Mr. Dodd,

I have delayed writing to you to let you know the results of my meeting with our legal advisor, as I was expecting further correspondence from you in connection with the serving of formal notices on the co-lessees of Archway 167 and Archway 141. However, I am able to tell you that the Brighton Archways Ventures have been advised that they are able to give you an assurance that, as in the past, no breaches of the lease will take place in the future. We give this assurance with confidence as we have always maintained that no breaches of the leases have taken place.

In addition to the question of immediate forfeiture of the leases we are concerned that the Brighton Entertainments and Publicity Committee may be considering refusing us first option for renewal on leases that we hold until December 25th 1968. As you know there is no question of Brighton Archways Ventures failing in their financial commitments to the council with regard to rent and rate payments. We have also carried out improvements to both Archways amounting to some $2,200. In view of these facts and that we feel we have been satisfactory tenants we are taking legal advice as to the proper action should the Entertainments and Publicity Committee make it known to us that they intend not to renew our lease.

I hope the above statement of our feelings and intentions has helped to clarify the various issues. I feel that these exchanges are most unwelcome and distressing for both the committee and ourselves and I sincerely hope that you will be instrumental in bringing the Entertainment and Publicity Committee and ourselves to a meeting so that we are able to work out a satisfactory settlement to our differences.

              Yours Sincerely,

        (Signed)   Barrie Biven

_____

To: Barrie Biven   6th February, 1968
From: W.O. Dodd, Town Clerk
Dear Sir,

141 and 167 King's Road Arches

Thank you for your letter of the 29th January and I note that you have consulted your own legal advisors in connection with the alleged breaches of the covenants in your two leases of Arches 141 and 167. However, as you know, the council is not prepared to accept that in the past there have been no breaches of these covenants and, indeed, it was precisely because of this view that they have instructed me to serve notices upon you under Section 146 of the Law Property Act, 1925. As intimated to you in my previous letter these are in the process of being prepared and should be served upon you and your co-lessees within the course of the next few days.

I note, too, that in addition to the question of the possible forfeiture of the leases you are concerned that the council might be unwilling to consider their renewal when they expire in December of this year. As far as I am aware, I am unable to dispute that you and your co-lessees have not failed in your financial commitments to the council with regard to the payment of rent and rates and I note that you say that extensive improvements to both Archways have been carried out. It may well be that in these respects the council would consider that you have been satisfactory tenants of these two Arches, but you do not need me to remind you that with regard generally to the activities which have been carried on by the Brighton Archways Ventures from these two premises the council regard the position as being far from satisfactory, particularly in view of the considerable volume of complaints that they have received. As I pointed out to Dr. Klein in previous correspondence, the council clearly would take very much into account in deciding whether or not these leases should be renewed, both the past history of the premises while they have been leased to you and their future conduct.

In your final paragraph you ask that I should endeavor to arrange a meeting between yourself and the Entertainments and Publicity Committee in an attempt to work out a satisfactory settlement to the present difficulties. The February meeting of the committee will be held tomorrow and I will place your request before them. I will let you know their decision as soon as possible.

Yours faithfully,

(Signed)   W.O. Dodd, Town Clerk

To: Mr. B. Biven   February 9th, 1968
    Dr. J. Klein
From: Mr. W.O. Dodd

Brighton Archway Ventures

141 and 167 King's Road Arches

Further to my letter of 11th January, in accordance with the instructions of the Entertainments and Publicity Committee, I enclose by way of service on you formal notices under Section 146 of the Law of Property Act requiring you to remedy certain breaches of covenants contained in the leases of Arches 141 and 167. Similar notices have also been sent to-day to your co-lessees.

The important parts of the notices appeared in sections 2 and 3:

2. There have been breaches of the said covenants
(a) in that the outside of the demised premises has been painted otherwise than in the manner stated in the said lease and without the prior approval of the borough valuer as to the color or colors.
(b) in that the lessees have used or permitted or suffered to be used the demised premises or some part thereof;

(i) otherwise than as an office for three-full-time social workers; and in particular
(ii) for the preparation of refreshments;
(iii) for the purpose of a sleeping apartment or for sleeping accomodation;
(iv) for the playing or broadcasting or amplifying of music or sound audible outside the demised premises, and;
(c) in that the leases have suffered to be done or committed upon the demised premises acts or things which have become a nuisance or annoyance to the owners or occupies of adjoining properties or to the neighborhood.
3. I hereby require you within 28 days from the date hereof to remedy the said breaches and hereby further give notice that unless this requirement is complied with within the time abovementioned I shall proceed to enforce the right of re-entry under the lease and shall take such further or other steps or proceedings as I may be advised:
Date the Ninth day of February 1968

(Signed)   W.O. Dodd
              Town Clerk, Town Hall, Brighton
For and on behalf of the corporation, the lessors of the said premises.

To: W.O. Dodd, Town Clerk   26th February, 1968
From: Barrie Biven, et al.
Dear Sir,
    We, as co-lessees of Arch Number 141 and Arch Number 167 of the King's Road Arches in the County Borough of Brighton, have remedied those breaches of the covenant as have occurred, and hereby assure the Mayor, Alderman and Burgesses of the Borough of Brighton that no breaches of those or any other covenants will occur for the remainder of this lease.
    (Signed) Barrie Biven
            Josephine Klein
            Gordon Leslie Brown (Temporary Treasurer)

From: W.O. Dodd   April 26th, 1968
To: Mr. N. Ashwell

"I wish to refer to the paragraph in your letter to the 'Evening Argus' on Thursday which stated that the Entertainments and Publicity Department assisted your venture by pasting up posters in the center of the town. So that you should be under no misapprehension, I must point out to you that this was done without the approval of a senior officer of the corporation. The matter was not considered by the Entertainments and Publicity Committee and if it had been, it would certainly not have been approved. Steps have been taken to remove the posters in question and instructions given that no further assistance of this kind is to be rendered."

Yours sincerely,
W.O. Dodd

To: Mr. W.O. Dodd   14th May, 1968
From: Nick Ashwell
Dear Sir,

Thank you for letter of 26th April, 1968.

Your letter has proved a point that we have been making for several months. Mr. Biven wrote to you on February 6th saying that he believed that the council was unable to adopt a neutral position in its dealings with the scheme. In your reply you said that:

" . . . the committee's decision has not been motivated by its attitude to the value of the work which Brighton Archways Ventures is doing . . ."

You now say that the committee would not give approval to our posters being exhibited, and this is before the committee has been confronted with our request. This shows simply that you must be sure that any decisions made by the committee about Brighton Archways Ventures must be motivated by its attitude to the scheme.

It does seem a pity that we are being hampered in our efforts to avoid Brighton being troubled at Bank Holiday weekends.

Yours Sincerely,
(Signed)   Nick Ashwell

To: Nick Ashwell   17th May, 1968
From: W.O. Dodd
Dear Sir,
   I do not propose to re-open matters which were more than fully gone over in our previous correspondence but I must repeat that the council's decision to serve notices upon you and your fellow lessees to secure compliance with the covenants in your two leases was taken as a result of cogent evidence that it had received that breaches were taking place. Legally, it could not have been otherwise. However, it would be superfluous of me to point out to you what can only be obvious, namely that a large number of members of the council have very decided views about the value of the work that the Archways Ventures is doing and about the character of the clientele that is attracted by the facilities which the Venture is providing. These views have been expressed publicly, in the Council Chamber and also in the local press and you will of course, have seen the report in yesterday's *Evening Argus* of the interview that the paper held with the chairman of the Entertainments and Publicity Committee. To what was said and to what is said above I have nothing further to add.

Yours faithfully,
(Signed)   W.O. Dodd

To: Mr. W.O. Dodd   30th May, 1968
From: Dr. J. Klein
Dear Mr. Dodd,

Mr. Ashwell has passed on to me your letter to him of 17th May. I note that you now believe you have "cogent evidence" that breaches of the lease were taking place. What new evidence have you? If you will look through your papers you will be able to remind yourself that the complaints were mainly against beats in general, wherever they were, that some of the complaints were peculiar beyond ordinary sanity, and that the Archways only came into the matter because that was where some of the beats were some of the time. Are you sure that mere repetition of the allegations has not inadvertently turned into "cogent evidence?"

The only matter in which we did not immediately conform was the painting of the outside. We still have photographs of these exteriors, as well as of some other exteriors along the seafront.

If you have material which leads you now to believe that you have cogent evidence, Mr. Ashwell would be glad to have it, for our records and for our eventual report . . .

                              Yours faithfully,
        (Signed)   Josephine Klein

———————————————

To: Jo Klein   31st May, 1968
From: W.O. Dodd
Dear Madam,

May I thank you for your letter of the 30th May although it in no way raises issues which have not been gone over more than fully in previous correspondence between my office and you and your co-lessees. To re-open the past investigation and enter into a debate by correspondence over the rights and wrongs of the issues at stake is something that I do not propose to do. In its futility it would be wasteful of both your time and mine. May I however make this one observation?

The Entertainments and Publicity Committee received a large number of statements and reports concerning events and activities on the lower esplanade in the vicinity of Arches 141 and 167. They carefully sifted through these, heard you and your fellow workers in reply to the complaints but remained satisfied that from what they had been told there was evidence to justify them proceeding with the service of the Notices which you later received.

That a great deal of the complaints were made against beats in general I would accept, but, ignoring this irrelevancy, there still remained more than adequate support for the action which the committee took.

Just as mere repetition of allegations does not turn them into cogent evidence, their denial does not automatically invalidate them.

> Yours faithfully,
> (Signed)   W.O. Dodd

To: The Lessees   13th June, 1968
From: W.O. Dodd
Dear Sirs,

167 King's Road Arches, Brighton

I enclose a notice in duplicate determining your tenancy of the above mentioned premises on the 25th December 1968. Will you kindly acknowledge safe receipt by signing on the reverse of the duplicate notice and returning it to me in the enclosed prepaid envelope.

A similar notice has today been sent to the other lessees.

> Yours faithfully,
> (Signed)   W.O. Dodd, Town Clerk

APPENDIX D
BANK HOLIDAY VISITORS

Day/night of each weekend	Numbers using sleeping centres at night			Number of sleeping centres used at night	Number of helpers working in archway and sleeping centres each 24 hr. day
WHIT 1966	approx. 1200			6	120
AUGUST '66	approx. 1000			8	105
EASTER '67	Male	Female			
Friday	70	10		4	46
Saturday	287	51		6	45
Sunday	298	54		6	52
Monday	20	5		3	25
	675	120	795		
WHIT '67					
Friday	10	0		6	59
Saturday	144	30		6	80
Sunday	217	29		6	73
Monday	30	6		6	45
	671	65	736		
AUGUST '67					
Friday	45	0		3	23
Saturday	140	16		5	30
Sunday	194	33		6	32
Monday	35	2		1	10
	414	51	465		
EASTER '68					
Friday	61	13		2	23
Saturday	165	26		5	51
Sunday	149	46		5	57
Monday	55	12		1	29
	430	97	527		
WHIT '68					
Friday	12	7		2	22
Saturday	136	17		5	32
Sunday	138	49		4	32
Monday	47	12		2	28
	333	85	418		

APPENDIX D CONTINUED
BANK HOLIDAY VISITORS

Day/night of each weekend	Numbers using sleeping centres at night			Number of sleeping centres used at night	Number of helpers working in archway and sleeping centres each 24 hr. day
AUGUST '68	Male	Female			
Friday	46	9		2	25
Saturday	93	27		6	42
Sunday	196	42		5	40
Monday	32	8		1	21
	367	86	453		
EASTER '69					
Friday	55	8		4	38
Saturday	220	23		5	51
Sunday	201	52		4	39
Monday	13	3		1	37
	489	86	575		

Appendix E

An Unusually Busy and Unproductive Night in Arch 167
By
Leo Jago

This night I felt like the Ringmaster of a three-ring circus. Vic described the performances as being like a firework display.

Soon after opening time at 8:05 p.m., a university student acting as a reporter for the newspaper *Wine Press* visited. She did not stay long as she only wanted to ask questions about the council threat to our lease. She had considered herself a volunteer worker but previous visits had taught her little of our aims and methods.

Shortly afterwards, Mrs. K. came in, closely followed by four members of another local church. Mrs. K. was an upright, grey-haired, well-dressed, severe sort of person. She had been part of several church projects that had attempted to work with the beatniks. Now she was independent and her mission to the beats was to proclaim to them that they were God's new chosen people who would spread the word of the second coming. I approached the quartet from the church and told them they were only welcome in the Archway if they did not "push." They thought that I was using the slang term "push" in connection with drugs and they were a little staggered that I thought they were pushing drugs. I explained that I was not accusing them of pushing drugs but made it clear to them that I considered the "pushing of religion" as unethical and unprofessional and that it was not allowed in the Arch. I worked to get them to understand that they must work with the kids at the level of whatever the kids presented. I was able to refer to Brother Mark as one who was prepared to let the kids dictate what they wanted to talk about. Mrs. K. was to the church people an example of how not to behave, and they were quickly able to sense the situation themselves and were rather embarrassed about her as a fellow Christian.

This conversation was interrupted by a telephone call from a member of the youth team at Radio Brighton who wanted us to be on a program called "Controversy," I told him I did not think we could do that and if he wanted to discuss it further he should phone Nick Ashwell at the office tomorrow.

The next moment Ian, Hamy, Ben, Bill and Millie made their appearance, all of them drunk, drugged, or both. They reeled about the Archway for some time causing eddies of concern and momentary terror, but doing no one any harm. Ian vomited, which called for a clean-up operation and gained him some sympathy for his condition. Bass made his way to the toilet where he, too, vomited. He was very quiet for the rest of the evening and sat very still. Millie staggered about for a while until at last she subsided onto a box and fell asleep.

Aaron provided the next diversion, he had apparently wandered outside and lain down on the pebbles at the edge of the beach where he was found by a cruising police patrol car. This caused a great stir as most of the people in the Arch came out to see what was going on, and it attracted passersby on the promenade as well. The police cleared the ramp up to the road as the Archway visitors were hanging over the edge and apparently annoying the police. They asked people to go back inside the Arch and their insistence on this caused side disputes. The police called an ambulance which added to the attraction. No doubt, our curious visitors, combined with the tension of waiting around for the ambulance, contributed towards the build-up of hostility between the police and the youngsters.

One time a policeman came to the door of the Arch and looked in. He did not come inside, no doubt repelled by the atmosphere of turmoil and agitation. The cause of the panic in the Arch was that Luke had collapsed on a box near the front. He was drugged with Mandrax and quite incapable of helping himself. A group of friends grabbed him and whisked

302

him to the back room and out of sight of any police eyes. At the sight of this pandemonium, Mrs. K. was fussing about and exhorting people to pray along with her. The confusion was too much for her. Luke's friends who carried him away did more to calm the situation than did her prayers.

During this time, Jamie was wandering about the archway, also drugged, falling about and draping herself over people. It certainly didn't help toward keeping cool when in the middle of organizing a stretcher party for Luke and trying to bypass a praying Mrs. K., a swaying Jamie hove into sight and flung her arms about me like a long lost lover. But she was less of a bother like that than if I angered her; tact and firm persuasion was necessary to free myself and set her staggering in someone else's direction.

After the ambulance and the police had departed there was relative calm for a while and I turned my attention to the various internal situations. Luke was a limp heap draped across two chairs, his head and arms hanging off one end and his feet splayed in an ungainly way in the other direction. I made some inquiries to find out what people thought we ought to do and whether they thought he was really in a bad way or just needed to be left alone. Leaving him was the general consensus, so he was left. However, my anxiety was raised again by the sudden appearance of Councillor C. and his wife, and Mike Edwards, a television news reporter.

Visions of embarrassing repercussions in Council meetings and lurid scenes on the "box" about the Archway flashed across my mind as I turned from Luke to deal with these visitors. The C.'s asked a few brief questions about Luke and how he came to be like that and then they left me with Mike. I spent some time with him, withdrawn from the general confusion, to explain that we were only prepared to have anything to do with telvision if it was on our terms. Any program to be made must cover the full range of the work — we were not interested in three-minute news spots. He was, in fact, very understanding about the difficulties of making a program about a project like ours and he said he would not be looking for sensational matter, like Luke, which would give a very one-sided picture of the work. We arranged to meet again when we could discuss, with other members of the team, the possibility of filming.

The arrival of Dave, a volunteer, with his van provided a solution to the problem of what to do with Luke, who was in no condition to get to his cabin on the houseboat at Shoreham. Jamie had also collapsed by now and they decided to take her along to the boat. Two of Luke's friends offered to help and the task of placing the inert Luke and Jamie in the van and getting them out at the other end needed more than Dave on his own. The difficulty of actually getting them in was complicated by the fact that they were not at all sure as to what was happening to them. They were not cooperative. The process looked more like loading firewood. Innes, still drunk, also decided to take a hand and that really created trouble as he wanted to take over and this angered the others who were also wanting to help. He pushed around a few people who he said were crowding him and getting in the way, while he was looking after Luke and Jamie. I moved in to see if I could calm the situation a bit and help to get them into the van before we attracted the attention of people and caused another crowd to gather. More worrying to me and Dave was the possibility of attracting the attention of the police. Innes felt that I was also crowding him so he grabbed hold of me and ran me up against the rails on the ramp. He recognized who I was and only threatened to punch my head in. I managed to convince him that I really only wanted to help him. Finally, we managed to get Jamie inside and shut the door on her. She appeared to be upside down but I thought she would sort out by herself. I was really anxious that the van disappear. Mrs. K. came out of the Arch at the moment and said, "I would like to help but I have a bus to catch."

I retired to the back of the Arch to talk to the television reporter, and was called again to the front to discover a potentially dangerous situation had arisen. Someone had slipped a hasp across the door and locked us all inside. The trouble was that Innes wanted to go out and the attempts by Geoff, a volunteer, to shake the door open had failed and Innes was launching himself against it in an effort to break it open. The door opens inward so he had a tough job. I tried to reason with him and get him to see that someone would eventually come along who wanted to come in and they would open the door. I wasn't making any headway with him and he had backed off from the door to get a real run at it when the door opened and about four people came in. They had seen the little stick in the hasp but did not really grasp the situation that they saw when they got inside. I went back again to Mike and relative calm.

Aaron returned as we were cleaning up, at about 11:30 p.m., and was hailed as the returning hero and surrounded by his few remaining friends. Innes and Cathy organized themselves to get Millie home. Like most people out on Mandrax, when she was walked around, she seemed to come to and was able to stagger along between them.

The cleaning up was accomplished by three volunteers who were able to see that I was engaged with Mike, the television reporter. The time of closing was given in the report as midnight; that indicated that I did not intend to hang about after such a night, even though we were not so punctual every night.

Three volunteers, Carolyn, Vic and Geoff, came back to my flat where we discussed the evening's events over a welcome cup of tea made for us by Carolyn. The discussion was centered on easing my worry about drugs being in the Archway and on finding a solution to the problem of people who came in after drugs, then fell asleep. A number of suggestions and considerations were made by the group. One was to put the drugged person and his friends out of the Archway on the principle that they disrupted the atmosphere, preventing any possibility of people enjoying themselves. It was also suggested that we call the ambulance for anyone that was unconscious. This would prevent any possible accidents due to overdosing. Young people loathe the idea of going to the hospital. With the possibility of a police enquiry we felt that they would stop running the risk of overdosing in the Archway. It was proposed that as one particular doctor was prescribing the drugs we should telephone him whenever any of the young people were unconscious and ask him to attend to them. It was felt that such a course would probably dry up the source of drugs fairly quickly. It was then suggested that if we were to visit the doctor and tell him what was happening, and point out to him that if pills kept going around, the police were bound to be asking questions as to where they came from. The doctor had already been involved in a court case in which a patient of his had been selling her prescribed drugs. The group also discussed the idea of finding a doctor who was informed about the use of drugs by young people and who was sympathetic to our work and who could act as an advisor.

At the end of the discussion, I decided to take the proposals and discuss them with Biven the next day before opening the Arch that night.

Selected Bibliography

Aichorn, A. **Wayward Youth**. London: Putnam, 1936.

Albemarle Report. **The Youth Service in England and Wales**, H.M.S.O. 1960.

Bartollas, Clemens, "**Runaways at the Training Institution Central Ohio**," Canadian Journal of Criminology and Corrections, Vol. 17, 1975.

Bassis, Edward. **Characteristics of Adolescent Runaways in a Community Residential Treatment Center**. Diss. Abstr. Intern 33 (11-13) 5505-5506, 1973.

Bestic, A. **Turn Me On Man**. New York: Award Books, 1966.

Biven, B. "**The Brighton Experiment**," Youth Review, Number 3, London, 1966.

Blishen, E. **Roaring Boys**. London: Thames & Hudson, 1955.

Blos, P. **On Adolescence**. Free Press: New York, 1962.

Cohen, S. **Mods, Rockers and the Rest**, in **Crime and Delinquency in Britain**. Eds W.G. Carson and P. Wiles. London: Martin Robertson Co., 1971.

Cox, D.M. **Youth Work in East London**. London: Young Women's Christian Association, 1970.

Ellis, R. **The Big Beat Scene**. London: Four Square Books, 1961.

English, Clifford. "**Leaving Home: A Typology of Runaways**," Transaction, Vol. 10(5), 1973.

Guardian Weekly. 6/9/91 "**The Other Side of Brighton Pier**."

Goetschius, G. and Tash, J. **Working with Unattached Youths**. London: Routledge and Kegan Paul, 1967.

Goffman, E. **Asylums**. New York, Doubleday Anchor.

Goldmeier, J. and Dean, R.D. **The Runaway: Person, Problem or Situation**? Crime & Delinquency, 19.4, 1972.

Gosling, R. **Sum Total**. London: Faber & Faber, 1962.

Hamblett, C. and J. Deverson. **Generation X**. London: Tandem Books, 1964.

Holden, H.M. **The Anvil Club**. Unpublished Report to Anvil Club Committee, London: 1960.

Holden, H.M. and Biven, B. "**Informal Youth Work in a Cafe Setting**. The Social Development of Youth Offenders:" Editor, J.B. Mays. Longmans, 1975.

Holden, H.M. "**Medical Care of Homeless and Rootless Young People**," British Medical Journal, Vol. 407, 1975.

Hunter, E. **The Blackboard Jungle**. London: Constable & Co., 1955.

Ince, D.E. **Contact**. Youth Service Information Center, 2, Leicester: U.K., 1971.

Kaplan. A. **The Conduct Of Inquiry**. San Francisco, Chandler Publishing Co, 1964.

Klein, J. **Working with Groups**. Hutchinson: London, 1961.

Laufer, M. and Laufer, M.E. **Adolescence and Developmental Breakdown**. New Haven: Yale University Press, 1984.

Leech, K. **Keep the Faith Baby**. London: S.P.C.K., 1973.

Leventhal, T. **Inner Control Deficiencies in Runaway Children**. Archives of General Pscyhiatry II, 1963.

Lewis, B.; Chisnal A.; Hall, A. **Unattached Youth**. London: Blond and Briggs, 1974.

Makarenko, A.S. **The Road to Life**. Moscow: Foreign Languages Publishing House, 1955.

Merton, R.K. **Social Theory and Social Structure**, London: Roultedge and Kegan Paul, 1957.

Miller, D. **Growth to Freedom**. London: Tavistock Press, 1964.

Milson, F. **Youth Work in the Seventies**. London: Routledge and Kegan Paul, 1970.

Moriarty, Daniel. "**Runaways: Psychological and Sociological Study**," Dissertation Abstracts International, Vol. 36(1-B), 1975.

Neill, A.S. **Neill! Neill! Orange Peel**. London: Tavistock Publications, 1926.

New York Times, editorial, 8/16/1991.

New York Times, 12/11/1983.

Salisbury, H.F. **The Shook Up Generation**. London: Michael Joseph, 1958.

Shellow, Robert; Juliana Schamp, and Elliot Liebow. "**Suburban Runaways of the 1960's**," Monographs of the Society for Research in Child Development, Vol. 32(3), 1967.

Skinner, H. **Adolescents Away from Home**. Annals of Academy of Political and Social Science, 236, 1949.

Smith, C.S. M.R. Farrant, and H.J. Marchant. **The Wincroft Project**. London: Tavistock, 1972.

Social Work, November, 1989. Editorial. "**Homelessness: Public Issue and Private Trouble**."

Stierlin, Helm. "**A Family Perspective on Adolescent Runaways**," Archives of General Psychiatry, Vol. 29(1), 1973.

Stierlin, Helm. **Separating Parents and Adolescents: A Perspective on Running Way, Schizophrenia and Waywardness**. New York: Quadrangle, 1974.

Turner, M.L. **Ship Without Sails**. London: University of London Press, 1953.

Thrasher, F.M. **The Gang**. Chicago: University of Chicago Press, 1927.

U.S. News and World Report, 1/17/1983. "An Endless Parade of Runaway Kids."

Walker, D. **Runaway Youth**. DHEW, September, 1974.

Whyte, W.F. **Street Corner Society**. Chicago: University of Chicago Press, 1943.

Wilkerson, D. **The Cross and the Switchblade**. Pyramid Books, New York, 1962.

Wilkins, L. **Delinquent Generations**. London: H.M.S.O., 1960.

Wollen, S. and Brandon, U. **Runaway Adolescents Perceptions of Parents and Self**. Adolescence 1, 2, 1977.

Yablonsky, L. **The Violent Gang**. London: Pelican Books, 1967.

References

Asch, S.E. (1952). **Social Psychology**, New York: Prentice Hall.

Elms, A.C., Milgram, S. (1966). **"Personality Characteristics Associated with Obedience and Defiance Toward Authoritative Command."** Journal of Experimental Research in Personality, Vol. 1 (no. 4), p. 282-289.

Kurtz, P.D., Tavis, S.V., Kurtz, G.L. (1991) **Problems of Homeless Youths**: Empirical Findings and Human Service Issues. Social Work, Vol. 36 (No. 4), p. 309-315.

Matza, D. (1964). **Delinquency and Drift**. New York: Wiley.

Seligman, M.E., Beagley, G. (1975). **"Learned Helplessness in the Rat."** Journal of Comparative and Physiological Psychology, Vol. 88 (no. 2), p. 534-541.

Seligman, M., Rosellini, R.A., Kozak, M.J. (1975). **"Learned Helplessness in the Rat**: Time Course, Immunization and Reversibility." Journal of Comparative and Physiological Psychology, Vol. 88 (no. 2), p. 542-547.

Shengold, L. (1989). **Soul Murder: The Effects of Childhood Abuse and Deprivation**. New Haven: Yale University Press.